Joe's Dash

Joe's Dash

From Million Dollar Drug Busts
to Multi-Million Dollar Collections
for Las Vegas Casinos

Linda Ellis
with Joe Dorsey

HUNTINGTON PRESS
LAS VEGAS, NEVADA

Joe's Dash
From Million Dollar Drug Busts to
Multi-Million Dollar Collections for Las Vegas Casinos

Published by
  Huntington Press
  3665 Procyon Street
  Las Vegas, NV 89103
  Phone (702) 252-0655
  e-mail: books@huntingtonpress.com

ISBN: 978-1-944877-41-5
$19.95us

Production & design: Laurie Cabot
Cover Design: Tanya Maynard
Cover Photos: Las Vegas skyline, ©Rich Legg; bundles of money,
©homeworks255
Photospread: page 4: San Diego heroin drug bust ©Rob Lampert;
page 10: Las Vegas Hilton ©VintageLasVegas.com; page 11: Golden
Nugget ©Chon Kit Leong | Dreamstime.com; page 11-13: Alad-
din, Dunes, Tropicana ©VintageLasVegas.com; page 14: Ron Lyle
©WikimediaCommons; page 16: Ellis Island ©Ellis Island

This is a work of creative non-fiction. All of the events in this memoir are true to the best of Joe Dorsey's memory, with some names and identifying features omitted to protect the identity of certain parties. Unless otherwise expressed, the details and opinions in this biography are solely as recounted by Joe Dorsey.

Joe's Dedication

To my wife, Karen Rose Dorsey, who blesses my life every single day.

And to those in law enforcement who put their lives on the line for me during my career and do the same for each of us every single day.

Joe's Acknowledgments

I'd like to use this section to acknowledge and salute all law enforcement, military and first responders. The respect and admiration you so richly deserve is sadly lacking in today's society. To those who risked their lives to save mine more times than I can recall and to those who do the same every day for all of us. Just know that for every one person who disrespects you or is not appreciative and grateful for your efforts, there are thousands of us that know the truth.

Many of the people who have influenced my dash have been mentioned in this book. The friends and family below are as much a part of my life and have inspired me.

Personal Acknowledgements

Mary Jo Porach, John Porach, Robert Dorsey, Kelly Dorsey, Theresa & George Cavanagh, Cindy & Gary Ellis, Christina Ellis, Anamarie Ellis, Michaela Ellis, Frank Ellis, III, Mary Jo Ellis, Pete Berger, Geri & Michael Rumbolz, Jack Pearson, Mike Hentigan, Jay McBride, Bob Williams, Vince Krolikowski, Jimmy Conklin, Paul Jaramillo, Dr. Jerry Schwartz, Dr. James Lovett, Dr. Arthur Fusco, Dr. Carlos Fonte, Dr. Scott Baranoff, Michelle Taylor, RN,

Arlyn Filamore, RN, Gay Echiverri, RN, Leslie Guarin, RN, Robert Kopecky, Father Doug Koesel, Sister Georgita Cunningham, Mary Cavallaro, Jodi Snyder (Rest In Peace), Ana Romo Zavala, Connie Stamper Silva

From day one, I was humbled that Linda Ellis was excited about helping me write my story. Her sincere interest enabled me to open up and relive some of the most difficult times of my life, while taking pride in my achievements. Through it all, we forged a great friendship based on mutual respect.

There are times when everyone needs someone to just open the door. Anthony Curtis, owner of Huntington Press, did not hesitate to do that for me. Without his commitment and belief in my book, and tremendous expertise, we would not have crossed the finish line. For this I will be forever grateful.

Deke Castleman, Sr. Editor of Huntington Press, helped educate me through the process and he ensured nothing was compromised as he connected the dots and tied everything together. His patience and talent through this journey was immeasurable and greatly appreciated.

My sincere thanks to Tanya Maynard for the phenomenal cover design. To Laurie Cabot for her incredible design work, and the hours spent wading through dozens of photos to produce a center photo spread that I am very proud of.

Contents

Author's Note

In 1996, I wrote a poem that became a world-renowned inspirational work, "The Dash." It's about that little line between one's dates of birth and death, the hyphen that ultimately represents every step we take on Earth.

One stanza from the poem, in particular, kept repeating itself in my mind throughout my journey learning and writing about Joe Dorsey:

> *For it matters not how much we own:*
> *the cars, the house, the cash.*
> *What matters is how we live and love*
> *and how we spend our dash.*

Each and every one of us has stories to share from this journey that I've dubbed the "dash." Yet have you ever wondered, as I have, why certain people seem to have a greater cache of unique life experiences from which to draw?

Sure, every dash has its share of loss and calamities, but the majority of us live routine and predictable lives. Thrill seekers don't wait for life to extend invitations; they create and conquer their own encounters in their own way on their own time. Others simply follow their path, which presents extraordinary circumstances. Joe Dorsey's, for example, includes jumping out of helicopters in violent storms to save lives, going undercover in narcotics operations, gathering body parts after a midair collision, raising two kids as a single father, and collecting millions of dollars of unpaid gambling debts overseas.

I have done my best to portray Joe Dorsey as he is — the real deal. He has no hidden agendas, he tells no lies, he doesn't put on pretenses. At work and in life, he's the type of man who leads by example. He is, by all accounts, an embodiment of the adage, "Actions speak louder than words."

He knows who he is. His friends and family know who he is. And God knows what's truly in his heart. What more can a man ask for than to be true to himself, his loved ones, and his God?

Early Years

Thursday's Child

Joseph Patrick Dorsey was born on a cold Thursday morning in March, 1943. The old nursery rhyme foretold Joe's life well: "Thursday's child has far to go." But only God knew at the time how true those words would be.

He joined two brothers and two sisters in a family that would eventually grow to 11 people, including three younger siblings and his grandmother, living in a three-bedroom apartment located in a low-income section of Cleveland, otherwise known as "the projects."

Joe's family was poor, but he didn't know it at the time. None of the children in his neighborhood knew their social or economic status or lack thereof. Not until he grew to become the young boy who wasn't invited to birthday parties, because he lived on the "wrong side" of town, did he begin to feel the sting of distinction.

Joe remembers how each of his younger siblings suddenly appeared. With each labor, when his mother went to the hospital, his older siblings explained her abrupt departure as, "She went to the store." He remembered thinking, "Every time she goes to the store, she buys a *baby*!"

Joe took his place in a long ancestry of Irish Catholics

who shared a common denominator: alcohol. To this day, the Irish and their whiskey are the subject of many jokes, but where there's smoke, there's often fire and so was the case with the Dorsey family of Cleveland.

The memories of children who grow up in an environment where alcohol is predominant in their parents' lives linger throughout their lifetimes: the muffled sounds of fights coming from the other side of the wall, the silent tears falling, the sudden violence, the unrest that hovered like an ominous cloud over happy times. Fortunately, our origins do not determine our fate. We can rise above our circumstances by seizing opportunities that make things better. And that's exactly what Joe did.

Mother

His mother, Mary, didn't wear the title of homemaker well. She didn't bake cookies, help with homework, or check behind ears. She never served as a dependable foundation for her children. She loved them as best she could, but she was an alcoholic.

Joe's mother was the designated disciplinarian, doling out the physical punishment. Joe vividly recalls one of his older brothers sitting at the dinner table tapping his fork against a glass. Mary asked him to stop, but he continued, which infuriated her to the point where she threw a knife, deeply piercing his arm. As for himself, she once hit him so hard that she broke her own knuckle. That was when she moved on to hairbrushes.

When his mother eventually left this Earth, Joe was in his early thirties. He hadn't seen or spoken to her in 15 years. When Joe's sister called to give him the news, he had little reaction, outwardly or inwardly. He felt as though his sister spoke of an acquaintance they knew, not the mother who had labored to bring them into this world.

Father

Joe's father, Joseph, for whom he was named, drove a truck, then a cab, and later went to work at a Cadillac plant where they made Army tanks. His grandmother and an older sister and brother also worked at the plant. Though Joseph's relationship with Mary wasn't always amiable, Joe and his dad had a solid bond.

According to Joe, Joseph was always cheerful. He was a good father, did his best to be a provider, and treated his eight children equally, providing a solid foundation for all of them.

Joe received a good spanking from his dad only once. One day, he made a makeshift toy out of a small metal index-card holder and a string. He was lying on the top of the bunk beds, swinging the gadget back and forth, when he accidentally hit his sister in the head, resulting in a small cut above her eye. The spanking wasn't nearly as painful as the fact that his father threw away the secret box in which he kept all his money: 15 cents. Though he pleaded, Joseph wouldn't tell him where he dumped the box.

Another time, however, also stands out in his memory. Joe's older brother was good at baseball; Joe looked up to him and watched his skills with the envy of a little brother. One day, Bobby was out playing baseball and Joe asked him, "Can I play?"

Bobby answered, "Sure. Just run home and get my glove."

When Joe returned with the glove, eager to play baseball alongside his big brother, he found out it was just a ruse and his brother had no intention of letting him join the game that day.

His father happened to be passing in his cab and saw Joe crying. He pulled up beside him and rolled down his window. "Got anything going on today, Joe?" Joe jumped in the cab and spent the entire day with his father, sharing hamburgers at the local bar and grill. (Joe still swears it was the best hamburger ever.) Later, a handgun slid out from underneath the driver's seat. Joe had never seen a gun before. No words were spoken about it, just a secret acknowledgement between father and son.

When Joe was around eight, his family moved out of the projects into a three-bedroom house in the suburbs. The house had a driveway, a back yard, and a garage—none of which he'd ever experienced before.

But when Joe was 11 years old and Joseph was 43, he suffered a fatal heart attack at work and passed away a little later at the hospital. Joe heard about it from one of his sisters. Ironically, his father's death saved his own life when much later, Joe recognized the early symptoms of his own heart attack from having listened to his sister talk about the numbness and pain their father had experienced.

Return to, and Escape from, the Projects

Following the death of his father, Joe, a sixth grader, found himself facing a future of walking a tightrope without a safety net. His father was his security, stability, and chief role model. Also, the death of her husband was the turning point in his mother's alcoholism.

With the life-insurance money, Joe's mother bought a new car, a bad decision. Their nice suburban home was foreclosed and the family had to return to public housing.

Soon, his mother took up with an ex-convict barfly named Johnny who, when he was drunk, often smacked Joe around. Joe was relieved when his mother and Johnny disappeared for days at a time, even though she didn't leave any food in the house for him or his siblings.

One night, his older sister Mary Jo, who had since married and moved out of the house, came by and saw the conditions in which her siblings were living. Together with her older sister Betty, they confronted their mother, insisting on taking their younger brothers and sisters away from her. Their mother resisted, but later it became clear that she didn't care about her children; she didn't want to lose her monthly government check.

Mary Jo, only 21 and recently married, took Joe and his sister Judy into her home, while Betty took the two youngest siblings, Julianne and Tim. Joe slept on the couch and on a cot in the apartment until Mary Jo and her husband Tom bought a house near her workplace, which had bedrooms enough for all. Even so, Joe wasn't the most well-behaved kid and taking him in couldn't have been easy for a young married couple. But they gave him a home, provided him stability, and likely saved his life — beyond the influence of childhood friends who chose poor life paths that Joe could easily have followed.

George was one of his best friends from the projects. Bigger and older than Joe, he was a burglar. Had Joe remained in the area, he most likely would have ended up on the same destructive trajectory as George and others. Indeed, one of Joe's other close childhood friends was later put to death in the Ohio state penitentiary.

Life in this home was very different than anything Joe had ever known. There were no drunken fights; there was an established routine. The transition took time, but he knew he had it good there. He began to make friends. When they asked him about where he previously lived, he lied. He was afraid the truth would change their attitude toward him and he would lose ground in this new life.

He attended the local Catholic high school, where the boys were separated from the girls. He had grown into a striking young man and the girls didn't fail to notice. It was standard practice that the girls asked the boys to prom. Meeting different young girls from various grades and schools, Joe eventually attended about 10 different proms throughout his high school years.

His brother-in-law, Tom, continued to fulfill the role as a substitute father until he became one himself. By the time his sister and brother-in-law began growing their own family, Joe was old enough to go into the service.

Military Service and Marriage

Into the Navy

Joe served a year in the Naval Reserves in high school, figuring he'd join the Navy after graduation. It was winter 1961, he was 18, and affording college was out of the question. But he learned about the GI Bill, which he could use to help pay for tuition. He would also get on-the-job training in a useful occupation.

The temperature was about two degrees in Cleveland with heavy snowdrifts everywhere when he headed downtown to the recruiting office. The recruiter asked him where he'd like to go to boot camp. Joe asked what his choices were and when he heard about San Diego, he envisioned palm trees and no snow. That day, he was on a plane for the first time. When he arrived at 9 p.m., he stepped into a balmy 61 degrees. Waking up the next morning, it was like he'd come to the Land of Oz.

Joe soon discovered that his time in the Naval Reserves, including boot camp and a year of service, facilitated his training. The 12 weeks flew by, with all kinds of new experiences for a Midwest boy in California. At the end, he was assigned as an Aviation Seaman Apprentice and reported across the bay at the Naval Air Station North Island for immediate duty at the Aircraft Maintenance Division. There, his duties involved pre-flight tasks such as performing visual inspections of aircraft, running the engines to ensure they were operating correctly, and fueling and cleaning the aircraft.

Joe worked with everything from jets and large transports to propeller-driven and small civilian-type planes. Some were from World War II and still in operation. One of the greatest benefits of his job was the opportunity to fly in them. But first he had to attend the Aviation Physiology Training Center at North Island. Training included indoctrination in high-altitude-pressure breathing, the use of survival and night-vision equipment, and the Martin/ Baker ejection seat — an actual ejection-seat simulator that "shot" trainees up the rails. One instructor described it thus, "The pilot will, in an emergency, shout, 'Eject! Eject! Eject!' and if you ask any questions, you'll be talking to yourself. The pilot will have already ejected."

Joe took every opportunity to go aloft with various pilots, some having flown in World War II and Korea and so skilled, they could make the aircraft do things he thought planes weren't meant to do. During one test flight, the T-28 flew straight up until it reached 29,000 feet. At that altitude, when the plane couldn't climb any higher, Joe could count the prop blades, because they turned so slowly, even at maximum engine power. The pilot then let the plane slide backwards and turned the aircraft toward the ground as it picked up speed. At that point, Joe relaxed. He could no longer count the blades on the prop after it resumed normal operation.

Test flights were usually flown over a military area

around El Centro, California, approximately 100 miles east of San Diego. The tests often included a "sand-blower" flight, in which the aircraft was flown just above the level of nearby sand dunes.

One evening when they were returning to San Diego from San Francisco in a T-33, the pilot asked Joe if he'd ever seen the lights of Los Angeles at night. When Joe answered yes, the pilot responded, "Not like this!" He turned the T-33 completely upside down. Afterwards, Joe thought, "You're right. I've never seen Los Angeles at night like that!" And he never did again.

Joe spent two years at North Island. While there, he met a young woman, Colleen Griffin. They were married in July 1962, when Joe was just 20 years old and Colleen was 19.

After North Island, he was transferred to Ream Field, a Naval Auxiliary Air Station in Imperial Beach, about 15 miles south. Ream Field was home to all the helicopter squadrons in the area. There, he completed a two-month training course on the state-of-the-art helicopter used in anti-submarine warfare, the Sikorsky SH-3A Sea King. After training, he was assigned to an anti-submarine helicopter squadron. In October 1963, the squadron deployed to the South China Sea aboard the aircraft carrier USS Hornet. Other than having to leave Colleen and his new son Bobby, he didn't mind, since he was going to sea and had only about a year left on his enlistment.

Life at Sea

The Hornet was famous for its actions in the Pacific during World War II. Whenever the aircraft carrier docked in Japan, the crew hosted an open house and thousands of Japanese citizens lined up to tour the ship.

The *Hornet* was in port in Japan on November 22, 1963, when President John F. Kennedy was assassinated. All military personnel assigned to the ship were recalled and ordered to put to sea as quickly as possible. Tensions were high in the immediate hours following the assassination and the Pentagon readied the military for possible action. But once the details from Dallas become known, personnel returned to normal peacetime duties.

The outpouring of affection by the Japanese people following the president's death really touched Joe. In the cities, black banners were spread over the streets and department-store windows. People openly sobbed during President Kennedy's televised funeral. Many people came up to the naval personnel to clasp their hands and bow in respect.

For the next few months, Joe's helicopter squadron steamed around the South China Sea with other squadrons that made up the *Hornet's* air wing.

Joe spent a lot of time at sea and loved every minute of it. Primarily, he worked the flight deck at night, 6 p.m. until 6 a.m., seven days a week. All types of aircraft surrounded him, engines running, preparing to take off. His work required a lot physically and he was in constant motion, maneuvering around all these catapulting planes and hovering helicopters. Disasters weren't uncommon: plane crashes on the flight deck, personnel blown overboard, jet-fuel fires — the flight deck of an aircraft carrier is one of the most dangerous work sites in the world. The most dangerous time for everyone involved was when the planes and choppers returned and had to land on a pitching heaving deck smaller than some parking lots, especially in nasty weather. Joe gave enormous credit to the pilots and their large *huevos*.

One time, an aircraft armed with rockets overshot the

deck and was dangling over the side of the carrier, held only by the arresting cable and tail hook. The Marine pilot was still in his seat, upside down; ejecting would have propelled him directly into the sea. A flight-deck sailor tied a line around himself, then crawled out onto the aircraft hanging over the ocean to retrieve the very grateful pilot. All the while, the aircraft was leaking fuel from a drop tank and the tail hook had to be cut to release the aircraft, which fell into the ocean.

Twice, Joe left the carrier on helicopter missions — one to the Marine Corp Air Station in Iwakuni, Japan, for special flight-crew training, the other a week-long trip in early 1964 to a base in Southeast Asia.

While at the base, Joe spoke with an intelligence officer about the current military situation in Laos and Vietnam. The officer mentioned a large buildup of North Vietnamese troops along the Ho Chi Minh trail, a military supply route running from North Vietnam through Laos and Cambodia to South Vietnam, all names that would become all-too-familiar to Joe and the nation in the months to come.

In February 1964, Joe flew off the aircraft carrier, stopping all over Southeast Asia on his way to the Naval Station on Treasure Island in San Francisco Bay to await his discharge. Right after he received his walking papers, he headed back to San Diego to see Colleen and his son Bobby, who was three months old when Joe last deployed.

During his deployment, Colleen and Bobby lived with her parents in Coronado. Arriving at his in-law's house, he saw the Christmas tree was still standing. It was February, but they'd left the decorations in place, so Joe could enjoy them when he returned. Bobby was now nine months old and had grown more than Joe had anticipated.

He was relieved to be home with his family and ready

for his next career move. But as he looked ahead, he also looked back. He was thankful for his time in the Navy and the experience he'd gained. He wished his shipmates Godspeed in their continued journeys.

Welcome to the Coast Guard

The same month Joe was discharged from the Navy, he received a letter from the Army requesting that he stop by their downtown San Diego recruiting office. He thought the letter was some sort of military mix-up, so he went to the office. The recruiter asked his name, glanced down at his list, and replied, "This is no mistake. Your name is right here." Joe's military specialty made him eligible for recruitment into the Army at the rank of warrant officer to begin training as a helicopter pilot.

"Nice offer ... bad timing," Joe thought, recalling his conversation with the intelligence officer about the trouble brewing in Southeast Asia.

The Army recruiting office was shared by the Coast Guard. When Joe finished speaking with the Army recruiter, a Coast Guard recruiter approached him, explaining that the Coast Guard would soon be getting new gas-turbine helicopters, similar to the ones on which Joe had worked during his Navy service. Offhand, he mentioned that the Coast Guard had no one enlisted with Joe's level of helicopter qualifications. Joe knew he had an edge. When the recruiter asked Joe what it would take to get him on board, he replied, "A written contract guaranteeing flight pay, my Petty Officer ranking in the Navy, and a guarantee to be stationed in San Diego for the next four years."

Those conditions made their way up the chain of command, then back down to Joe, all being met. A few weeks later, Joe received his orders and reported for duty.

Air-Crewman Responsibilities

Joe was assigned to air-crewman training on the Sikorsky H-19 helicopter. This was an older model, having served the Coast Guard since 1951, but it was well-maintained and operated by some of the best pilots with whom Joe had ever flown. He trained from June to October 1964 and was certified as an air crewman of the H-19. Later, Joe was certified on a number of other aircraft, including the HU-16E Albatross, a twin-engine propeller-driven sea plane used on extended search-and-rescue missions (eventually replaced by the famous C-130 Hercules).

At one point, Joe and a group of other airmen were deployed to the Sikorsky helicopter manufacturing plant in Stratford, Connecticut, where they received intensive training on the new HH-52 Seaguard helicopters. The highlight of the trip was meeting Igor Sikorsky, the designer and pilot of the first viable American helicopter in 1939. Sikorsky's contributions to the design and production of helicopter and fixed-wing aircraft are legendary.

Desperate Situations

As a Coast Guard air crewman, Joe was responsible for: preflight inspections; weight and balance issues; communications, radio, and navigation systems; rescue equipment; search-and-rescue, hoist, and towing procedures; engine analysis; troubleshooting emergency repairs and emergency crew survival, and much more.

A lot of the job was technical, but Joe also performed numerous rescue operations that required nerves of steel. One such incident was a night rescue of a sailor from a vessel breaking into pieces off a rocky Mexican shoreline. Heavy rains and high winds combined for low visibility and high instability. The situation was worsened by the loss of the vessel's radio transmitter. Only a lucky break on the visible search allowed Joe and his helicopter pilot to locate the stranded craft. It took two tries of the pilot being directed by Joe to position the aircraft and Joe lowering the rescue harness, but the sailor was lifted into the air just before his sailboat disintegrated. Fortunately, the man wasn't badly injured.

In another emergency call, four teenagers were trapped on a ranch, surrounded by backcountry forest and brush fires. The Coast Guard was now flying the new Sikorsky HH-52 amphibious helicopter that could land in the water to complete rescues. Through thick smoke, Joe spotted the four teenagers in a pond clinging to a small dock. The pilot had to assume the pond was deep enough for a landing and set down as quickly as possible near the teens. Joe pulled them onboard and the pilot turned the helicopter around in the water to face the wind. By this time, the fire had surrounded them. As the helicopter lifted off, its rise was slow because of the extremely hot air. The aircraft shuddered as it labored to ascend from the pond.

Joe watched the tailpipe temperature gauge moving toward 696 degrees Celsius (1,284 degrees Fahrenheit), the maximum operating temperature of the engine. It got very close to the limit, but as they gained lift, their air speed increased and they passed safely through the smoke and flames. All gauges returned to normal and the pilot landed at a nearby safe location.

Joe knew the teens had been traumatized and when they hugged him with tears streaming down their faces and thanked him for saving their lives, he told them their own quick thinking was the reason they survived. Entering the pond gave the helicopter crew time to get them out. He said, "You're as responsible for your survival as we are." Joe knew that victims often blame themselves and, in this situation at least, they were blameless survivors.

Joe also participated in many emergency calls in which victims, unfortunately, didn't survive their ordeals. In those events, he recovered their remains and delivered them to the coroner at the base. Many of the calls involved military aircraft declaring emergencies on land and over the ocean and, sadly, most of those calls were for recovery only. Many of those crews were victims of tragic and violent aircraft crashes, but civilians weren't immune from them either. During one six-month stretch, every call—and there were many—to which Joe responded had no survivors. He was given the call sign, "Dirty Joe the Body Snatcher."

The Coast Guard often launches search-and-rescue missions when no one else will go, placing personnel in unpredictable and dangerous situations. When the emergency calls come in, no one knows what perilous circumstances the rescuers will enter. And no one is guaranteed a safe return. From time to time, Joe and his colleagues had to rescue their own from aircraft downed during operations.

On one occasion, Joe and a pilot were conducting a night search off the coast when a fog bank suddenly enveloped them. They headed back to base, but the closer they got to land, the denser the fog grew. They were also facing a low-fuel situation. They requested assistance from the Naval Air Station at North Island.

North Island vectored them out over the ocean and

turned them around, so they could attempt an instrument approach where fewer buildings and obstructions cut their landing risks. Doing so, their fuel fell to the lowest level Joe had ever seen. Visibility was down to zero and they knew they had one shot only.

Ground Control Approach finally ordered them to stop forward motion and hover. They complied and were told to set the helicopter down. Unable to see a thing, the pilot slowly took them down to land, without even the guidance of runway lights. A ground-support vehicle appeared out of the fog and they'd just started taxiing behind when the helicopter suddenly shut down. They were out of fuel. If that had happened less than a minute earlier, they wouldn't have made it.

Another task on the Coast Guard's agenda was ocean-survival training for flight crews of commercial airlines with overwater routes. Crews watched instructional films and were then taken about two miles offshore, where Joe and others demonstrated live helicopter rescues. The flight crews were then transferred to a 30-man raft with an instructor and shown how to operate all the survival equipment kept in the raft. Joe jumped from the helicopter into the ocean to display how to enter the raft from the ocean, using boarding ramps.

On one such occasion, Joe noticed a B-25 from North Island circling overhead. The aircraft's circling pattern wasn't unusual, but the length of time was. Routine procedure dictated that all area aircraft and air stations were notified of Coast Guard training drills. While Joe was chatting with a flight attendant, she pointed toward land and yelled, "Look!"

Joe saw the B-25 descend and crash into the ocean.

The Coast Guard helicopter and a nearby cutter

responded immediately to the crash site. They later learned that the B-25 hadn't been informed of the training exercises and was justifiably circling the site in due diligence. Unfortunately, the pilot forgot to switch fuel tanks and they ran out of fuel.

The flight attendant asked Joe, "Was that part of the demonstration?"

Joe responded, "No. The Coast Guard isn't in the habit of crashing perfectly good aircraft to demonstrate ocean-survival techniques."

In 1966, a Coast Guard pilot told Joe that a program had been created in which ten Coast Guard pilots would be assigned to the Air Force rescue squadrons in Vietnam. He explained that the Air Force had acquired modern helicopters, but lacked skilled and experienced aviators. This pilot was considering volunteering for the mission and wanted to know if Joe thought he was good enough—not just to qualify, but to survive.

"I would fly with you here or there," Joe responded. "You're one of the best pilots I've ever flown with and I'd say that about you and only a handful of others."

The pilot volunteered, was selected for the program, and was sent to Vietnam for a year's tour of duty. After many years, Joe looked him up and learned he made it back home with a chest full of medals. Joe was relieved, as he'd felt a little responsible for his volunteering. That pilot reached the rank of Admiral before retiring after a distinguished career.

Of the ten Coast Guard helicopter pilots assigned to Vietnam, only one was killed in action: Lt. Jack Rittichier. A mere 11 days after reporting for duty, Lt. Rittichier was awarded the first of two Distinguished Flying Crosses for rescuing four Army helicopter pilots from two downed aircraft. If this isn't a testimony to the quality of the pilots in the Coast Guard, nothing is.

Joe received three Sikorsky Helicopter Rescue Awards, rescue emblems signed by the aviation pioneer Igor Sikorsky bestowed for skill and courage while participating in a life-saving rescue mission. But ask him and he'll tell you that no award takes the place of the face of a person rescued within minutes or even seconds of losing his or her life. On many occasions, he witnessed the victim's look of terror transform to a look of gratitude.

Joe loved his career in rescue operations. His intense training and fortitude paid off countless times, because to him, failing was never an option. In 1967, he was named Aircrewman of the Year. To this day, Joe is unable to describe the sensation of knowing that you've saved another person's life. To be directly responsible for ensuring someone wakes up the next day and has an opportunity to live life brings a unique satisfaction.

At times, he was frightened beyond words and after responding to many no-survivor callouts — especially military-aircraft crashes — he knew that any one of them could have been him. After serving his four years, Joe left the Coast Guard with a modest sense of pride, knowing he'd done a good job.

And he was on his way to a much "safer" career — as a San Diego police officer.

Law Enforcement

A Committed Applicant

In July 1968, Joe was employed at the San Diego utility company in a position with good prospects. With his military background, however, he also believed strongly in the mission of law enforcement and its role in society. But it wasn't only his moral code that prompted him to apply to become a recruit with the San Diego Police Department. More than 1,200 applications would be submitted, out of which only 80 individuals would be selected to start the next class. Joe wanted to beat the odds.

The series of recruiting tests included written and physical examinations, a stress interview, a polygraph exam, an interview with the deputy chief of police, and a psychological evaluation.

About a month later, he was notified that he'd been rejected — not for failing any of the tests, but due to his height. Joe stood five-eight, an inch shorter than the minimum height requirement.

But a month after that, in September 1968, he was again contacted by the San Diego Police Department, which had lowered the height requirement for police officers to 5'8", permitting him to continue with the application process.

Joe was concerned with only one part of the process: the hearing test. He'd suffered high-frequency hearing loss while working on the flight decks of aircraft carriers and spending hundreds of hours flying in helicopters. He'd also been denied a position as a gas-turbine test-cell operator for a company that made auxiliary power units for commercial aircraft, because they were afraid that additional exposure to the noise of the engines would exacerbate his hearing problem over time.

A San Diego County doctor performed the physical exams for the police department. Joe assumed the hearing test would involve putting on a headset and responding to various frequency signals. But the doctor told him to walk to the other side of the room, face the window, and whenever he heard the doctor call out numbers, to raise his hand. Joe thought the doctor was joking, so he turned to look at him. The doctor instructed him to turn back toward the window as he started speaking numbers in a whisper. Joe raised his hand and the doctor said, "You're hearing is fine. You pass."

Surprised and relieved, Joe then participated in the stress interview. Three police lieutenants tried to fluster and excite applicants. For example, one lieutenant questioned Joe about his height, doubting his ability to take a larger person into custody who was resisting arrest. Joe responded, "I'll just make sure I'm number one in my defensive-tactics class," to which the lieutenant responded, "I'll hold you to that." Later, Joe would go back and tell this lieutenant that he did as he'd intended — finished number one in that class.

Finally, the deputy chief reviewed Joe's test results, stood up, shook Joe's hand, and welcomed him to the San Diego Police Department.

Up until that point, Joe hadn't been entirely convinced that he wanted to be a cop. But he was proud that he'd passed all the testing and evaluations and was one of the 6% of applicants accepted. As he was walking out the door, he was congratulated by the chief's staff member in charge of recruit training. Any lingering doubts were dispelled and Joe was sure that this was the right path for him.

The Police Academy and Rookie Time

Joe figured his eight years in the military had prepared him for the police academy. He was partially right, but there was much to learn.

The training began with 12-hour days over three weeks, during which new recruits received instruction in firearms, the California Penal Code, and advanced first aid. They then spent four hours a day, six days a week, in the academy classroom and eight hours a day with a Field Training Officer (FTO) in patrol cars, working with several different FTOs.

The FTOs shared a wealth of experience with Joe. One knew the penal code inside and out. Another coached him in the amount of force necessary to subdue a subject who was resisting arrest. A third instructed him in effective report writing, often saying, "The way to plainclothes detective is through a well-written report."

The academy program involved all aspects of a police officer's duties and lasted 12 weeks. Once completed, graduates were assigned to patrol and traffic shifts and remained on probation until the first anniversary of their admission to the academy. A new officer could be immediately terminated with no explanation. During that first year, various shift commanders monitored the activities and problem-solving abilities of the new officers and determined shift assignments. As rookie officers, they were assigned the least desirable shifts and days off, which were allotted by seniority and performance. However, they also began to feel the camaraderie of other officers.

Uniformed Patrol

First Night on Patrol

Joe was assigned to foot patrol in a business district in East San Diego from 8 p.m. to 4 a.m. His objective was to prevent burglaries after the businesses had closed. The job consisted of a lot of door shaking and doorknob twisting, finding a surprising number of businesses that neglected or forgot to lock their doors or set their alarms after closing.

Around 2 a.m. on his first night on foot, he observed a subject entering the front alcove of a jewelry store. He followed, made contact, and began questioning him as to why he was window shopping at that time of night. Another foot-patrol officer, also working his first night on a nearby beat, showed up. Joe asked the subject for his identification and as he removed his wallet from a rear pocket, he exposed a blue-steel handgun tucked inside his waistband.

"Freeze!" Joe ordered the subject. "He's got a gun in his waistband — get it!"

The suspect reached for the gun. Joe drew his weapon and stuck the barrel into the subject's neck. Simultaneously, the other office grabbed the gun.

In hindsight, it was as though the incident unfolded in slow motion. Joe knew he'd drawn his weapon, but didn't remember doing it. He later attributed his quick reflexes to the great training he'd received. The two rookies handcuffed the subject, who was charged with carrying a concealed weapon.

When the patrol car pulled up to transport the prisoner, one of the officers said, "You know, I've been on the department for two years and I have yet to arrest anyone for carrying a concealed weapon. You've been on the street alone for six hours and you arrest one! It looks like you're going to have a very exciting career."

When Joe returned to the station, his sergeant told him he'd done a good job and that his report was well-written. Not bad for a first night.

"Call the Captain"

Joe patrolled various neighborhoods for a year, which included businesses, single-family houses, and apartments. He made a conscious effort to become familiar with the business owners and residents on his beat and became especially friendly with one mother and her 20-year-old daughter, who was paralyzed from the waist down and used a wheelchair. This hardworking mom waitressed on the midnight shift in a downtown coffee shop.

Then, on Christmas morning, he received a radio call: "Call the captain." Joe learned that he'd been assigned to make a death-notification visit to a resident in his area whom he knew well. This was the hardest duty for any cop, but as he learned the details, his heart sank. Being Christmas, he suspected that this would be the saddest notification he'd ever have to make.

He first went to the building manager's apartment to inform her of what happened and ask that she bring the key and accompany him to the disabled girl's apartment. The manager entered first and explained to the girl that a police officer was there to talk to her. While fighting to hold back his own emotions, Joe told her that her mother had been struck by a car and killed while crossing the street on her way home.

Joe's heart ached as he watched the daughter experience sheer and utter shock, then pure agony—all nearly bringing this tough cop to his knees. He stood by her as her grief unfolded, experiencing vicariously the terror of this poor disabled girl who was now totally alone in this world. Joe knew they had no relatives in the area. On the spot, he turned his sorrow into a vow that he would find a way to help her.

The apartment manager had known the girl since she was 12 years old and offered to look after her until a family member or viable alternative could be identified. In the next hour or so, the girl remembered the name of a relative who lived in Pennsylvania, so Joe got on the phone with the state police, trying to locate a person or an agency to offer care. The fact that it was Christmas morning made his job more difficult.

On his way back to the station, Joe stopped at a church. The silence was palpable as parishioners watched him enter in full uniform, a humbled authority figure seeking solace on a sacred day. Later, Joe got a call that the girl's relatives had been found and they were making preparations to travel to San Diego.

The girl, and her mother's remains, were turned over to the relatives' care. From that day on, when Joe worked a patrol car on Christmas, his heart skipped a beat whenever he heard the radio dispatcher's words, "Unit one, call the captain."

That same year, Joe responded to a similar call, a welfare check on several children in their home. The house was in complete disarray, with rancid food and human feces scattered throughout and evidence of drug use. The four kids ranged from five to 12 years old and Joe learned that the mother hadn't been home for some time. As he searched for other signs of child abuse and abandonment, he couldn't help but be reminded of his own childhood. The more Joe uncovered, the more he knew with certainty that these children must be removed from the deplorable conditions, even though the emotional toll on them would be substantial.

He sat down with them and said, "Listen, you guys, I know you're upset. In fact, I know exactly how you feel. Believe it or not, I went through the same thing when I was your age. Leaving your house will be a good thing for you, just as it was for me. The help I got when I was young, like the kind you're getting today, is what enabled me to become a policeman." With that, he took custody of the children and personally transported them to a receiving facility, where they'd receive badly needed attention.

After they arrived, he promised he would return to make sure they were okay. But the staff told him that he should wait at least a week before visiting, to give them enough time to settle in and adjust to their new surroundings.

Those kids remained on Joe's mind every day. When he finally returned to the receiving home and saw them, he barely recognized them. They were clean and obviously well-nourished.

Before Joe left that day, one of the supervisors thanked him for caring so much. Joe said, "Not too long ago, I went through the same exact thing."

The War Comes Home

One afternoon, Joe was dispatched to a residence in an upper-middle-class neighborhood, where he learned that a woman was sitting alone in her kitchen in obvious distress — with a 45-caliber semi-automatic pistol on the table next to her.

As Joe was looking through the window, the woman saw him and started explaining to him that her son, an only child in his early 20s, had been drafted by the Army. He had answered the call of duty against her wishes and deployed to Vietnam. He was killed in action earlier that week. She wanted to speak to General William Westmoreland, the commander of the U.S. forces in Vietnam, before she took her own life, which to her was no longer worth living.

Joe asked her to surrender the weapon, but she refused. So he ordered her not to reach for the gun, which would not only put them both in danger, but then he wouldn't be able to help her. She agreed.

Joe called for backup. When a sergeant arrived, they formulated a plan. Joe kept the woman occupied in conversation through the open window, while the sergeant found the front door unlocked. He then went next door and used the phone to call the captain, who agreed to pose as an aide to Westmoreland and explain to the grieving mother that her son had died a hero, saving the lives of his comrades in the Mekong Delta.

The captain called the woman and she quickly answered the phone. Thus distracted, Joe reached through the window and secured the handgun.

The captain explained that the general wasn't available, but as his aide, he could tell her that if it hadn't been for her son's actions, other mothers would have received the same notifications about their own sons.

As she ended the conversation with the captain with a sorrowful but proud thank you, Joe and the other officer gently took her into custody, then transported her to the inpatient psychiatric unit of the county hospital, where she was committed for a 72-hour emergency evaluation to determine if she was a threat to herself or others. Joe was hopeful she would get the help she desperately needed and deserved, after the tragic loss of her only child in the service of his country.

COP (Community-Oriented Police) Work

Joe arrested a crazed husband with a full-size axe trying to batter down the door of his apartment. His wife had locked him out, afraid for her life. Statements from neighbors corroborated the wife's account that her husband flew into dangerous rages and became violent quickly.

Joe and his backup arrested the husband and informed the neighbors that he would be charged with assault with a deadly weapon and attempted murder. Since it was late afternoon on the Wednesday before Thanksgiving, they could rest easy. Bail would most likely not be set until the following Monday.

On Thanksgiving Day, Joe worked an emergency detail at the jail, which was short-handed. There, he received a call from one of the neighbors of the axe-wielder, telling him that the husband had returned to the apartment building and was threatening people.

Joe checked the release log and confirmed that the suspect had been released on his own recognizance by a judge known to grant ROR releases without suspects posting any bail. Joe also knew where to find a list of home phone numbers for all the local judges. He told the man on the phone that he'd call him back, then dialed the number listed for the judge who released the axe-wielder to make sure it was accurate. It was.

He then re-contacted the neighbor and said, "I'll give you

the judge's home number. You can hand it out to all your neighbors who are trying to have a nice quiet Thanksgiving dinner with family and friends. But you have to abide by one condition—that you don't tell anyone how you got the judge's number."

About 90 minutes later, the man called back to tell Joe that county marshals had taken the husband back into custody. Obviously, the ROR had been rescinded.

The marshals soon showed up at the jail to rebook the suspect. Joe was still there and the husband remembered Joe being in on his arrest the previous day. Joe turned to the suspect and told him sternly, "You don't fuck with my people." Then he told the jail sergeant, "Put his sorry ass in my cell block, so every time he sees me, it'll piss him off more."

Joe returned to the booking area and the sergeant asked him what was going on.

He replied, "Just doing a little Community-Oriented Policing—my way."

The sergeant smiled and shook his head. "Joe, I don't even want to know."

Joe answered, "I knew you wouldn't."

Joe bet the judge was scratching his head at his own Thanksgiving table as he wondered, "How did all those people get my home number?" Little did he know it was a simple matter of "patrolman justice."

No Ghetto

While working in Logan Heights, a predominately African American community, Joe carried with him an old photograph of the projects where grew up. Whenever he was berated for being a white cop working in the "ghetto," he responded, "Ghetto? I don't have any idea what you're talking about. This is a regular residential neighborhood. Here, look at this." After showing the photo, he often got a response such as, "Man, you were poor."

One time, a young punk was telling Joe how tough he was and how Joe had better watch out for him. Joe took out his photo. "Tough? Hell, I knew a sixteen-year-old girl in the projects I grew up in who could whip your ass." The punk's attitude quickly changed.

Soon, Joe noticed how other folks in the neighborhood changed their attitude toward him. When one young guy introduced him to another, he said, "Man, this is that poor cop motherfucker I told you about."

As word of Joe's own "ghetto" childhood spread, work in Logan Heights got a little easier for him.

Joe and his partner were working Unit 16, the toughest area of Logan Heights, when they received a radio call about a man breaking into his ex-girlfriend's apartment. They quickly drove to the location and found the young woman on the street in front of her apartment building. She told them her ex was high on drugs and had punched her in the face. She ran from the apartment in fear, leaving him inside alone. Joe clearly saw physical trauma on the woman's face and believed she was telling them the truth.

Joe and his partner had to force their way into the apartment, but when Joe stumbled inside the doorway, he saw the man standing to his right — then felt something strike the left side of his chest. The ex-boyfriend was holding a 12-inch butcher knife. The suspect ran deeper into the apartment.

Cautiously following, they found the bedroom empty. Looking out the open window, they saw him sprawled on the ground below. He'd jumped out of the second-story window and did a belly flop on a cyclone fence. Joe then looked down and noticed a slash mark across his badge, which had saved him from a serious knife wound.

Joe rode in the ambulance as the man was transported to the hospital. Along the way, the irony of the situation struck him. What a crazy profession he'd chosen! He was now attending to a gravely injured man who had just tried to kill him. But without hesitation, Joe switched roles from defending his own life and protecting an innocent citizen to doing what he could to save the life of this potential murderer.

Most Dangerous Radio Call

Most people believe armed-suspect calls are the most dangerous a police officer receives, but in fact, the most dangerous is a 415 Disturbance. These come in all types: Barking Dog, Loud Music, Yelling. But the most perilous an officer must recognize and prepare for is the Family Disturbance.

Cops respond to hundreds of 415 calls during their careers and more officers lose their lives during these situations than any other type of radio call. In many of these events, police enter a combat situation. Often enough, the *victim* of a domestic assault comes to the aid of the assailant, especially if they're related. This is when law enforcement becomes the enemy and, on too many occasions, the victim. One in particular stands out in Joe's memory: Two officers arrived on the scene and spoke to a homeowner, the subject of the complaint from a neighbor; as they were returning to their patrol car, the man shot both officers in the back, leaving them to die in his driveway.

One of Joe's Family Disturbance calls took a similar twist. When he arrived at the house, an elderly woman came running out screaming, "He's going to kill his sister!"

From inside the house, Joe heard a girl screaming. He ran in to the living room where he saw a young female adult on her back on the floor, facing an adult male who was bent over her punching her in the face with a closed fist. Joe grabbed the brother by the hair and pulled him off. But while Joe was positioning him to apply a standard police sleeper hold to render him unconscious, he felt his night stick being pulled from its holding ring on his belt. When he turned, the sister was coming at him, holding his nightstick like a baseball bat. She swung it right at him, but he managed to maneuver her brother between himself and the bat, which struck her brother hard in the head.

As she approached again, Joe spun her around and subdued her. Before either of them regained consciousness, he put them both in handcuffs. The mother frantically begged Joe to release them, but Joe told her that once he was forced to put his hands on them, they were under arrest.

Lessons from a Field Training Officer

During Joe's third year of working patrol, he was selected as a Field Training Officer (FTO). Just as he had worked under the supervision of an FTO in his academy days, he was now tasked with supervising police recruits. At this time, most of the recruits were former military who had returned recently from service in Vietnam.

Joe knew he had to impress on his recruits that they had to carefully evaluate situations *prior* to taking action. More than likely, they'd be assigned to a one-man patrol car and there would be no radio contact once they left the vehicle. It was, therefore, imperative that every call be thoughtfully assessed and back-up summoned (and waited for) if warranted before the rookies took any action.

An example of this advice played out in Barrio Logan when Joe was working a swing shift with a recruit. They were driving through a residential area when two men driving in the opposite direction passed the patrol car and one yelled loudly, "Fuck you, pig!"

The recruit urged Joe to turn around. "Let's get those guys!"

Joe knew the situation presented a great learning opportunity for the new officer.

Joe made a U-turn and slowly followed. They watched the men park and enter a back yard where a large loud party was well under way. He drove past and parked several houses down, facing the opposite direction, but keeping the subjects' vehicle in sight through his rearview mirror.

He then assessed the situation for the benefit of his recruit. "Did you see the party when we first drove past? These are details you need to notice. I figured the guys in the car who yelled at us were headed there and they were. If we'd confronted them before they got to the party, as you wanted, we were this close to a hundred drunk and potentially hostile people. Now. How many rounds of ammo do we have between us?"

"Thirty-six."

"Right. How far do you think that would get us against a hundred attackers? I can tell you that plenty of cops have wound up in the hospital because they simply reacted — and didn't stay calm. You have to learn to control your gut response when someone offends you, which will happen a lot. Always be aware of what's happening around you and decide on a course of action *first.*" Then Joe explained what their course of action would be.

They watched the vehicle and luckily, they didn't receive

a call to report elsewhere before the two male subjects left the party and walked toward their vehicle. One of them tried unsuccessfully to take the keys away from the other. Joe knew this probably meant the driver was intoxicated. Joe pulled out and followed the suspect's car.

"Why haven't you stopped them yet?"

"Watch and learn."

Joe was aware of what the recruit wasn't: The suspects would soon cross over into the adjacent city's jurisdiction. Right at the border, he activated the lights and siren and pulled the men over while calling for backup. As they made contact with the suspects, the other city's police unit arrived.

In front of the other officer, Joe told the driver he was stopped for suspicion of driving under the influence. "I saw your friend try to take the car keys."

At that point, the passenger shouted to the driver, "Damn it! I told you that you shouldn't drive, because you're drunk!"

The driver responded, "Well, so are *you!*"

The neighboring city's police officer arrested the driver for DUI and the passenger for being under the influence. Right afterwards, Joe walked over, stuck his head in the window of the front seat of the other cruiser, and said to the two in the back seat, "That's 'Fuck you, pig, *sir!*'"

When Joe and the recruit returned to their patrol car, they reviewed the details of the incident.

"First, we let the suspects travel out of San Diego before making the stop. Second, we got the men to admit they were drunk in front of the other officer, who then had no choice but to arrest them. Third, we'll get credit for the arrests, but we won't have to fill out all the paperwork." Joe asked, "*Now* do you see why we didn't chase after them when they insulted us back there?"

"Yes, sir!" the recruit said.

Joe smiled. "Don't ya just love it when good police work happens?"

As an FTO, Joe found that recruits, anxious to jump right into their new career, always wanted to drive the patrol cars. As a rule, Joe allowed them to drive the last three days they were assigned to him.

Once, when he and a new recruit were assigned to a police ambulance unit (a station wagon during this time in San Diego), the young recruit persistently nagged Joe to let him drive. Finally, Joe let the rookie drive, instructing him to head to a nearby car wash prior to going into service. "Nobody wants to travel to the hospital in a dirty ambulance."

The novice asked, "Do you really think people care?"

"Probably not, but I'm not going to the hospitals in a dirty ambulance. It's all image, kid."

Shortly after, the recruit pulled up in line for the car wash. Suddenly, the vehicle behind them crashed into the back of the ambulance, hard enough to break the tailgate window.

"Holy shit!" the recruit yelled, looking at Joe.

Joe said, "Thank you for saving me from a two-day suspension."

"What?"

"If I'd been driving, it would've been an automatic suspension for me, regardless of whose fault it was."

"Really?"

"Yep. Either a suspension or working a day without pay."

This was one of the unfair policies that prompted Joe to run for a position on the Police Officers Association Board of Directors years later.

Joe trained many recruits. In the years that followed, some of them rose to the rank of deputy chief of police.

Single Fatherhood

Around this time, Joe's wife Colleen announced that she was leaving to go "find herself," an expression that was going around in those days and had its roots in the so-called sexual revolution of the '60s. After discussing her issues and their problems together, Joe realized that what she really wanted was just to be single again.

He told her he wanted to keep custody of Bobby, who was eight at the time, and their daughter Kelly, who was five. Though he anticipated resistance, she agreed fully—and moved out the following weekend.

Joe immediately found a housekeeper to fill in the gaps. Rosita was a Mexican national who had a green card, permitting her to work in the U.S.; she was as dependable as they came and Joe and the children soon settled into a new routine.

Joe understood the issues Colleen had with him and his job. But due to his own precarious childhood, he could never fathom that she left her own children. In fact, three months passed and she didn't even contact them, let alone see or take them. Joe kept calling and asking her to visit and take them out, but she came up with one excuse after another. Finally, he confronted her with the fact that she was living with another guy, an officer in the Navy.

"How did you find that out?" she demanded.

"You know, Colleen, I'm still a cop. And what cops do best is investigate. How long did you think you could keep this a secret from me?"

Joe never asked her for a dime of support; he even

offered to pay for her to take Bobby and Kelly on weekend afternoon outings. Finally, during one of their conversations, he realized that everything about her had changed. He later learned that after a car accident, she was prescribed valium for a neck injury. Eventually, she became addicted. Then it began to make more sense to him: Long-term use of the drug changes personality traits and addicts lose interest in things they once cared about, even their own children.

Then, Rosita returned to Mexico and it became intensely challenging for Joe. A friend's daughter had to spend the night as he was working the graveyard shift; then he rushed home to get Bobby and Kelly dressed, fed, and off to school. He managed to sleep for about four hours until Kelly returned; Bobby was in the third grade, but Kelly was in kindergarten, so she attended for only a half-day. He got up and attended to the parenting. That included finding out that kids can handle fast food only for so long; Joe taught himself to cook during this time. At 6 p.m., Joe started three hours of college classes, then began his shift at 10, got off at 6 a.m., and started the whole thing all over again.

Some friends watched Joe for a while, then got together to lend a hand. The wives volunteered to handle the kids during the day, while Joe got an eight-hour stretch of sleep.

Joe says he'd do it all over again. He understood how difficult this time was for him, but from his own childhood, he knew it was *much* more difficult for Bobby and Kelly to understand at their ages. Finally, Joe found another live-in housekeeper and their lives became somewhat normal again. Fortunately, he was blessed with wonderful children.

After a while, Colleen improved. She got help for her valium addiction, started taking the children once a month for a weekend, and became more caring. As the children grew, it was obvious that Kelly needed to be with her mother.

Joe and the children decided that Kelly and Bobby would live with their mother now that she was well and could be depended on to be a responsible parent, with the help of her husband, the naval officer she'd left them for. Joe saw his children on weekends.

Secondary School Task Force

In January 1972, Joe was assigned to a specialized uniformed unit, the Secondary School Task Force. Sixteen uniformed police officers were assigned to junior and senior high schools throughout San Diego. Eight two-officer teams patrolled two high schools and two junior highs. Team members received specialized training in child psychology and juvenile crime and worked directly with the Juvenile Detective Unit of the San Diego Police Department.

Joe wasn't sure about this effort. Over the previous few years, he had worked every area of San Diego, from the Mexican border to La Jolla, arresting some really bad perpetrators. Babysitting a bunch of school kids? He was cynical.

School administrators and counselors proved great to work with, but team members had to win over the teachers and students. Quite a few teachers weren't happy about the teams' armed presence. After all, this was the era in which police, who manned the barricades at anti-war demonstrations in full riot gear, weren't especially popular with citizens.

Task-force officers attended the schools' combined government classes, speaking and answering questions about their jobs and various aspects of juvenile and criminal law. As time and contact with the students went on, the cops noticed a growing acceptance of the teams' presence in the schools. Teachers, students, and Joe became more relaxed. The officers still arrested some students for various crimes, mostly narcotics offenses. But they were also more open to asking questions and the officers were able to quell rumors relating to their activities and the various arrests. Students benefitted from hearing both sides of the story. In a short time, the students began to trust the officers and actually confided in them as they learned that the task-force members would never disclose a student's name related to their various law-enforcement activities.

One night, a student was shot by police while committing a crime. Prior to reporting to their schools the next day, task-force officers were briefed by homicide detectives working the case. The officers arrived at their respective schools with knowledge of the facts. The students were better informed than their parents concerning the event.

Trust continued to grow and students began coming to the officers with information about activities occurring off-campus that concerned them. One case involved a junior high student who reported a man lurking at a school bus stop over several mornings. Joe and his partner went to the bus stop the next morning and confronted the man. They learned that he was a registered sex offender of children on parole. All the students waiting for the bus witnessed the man being handcuffed and taken away.

Joe and other officers went to the junior high to assure the students that the man was in jail for violation of parole. They answered questions from students who wanted to know the circumstances of the man's arrest.

Though the teams were assigned to specific schools, the officers operated as a whole team for all the designated schools. If word got out about a scheduled gang fight, all 16 cops and eight cars converged on the location. The activities of the officers clearly prevented criminal activities both on and off campus.

Joe was promoted to detective in 1972 and left the task force. But he and his partner were included in that year's yearbook pictures, which he considered a great honor.

The formation of the Secondary School Task Force by the San Diego Police Department was ahead of its time, and was successful because of the cooperation of everyone involved. As the public debates solutions to the violent acts committed against students today, too often by students, Joe believes that providing armed law enforcement at schools is a critical step in controlling the continued school killings around the country. And he doesn't know a single cop who wouldn't welcome the chance to stop these horrific school crimes.

Promotion to Detective and Burglary Detail

A promotion to detective required a minimum of four years in uniform, a recommendation from the Patrol Commanding Officer, and an interview with the Detective Division Commander. Joe was asked by the commander if he would work the Vice Unit and he replied honestly that he'd prefer to do felony investigations. The commander thanked him and Joe figured he'd just thrown away his opportunity by refusing the offer to go to vice. But lo and behold, Joe was promoted to detective in the Burglary Detail on his fourth anniversary with the police department. Joe spoke with the commander later and said he thought he'd blown his chance of making detective after passing on the vice offer. The commander replied that he wouldn't have wanted that assignment either!

The burglary unit investigated property crimes such as petty theft, shoplifting, grand theft, and breaking and entering of homes and businesses. Newly promoted detectives typically got assigned to burglary and worked specific districts. Joe was assigned to the Harbor and Pt. Loma areas of San Diego.

Burglaries are hard to solve. Usually, there are no witnesses and very little evidence is left at the scene. Residential break-ins generally occur during the day when family members are gone. Business break-ins occur after the business closes at night, or early mornings. Some of the reported burglaries are actually inside-job insurance frauds.

Burglaries are often solved by the arrest of a suspect for a particular break-in. The suspect might want to cut a deal and admit to other burglaries.

One such suspect was named Murphy, a 45-year-old career burglar. Detectives, including Joe, arrested Murphy for an apartment break-in and he agreed to take them to all the locations he had burglarized and disclose what he had taken from each site. Murphy led the detectives to more than 150 locations that he'd burglarized over a two-year period, often committing more than one per day.

Murphy explained his tactics on entry and how he used the phone at each location to call his fence (the person interested in buying the stolen property). While on the phone, Murphy described items at the location and the fence indicated the ones he'd buy. "No sense lugging around stuff I couldn't sell," Murphy admitted.

Murphy loaded the items into a vehicle and drove a few blocks, where he'd parked another vehicle that was never at the crime scene, so it wasn't seen by any possible witnesses to the break-in. He parked the vehicle containing the stolen property and drove off in the second vehicle. Two days later, he returned and, if the police hadn't found the vehicle used in the burglary, he drove it directly to his fence and sold the stolen goods.

Murphy was not only infamous, he was the best thief Joe had ever met. With his confessions, detectives were able to close all 150 city-wide cases. Murphy's description of the property he stole matched the burglary reports given by the victims. He'd done prison time before and was headed back after this arrest. He used that time to quit his addiction to heroin. By cooperating with the detectives, Murphy's sentence was reduced by half.

Occasionally, Joe was assigned a petty shoplifting case. Perpetrators were taken into custody by patrol officers, then brought to the Burglary Unit for processing by a detective.

Once, a patrol officer brought in an 18-year-old girl with a six-month-old in a stroller. She'd been caught at a department store after concealing a man's shirt and some diapers, all worth about $12. The arresting officer explained that she'd cooperated fully, explaining that she took the items because her military-dependents check had been delayed. Her husband was on his way home from being deployed on a ship off the coast of Vietnam for nine months. She wanted to give him the shirt as a Christmas gift.

She hadn't been charged yet, so Joe had two options. He could arrest the woman and put her in jail, placing the baby at Hillcrest Receiving Home. Or he could take a report and have the city attorney issue a notify warrant.

Joe asked the officer to contact the store manager and request that he drop the charges, assuring him the stolen items would be returned. The officer made the call, then returned and informed Joe that the manager would not drop the charges. He wanted to send a clear message to all shoplifters that there was no mercy at his store.

Joe's sergeant said, "Joe, do what you think is right."

Joe called the store manager and offered to pay for the items due to the extenuating circumstances and the fact that Christmas was 10 days away.

The store manager was having none of it.

After a little back and forth, Joe said, "After reviewing the case, I believe the evidence isn't strong enough to prosecute, so *I'm* dropping all the charges. You'll get your twelve dollars."

Joe returned to the interview room and told the woman she could keep the shirt and diapers, as they'd been paid for. "But don't shop at that store again."

As Joe returned to his desk, the sergeant stopped him and handed over a wad of bills amounting to more than $100. The other detectives had all kicked in and wanted Joe to give the money to the woman with a Merry Christmas message from the Burglary Detail.

Joe asked the patrol officer to give the woman and baby a ride to her car. She told them she didn't have a car and used the bus for transportation. So Joe asked the officer to take them home, regardless of how far away she lived.

Joe recalls this being a very nice Christmas. Cops really do care.

4

Narcotics

Narcotics Task Force and San Diego's Unified Approach

After only six months working in the Burglary Unit, Joe was transferred to the Narcotics Unit of the police department. He wasn't sure why. Most new detectives spent a year or two in Burglary. Also, while in uniform, he hadn't made a significant number of narcotics-related arrests, though he did send some viable informants over to their unit. At first, he thought he was being transferred because he did something wrong, but the Investigations Division Inspector who recommended Joe for Narcotics soon told him, "Your arrests didn't matter. What mattered was you were very good at turning suspects into confidential informants and handing them off to Narcotics detectives, who made large seizures based on the CIs' information. I knew I needed to put you in either Narcotics or Community Relations, due to your unique abilities at persuasion."

Still, Joe was understandably nervous. Going undercover is like learning to swim by jumping into very deep water. He had no experience and knew he could easily get himself killed.

He didn't buy new clothes; he simply wore what he did when he was off-duty. He tried growing facial hair, but hated it. He also knew that if he looked like a low-level street seller, he wouldn't be able to rise above that level and he wanted to be the guy who had the wares and the cash to buy large quantities from the suppliers and cartels.

The day he reported to Narcotics, Joe was sitting in the reception area waiting to be admitted to the unit, when a man in street clothes came in and sat down near him. As they waited, the guy looked at Joe and said, "I know you. We've met before."

Joe looked at him and said, "I'm really sorry, but I don't remember meeting you."

The man stuck out his hand. "I'm Gary Gleason."

Joe shook his hand. "Joe Dorsey."

"Well, Joe," Gary said, "you might not remember me, but I'm sure you'll remember the occasion."

Gary explained that they'd met when Joe was in the Coast Guard, part of a helicopter operation to recover the remains of two people from a downed World War II military aircraft in the ocean.

"Now I remember," Joe said. "You were one of the two Navy SEALs who recovered the bodies."

"That's right. Small world, huh?"

Gary was also a San Diego cop being assigned to Narcotics, though their paths hadn't crossed again until that day. As luck would have it, the two new guys to the unit became partners.

They soon learned that the Narcotics Unit was severely underfunded. Most of the equipment was long outdated and personnel often borrowed funds and equipment from other agencies. Joe and Gary were assigned a former fire-department high-mileage car, repainted. The vehicle's doors, hood, and trunk couldn't be opened while in the middle of a drug deal, because the city had sprung for a cheap paint job. Any unexposed area on the vehicle was still fire-engine red. So they could use the cars on street-buy cases only.

Fortunately, shortly after Joe and Gary signed up, the police department's Narcotics Unit merged with the Sheriff's Narcotics Unit and the newly established federal Drug Enforcement Administration (DEA). Thus, on October 15, 1973, the San Diego County Integrated Narcotics Task Force (NTF) was established, with full funding from the DEA.

The city and county narcotics detectives were deputized as U.S. Marshals, sworn to enforce federal laws. DEA agents were deputized as San Diego County Special Deputies, sworn to enforce state laws.

Police and federal officials wondered how well the personnel from these three separate and very different agencies would work together. Joe, as one of the guys on the street, knew that an undercover narcotics agent, well-known at the time as a "narc," focused first and foremost on making sure a deal didn't go bad. The first agent through the door could save your life and the type of badge he wore didn't matter. The group of men selected from the various agencies and departments for this new task force bonded quickly and dispelled all management concerns. They all identified as NTF agents and that was what mattered.

Perks were better at the NTF than at the SDPD. Federal rules applied, including paid time-and-a-half overtime, which the detectives lacked at the police department. They also drove brand-new undercover vehicles that were leased every year, each equipped with state-of-the-art radio systems.

As the NTF developed, it grew in size as well. Other agencies joined the operations, including the federal Bureau of Alcohol, Tobacco, and Firearms, the Internal Revenue Service, the U.S. Marshals Service, the U.S. Attorney's Office, the California Bureau of Narcotics Enforcement, and nearly every police department in San Diego County.

Gary Gleason and Joe were great partners and, given the right equipment and manpower, they both excelled in their positions. As time passed, Joe and Gary received many awards from the DEA — only without the bonus check DEA agents received with *their* awards.

After a year on the NTF, the two were summoned to the Senior DEA Executive's office and asked to consider joining the federal force. "Since you both have been part of the NTF for more than a year, you'll be considered federal agents seeking a transfer," the senior executive explained. "So the usual requirements to join the DEA will be waived — no tests to take, no prerequisites imposed. The only requirement will be to attend the DEA Academy in Georgia."

Joe asked, "If we accept, after training, will we be reassigned to San Diego?"

"I'm sorry, but I can't guarantee that will happen."

All Joe could think about were those miserable winters he'd endured as a kid growing up in Ohio. He'd lived in San Diego too long to consider working in the Northeast or Midwest. Both Joe and Gary politely declined the offer and thanked the executive.

And Justice for All

Joe was busy writing a report at the NTF when the phone rang. Being lunchtime, he was the only agent in the office, so he took the call. A deputy district attorney was trying to locate an agent who was expected to testify as an expert witness in an upcoming narcotics case.

"Sorry, but I don't know his current whereabouts."

"I need someone now. Are you court-certified as a narcotics expert?" the deputy DA asked.

"Yes, I am."

"Can you testify in this case?"

"I can."

"And can you be at the courthouse by one p.m.?"

"Today?"

"Yes."

That gave Joe less than an hour, but he agreed. When he pressed for more details about the case, the deputy DA said he'd be fully briefed when he got there.

While en route to the courthouse, Joe realized that Judge Crawford, with whom he had previous experiences, would be presiding over the case. His first experience with Crawford occurred when Joe was in uniform. Headed to court one day to testify, he was crossing the street in front of the courthouse when Joe noticed a driver parked in the red zone exiting his vehicle. Joe told the driver that he was risking a citation or having his vehicle towed.

The driver heard him, but walked off without any acknowledgement.

Then Joe felt a tap on his shoulder and turned to find Judge Crawford. "I saw that exchange. I want you to take the driver into custody, bring him to my courtroom, and have the vehicle towed."

When Joe did so, the judge sentenced the driver to five days in jail, commencing immediately.

Joe's next contact with Judge Crawford was a radio call he received while on patrol, instructing him to appear in the judge's chambers. When Joe arrived, the judge instructed his bailiff to escort a man into the room. "I'm sick and tired of seeing this guy's drunk ass in my courtroom. I want you to drive him to the East County limits and dump him off."

"Okay, Judge, but the East County line is in the middle of the desert and this is July."

"That's right, Joe." He turned to the man and said, "Good luck."

Joe called his captain for further direction and was told to comply with the judge's orders.

Joe drove the man east for about 80 miles, where he found the closest relief from the heat at a truck stop. He advised him to catch an eastbound ride, warning him that if he came back to San Diego, he'd most likely end up in the same judge's courtroom and sentenced to some serious time behind bars.

Rumors circulated about Judge Crawford's no-nonsense attitude. Joe learned the judge had been in the Army Air Corps during World War II, was shot down over Europe, and was a prisoner of war for many months. One of Joe's favorite movies, *And Justice for All* starring Al Pacino, was rumored to be based on the antics of Judge Crawford.

Joe recalled his previous encounters with Crawford as he entered the courtroom to testify. The DA called Joe to the stand without sharing any information about the case. All Joe knew was that he was testifying as an expert witness.

The DA held up a kilo of marijuana recently smuggled across the border and still in its original packaging. The DA then asked Joe, confident he knew what the response would be, "In your expert opinion, is this enough marijuana to qualify for the charge of possession for sale?"

To the DA's dismay and astonishment, Joe answered, "No, sir."

The DA began to stutter in frustration and asked Joe why he would answer that way. Joe explained that only if the kilo had been broken down into smaller packages, commonly known as "lids," could he honestly testify that it would qualify as possession for sale.

The DA asserted, "How can you possibly render an opinion like that?"

Joe responded, "I see three defendants, each charged with possession for sale and each owning a third of a kilo, which is not an excessive amount for personal use."

The DA, not willing to accept this response, continued to press Joe until Judge Crawford stopped him. "I know Joe Dorsey. I've worked with him on other matters. I believe he's rendered the correct opinion—any expert coming into this court and testifying differently could very well end up in a holding cell, on my orders. I hereby find the three defendants not guilty. They will be released immediately."

As Joe left the witness stand, the judge thanked him, but then did something he'd never seen or heard a judge do. "Joe!" Judge Crawford called.

Joe turned to look back.

The judge told him, "Be careful out there," and *smiled*, a very infrequent occurrence for Judge Crawford.

Close Call

He and Gary Gleason worked four years together in what Joe describes as a "wild ride."

On one case, Joe and fellow narcs were outside a dealer's house while Gary, working undercover, was inside buying several ounces of cocaine. The dealer started a fight with Gary. Hearing the ruckus, the narcs outside knocked the door off its hinges. As he rushed in, Joe noticed a gun protruding from behind the kitchen door, aimed in Gary's direction. Joe shouted, "Drop the weapon!" The suspect had pushed open the swinging kitchen door just enough to aim the gun. When he tried to pull the gun back, his hand blocked the door from swinging back toward him and the gun was still aimed at Gary.

Joe began squeezing the trigger of his service weapon. As the hammer retracted, another agent jumped in front of Joe, directly into the line of his fire. Joe immediately raised his weapon toward the ceiling in the event it fired.

The agent pulled the trigger of his own gun and it misfired.

Meanwhile, the suspect behind the kitchen door managed to drop his gun and withdraw his hand. Joe and the other agent busted through the door and wrestled the suspect to the ground.

The NTF seized several ounces of cocaine and 1,000 pounds of marijuana.

Paraquat

During the time Joe was assigned to the NTF, every San Diego police detective was required to spend one week per year working in the narcotics evidence room at police headquarters. There, evidence was impounded and substances were tested to verify unlawful possession by suspects arrested by the Patrol Division.

While working in the evidence room, Joe received a call from a man inquiring about the Mexican government spraying the marijuana fields with paraquat, an herbicide widely used to control weeds. Joe confirmed the practice. The caller then asked how he could determine if his marijuana had been treated with paraquat.

Joe explained to the caller that his pot would have to be tested.

"Can you test if for me?" the caller asked.

"Sure," Joe replied. "We can do that."

"What do I have to do?"

"Just bring your stash to the police station at Market & Pacific Coast Highway, park in the front lot, and ask the uniformed officer in the business office to call Detective Dorsey." All the while, Joe was trying to keep a straight face. *This guy can't be so stupid. Can he?*

Around 90 minutes later, the man showed up, a young guy about 21. Joe asked to see the weed, so he could test it for paraquat. He expected the young man to pull a plastic baggie of marijuana out of his pocket, but instead the guy said, "It's in the trunk."

Joe got a uniformed officer to accompany him outside.

When the man opened his trunk, to their amazement, they saw about 30 kilos of marijuana. Joe and the officer immediately arrested the guy, who proceeded to protest about entrapment.

"No. There's no entrapment here. You brought the kilos to a location you'd clearly been informed was a San Diego police station. You also parked in front of a building displaying the sign San Diego Police Department."

The young man was charged with possession of marijuana with intent to sell and booked at the county jail. Joe proceeded to the DA's office and presented his report to a newly appointed deputy DA, who was reluctant to believe someone could be that clueless. Just then, the senior DA, whom Joe knew well, showed up and the junior DA asked what he should do. The senior DA said, "Listen, Joe Dorsey could sell ice to an Eskimo in January. Issue the complaint."

A few months later, the young man pled guilty, securing his place at the top of Joe's list of dumbasses.

Confidential Informants

Confidential informants, known as CIs, do exactly what their title implies: They share information, confidentially. Reliable CIs are a valued and important part of police work.

CIs become informants for many reasons. Often, a CI is an everyday citizen, considered reliable by the courts, who performs a civic duty. Others become informants to seek revenge, using their information as a tool to personally hurt someone else. Criminals will become CIs as a shrewd way to eliminate their competition. Other CIs intentionally infiltrate law enforcement to gain information about their activities and active cases. Perhaps the most common is an individual working off a pending criminal charge.

One afternoon, a citizen called Joe's office to report suspicious activity on a desolate street near her house, only three miles from the Mexican border. Joe arranged to meet with this CI at her home. She explained to Joe that on many afternoons, she witnessed a man park a vehicle across the street and walk away. She didn't recognize him and didn't think he lived in or around her neighborhood. Then, after dark, people approached the car carrying big green duffle bags. One person opened the trunk, the eight or so people all placed their bags inside, the trunk was closed, and everyone dispersed.

A second vehicle arrived, usually within two days, and a different man drove the first vehicle away, blending in with the daytime traffic. This was repeated many times a month.

Law enforcement often received calls about parked and abandoned vehicles in residential areas close to the Mexican border. The cars were classified as "suspicious." Officers searched the vehicles, seized any narcotics, and arranged to have them towed. Any activity taking place around these abandoned vehicles, such as the CI reported to Joe, was deemed unusual.

The CI agreed to alert Joe the next time she observed the routine on her street. Soon after their meeting, she called him and reported a parked vehicle she believed would be loaded with the duffle bags that night. Joe and other agents set up surveillance in the CI's home and in an RV parked as close to the suspicious vehicle as they could get without being discovered.

Surveillance confirmed the facts exactly as the CI had conveyed them to Joe. The agents watched as people loaded the vehicle's trunk with the duffle bags. Joe suspected them to be undocumented immigrants, or "illegal aliens," as they were known at the time. Many of them paid $2,000 to $3,000 to be led across the border by a guide, commonly known as a "coyote." The illegal aliens carried the duffle bags containing controlled substances, which meant even more money for the coyote.

On the second day of surveillance, someone arrived in the afternoon, unlocked the parked vehicle, and drove away. Joe and other agents followed the car to a residence in the Mission Hills area of San Diego. The man entered the garage and the agents waited, giving sufficient time for the suspects to remove the dope and transfer it into the resident's possession. Then they knocked down the door and found large amounts of marijuana, cocaine, and cash. Having waited to move in, the agents gave the suspects enough time to open the duffle bags. The drugs were in plain sight, so a search warrant wasn't needed. They arrested three people.

The case went to trial and, as usual, the defense wanted to know the identity of the informant. Joe refused to identify her for her own safety. He informed the federal judge that the person was a citizen CI and explained that she could be in danger of a drug cartel's retribution, living so close to the border. Joe would rather have the charges dropped than put the CI in danger. Joe believed that, with the charges dropped, the smugglers would continue their activities and be apprehended again. The judge held an in-camera hearing with the CI and ruled that she was, in fact, at risk. He would not release any information about her to the defense. All the defendants pled guilty at a later date.

CI Revenge

As mentioned, some individuals become informants to seek revenge. Such was the case with a CI who called to report that she was aware of a large smuggling operation originating in the Middle East.

An agent met with her and she explained that her boyfriend was the head of an operation to smuggle a ton of hashish into the United States. She was informing on him as payback for infidelity. Over the next five years, the agent worked on multiple cases stemming from this CI's information. Joe heard that the agent's efforts yielded indictments of around 60 people on conspiracy and narcotics-smuggling charges involving this one case.

One day a young woman called Joe, telling him that she wanted to become a CI. Joe met with her to evaluate her reasons and learn more about her offer. He couldn't help but notice how beautiful she was.

The young woman relayed her story to Joe. Five years earlier when she was 16, she was given narcotics by a dealer in northern California, who soon became her boyfriend. But once she was dependent on him, he pimped her to dealer after dealer, using her to further his own illegal activities and make more money. Through sincere tears, she explained that over the next three years, she became addicted to almost every type of drug imaginable. She finally made the decision to sober up and had been clean and straight for a year. Now she felt ready to handle being exposed to drugs again and wanted to expose all the dealers in the area.

Joe told her that the NTF didn't work cases involving street-level dealers and she insisted that she could work her way up the ladder to the highest levels of wholesalers and importers.

The very next day, after she passed two small test cases with flying colors, Joe thought, "Look out, dope dealers. This lady is going to be the best CI I've ever seen!"

And she was. She called to tell him the exact address of a dealer who was holding a pound of heroin. Joe obtained and served a search warrant and seized 16 ounces of heroin. Just like clockwork.

One time she called Joe. "I've got two guys ready to sell ten gallons of hash oil." Joe let her know that the flash roll (money agents used to show the seller) they needed for the transaction was in use by another narcotics team.

She replied, "We don't need it. The deal is in two hours."

Joe was still worried about the lack of cash when he met with her and the two dealers. But they opened the trunk and there sat two five-gallon water jugs filled with hash oil, just like she'd said. The whole thing took two minutes from start to finish.

Joe worked many undercover cases that began from the confidential information this CI provided. Not once was her information unreliable. Every call produced a dope dealer.

One afternoon she called Joe and said she'd just spoken to a dealer up at Lake Tahoe who had a kilo of cocaine for sale. Joe wasn't sure if the South Lake Tahoe police department had a narcotics unit, so he said he'd get back to her. He called Lake Tahoe and learned that they did have a small unit. Joe believed this bust wouldn't require much manpower, so he asked the local detectives if they could come up with $1,000 cash to purchase a sample and complete a buy bust. This involved giving the suspect the money, allowing him to furnish a sample half-ounce of cocaine, then placing him under arrest and seizing the remaining kilo of cocaine. The Tahoe detectives agreed.

Then he contacted his CI, who introduced Joe to the dealer over the phone. Joe told the dealer that his buyer, Phil, could be there within an hour to verify the cocaine's purity and purchase a half-ounce sample. If the product passed Phil's inspection, he'd buy the remaining kilo at the agreed price.

The deal took about two hours. The cops arrested the dealer, seized a kilo of cocaine, and Joe never left his desk.

Joe continued to depend on the reliable information he received from this valuable CI. Their collaboration resulted in the cessation of major drug operations in and around San Diego and Tijuana. She also assisted with a Bangkok case involving two kilos of Chinese white heroin, during which a former law-enforcement officer was arrested by the federal police in Thailand.

After a couple of years, he started to become concerned about her safety and explained that her involvement in so many cases increased the chances she'd become known among the dealers. He advised that perhaps the time had come for her to stop working as a CI before his only option, if she were identified, was the Federal Witness Protection Program. Joe had used the program for other CIs and told her the program would be highly intrusive in terms of how she lived the remainder of her life.

She left San Diego to attend college, using some of the money she accepted as payment for the risks she'd taken to fight the growing drug epidemic. Joe prayed that God would protect this lovely young woman who had found the strength and courage to turn her life around. And he reflected how, as an agent working undercover, it was always vitally important to evaluate a potential informant's motives, because lives literally depended on their reliability.

CI Infiltration

Some people become informants with the sole intent of gathering intelligence information on law-enforcement activities and investigations. They subsequently share details with the drug dealers for whom they work. This tactic is referred to as "CI infiltration."

Joe worked with such a CI, who offered information and made introductions to facilitate deals. This CI revealed to Joe the location of many dealers, which resulted in record-breaking heroin seizures and convictions of big-time dealers associated with large heroin trafficking operations.

But on one occasion, another citizen informant alerted Joe to the fact that the CI was also an infiltrator, working both sides of the fence. This was a dangerous situation. In undercover work, a dealer typically arrived with the narcotics, ready and anxious to close the deal and receive a bag full of cash. However, if the CI's information wasn't correct, or if the CI was compromised, and the agent's instincts didn't trigger a warning about the deal, the dealer might very well show up with others intent on robbing and possibly killing the undercover agent and those working with him. This scenario happened all too often in San Diego, where dealers and buyers flocked from all over the world due to the city's proximity to the Mexican border.

Joe knew the infiltrating CI's habits. So he proceeded, but with great caution. During the initial part of the deal, Joe caught the rogue CI by surprise, cutting off his double-dealing and getting the information the narcs needed to raid the dealer's house. There, they found kilos of cocaine and 600 kilos of marijuana.

During the raid, Joe saw a photo on a table that showed a man and the arrested female homeowner standing in front of an elementary school. He recognized the school; his own children were enrolled there! Joe gave the photo to an agent and requested he ask the arrested homeowner about it. The woman told the agent she was the president of the school's PTA.

Joe immediately separated himself from the case. The last thing he wanted was to put his children in danger. He updated his supervisor and the other agents, then immediately left the scene.

Narc Duty

Prisoner Exchange 1977

President Jimmy Carter signed a prisoner-exchange treaty in 1977, an agreement securing the release of 577 Americans imprisoned in Mexico. Most of these prisoners had been arrested for narcotics-trafficking offenses.

The first group of 66 prisoners was scheduled to arrive in San Diego and processed in the Customs area of the San Diego airport, with much media fanfare.

Joe reported to the airport as instructed to assist DEA agents with prisoner processing. On his way in, he noticed the area outside Customs was congested with reporters, news crews, and politicians all on site to report and use the publicity to their advantage.

Joe wove through the crowds and media equipment, making his way into the processing area where prisoners were being screened through the DEA database for outstanding criminal warrants. Once cleared, prisoners were transferred to the Metropolitan Corrections Center for further processing.

Joe, along with most of his fellow narcotics agents, believed the whole prisoner-exchange treaty was just a political move on the part of the president. They thought it sent the wrong message to dealers and smugglers and that the number of American traffickers would increase substantially if the main deterrent, being sentenced to a Mexican prison, was no longer a threat.

After a while, Joe took a break from the processing area and walked out onto the airport tarmac. There, he saw a Marine Corps Honor Guard. He spoke to the senior member who explained that the Honor Guard was there to receive the remains of a Marine killed in Vietnam.

Joe stood at attention and stared at the flag-draped coffin as it was transferred to the Marine Corp vehicle. As a veteran, Joe was moved as he observed the Marines handle the coffin with precision, respect, and care. He paused for his own moment of silence.

When he returned to the madhouse of crowds and news media, he suddenly found himself angry as the comparison struck him. News crews, politicians, and attention-seekers were all focused on a group of drug dealers re-entering the country in a political exchange. Yet on a nearby tarmac, the flag-draped coffin of a fallen Marine rested solemnly and alone. Joe couldn't help but wonder about the irony.

Where was this young man's fanfare?

Joe returned to his duties at the processing area. He helped force a passageway through the crowd, then encountered a camera crew and reporter setting up to interview a person of some importance. While Joe pushed his way through the news crew, the interviewee yelled, "Hey, we're trying to do an interview here!"

In response, Joe unloaded his thoughts about what he'd just seen out on the tarmac — a Marine who died in service to his country hadn't received even a gesture of gratitude, while dealers who were killing American youth with drugs were given an elaborate welcome.

What angered Joe even more was that the event was purposely held to get the prisoners home by Christmas. He couldn't help but think of all the people who, due to the actions of these prisoners, had overdosed and wouldn't be coming home for Christmas or any other holiday. Thoughts of these traffickers and dealers led him to recall a beautiful 16-year-old Latino girl, lying dead in her own vomit with a makeshift tourniquet on her arm and a syringe protruding from her vein.

A half-hour later, he received a page to call the Chief of Police, who told him he understood Joe's feelings, but asked him to steer clear of the interviews and politicians on site.

The plight of Americans in Mexican prisons subsequently turned into a human-rights issue. Joe was frustrated over the fact that no one considered the human rights of the thousands overdosing every year. If prison was so bad in Mexico, he argued, why did 20% of Americans held in those prisons want to stay behind? Many of them had outstanding arrest warrants in the U.S. for drug trafficking or they had relatives in Mexico to harbor them upon release. Some just wanted to see what happened to other American returnees.

Dealing drugs is a dangerous business. Joe's opinion was that traffickers should be thankful the U.S.' southern neighbor isn't Singapore, where the penalty for trafficking is life in prison or death. There, the trial and death-sentence appeal process usually last three years, compared to 30 or 40 years in the U.S.

One Big Dope Case

In September 1976, Joe and NTF agent Chuck Jones were working in the office when Jones took a call from an FBI agent. He and another FBI agent were having breakfast at an Ocean Beach restaurant when they overheard two men discussing a heroin deal with a supplier in San Diego.

The FBI agents heard that the dealer was in San Diego, having driven back from New Orleans to return an ounce of heroin he'd previously purchased. The dealer claimed the heroin was low-quality and planned to have the San Diego dealer provide a replacement of better quality. Joe and Chuck wanted to thoroughly investigate the situation, but they had very little to go on. They strongly suspected that this wouldn't lead anywhere, but they had to try. An ounce of heroin was a sufficient amount to warrant their investigation.

They began contacting informants to determine if anyone knew about a previous bar owner in San Diego who was from New Orleans. About an hour into their initial investigation, an informant contacted Joe with the address where the dealer was staying, a single-family residence. After a thorough records check, the detectives found no association between the residence and any drug dealing. They drove to the house to physically investigate and found a car in the driveway with Louisiana license plates.

For the next two days, agents had the house and car under surveillance. On the third afternoon, two men removed a spare tire from the vehicle. Assuming the heroin was being transported in the spare tire, the surveillance personnel believed the suspects would soon leave for New Orleans. But just as the agents felt the investigation was making headway, they were instructed to cease surveillance. The bosses had concluded the amount of information uncovered to date didn't justify the overtime. The next morning, the vehicle was gone.

So NTF notified the New Orleans DEA task force, sharing all the information they'd gathered. The New Orleans task force found and arrested the men.

A few days later, New Orleans DEA called Joe to say that one of the men was willing to cooperate and return to San Diego to purchase additional heroin from the supplier there. The new confidential informant soon showed up in San Diego, accompanied by a DEA agent and a New Orleans police detective assigned to the task force.

Joe and Chuck met with the informant to gain all information about the dealer. Jones went undercover with the informant at a hotel in Mission Valley, where they placed the order for an ounce of heroin to be delivered to their room. When the supplier delivered the heroin, he was immediately taken into custody.

Loyalty among drug addicts is scarce. The supplier soon agreed to contact his source for the heroin to purchase six more ounces. When the source delivered them to the hotel room, *he* was arrested.

A convicted felon currently on parole, he knew that if he didn't cooperate, he'd be put away for a long time. After some persuasion, he agreed to order a kilo of heroin from his wholesaler. He also divulged the address of the main supplier. When surveillance of that address was in place, the agents directed the ex-felon to order a kilo of heroin from *this* supplier. Gary Gleason watched a man and woman leaving the house and followed their car. When the couple arrived to meet the ex-felon, NTF agents moved in to make the arrest. They found the kilo of heroin and two handguns in their vehicle.

Joe obtained a federal search warrant for the couple's house. There, the agents seized 12 rifles, one with a mounted starlight scope, and shotguns, some with sawed-off barrels, along with 12 handguns, hundreds of thousands of dollars in cash, and diamond jewelry.

But the agents couldn't dispel their collective hunch that more was hidden in this house. Gleason's meticulous and well-known search techniques were put to good use. While searching the attic, Gleason called out to the other agents, asking for help with removing a large dog food bag. Before the bag was even opened, the agents could smell the heroin, which turned out to be 13.5 pounds of uncut heroin worth millions in street value, badly hidden in the dog-food bag. Gary also uncovered hundreds of thousands of dollars of cash.

The agents notified their supervisors of the haul, who immediately drove to the location. They also called a great friend of the task force, Bob Lampert. Bob had been a reserve officer with the San Diego Police Department and was an award-winning photojournalist for the number-one news station in the area. He showed up and took the now-famous photo of all the agents involved in the case, along with the seized contraband. Bob's photo from that day hangs on the wall of the DEA Museum in Washington, D.C.

From surveillance to seizure, the entire operation took 10 days. The arrests shut down a major heroin supplier and his entire organization throughout California and Mexico. And it all started with two FBI agents overhearing loose talk in a diner — and Joe's CI tracking down a heroin buyer.

Joe and Chuck Jones received awards and recognition by the DEA administrator. This quote from the *San Diego Union* dated February 11, 1988, is displayed above a photo of Joe and Chuck's NTF heroin case displayed in the DEA Museum:

"There are no victory parades in the war on drugs, no public acclaim for the men and women who wage an anonymous battle against impossible odds over five continents. They fight in the back alleys, corporate board rooms, jungles and on the high seas. They are heroes in the best sense of the word and they deserve the thanks of every American."

Quick Thinking

Good undercover agents are quick to improvise. They study their targets in advance and constantly read the signals in the field. Life holds little value in the drug world and law-enforcement personnel face extreme risk. Joe made it a point never to forget those facts — and they came in handy one Saturday night.

He received a call from agent Stan Furce (who later became the DEA attaché in Tokyo and helped Joe immensely during his career) asking if he could go undercover for a relatively simple introduction to a dealer who was offering to sell a million amphetamine pills. All the agent could tell Joe was that the meet was to gather intelligence, no money would change hands, and the intelligence gathering would be in front of a residence.

Joe went to the location. A man coming out of the house

told Joe his boss was en route. The two were making small talk when out of nowhere, the guy asked Joe, "You got a gun on you?"

Joe said, "No."

"Well, I do!" He pulled out a stainless-steel 357 magnum and stuck the barrel firmly into Joe's chest. "I have to search you."

The agent covering Joe couldn't see what was happening from his vantage point in the dark. Joe knew he was on his own.

Wearing a waist-length jacket, Joe placed both hands in his pockets and pulled the jacket above his head to expose his waistband. As he slowly turned around, he released the safety of the 25-caliber semi-auto pistol inside the pocket of his jacket and positioned himself so that the gun was aimed at the man's left eye. He figured that if he had to fire through the jacket with the small-caliber pistol, he needed to hit the eye socket to ensure the guy went down.

When the man was satisfied that Joe was unarmed, he placed the 357 back in his waistband as quickly as he'd drawn it.

Joe lowered his arms and removed his hands from his pockets. "Man, you must be using too many of those amphetamines. You're acting paranoid."

"Look, in this business, you can't be too careful. A lot of narcs are out there arresting dealers."

"Oh yeah?" Joe started walking away, saying, "See you later!"

Just then, the apparent "boss" pulled into the driveway and asked Joe where he was going.

"I'm leaving. I won't do business with a paranoid meth freak who just stuck a three-fifty-seven in my chest."

"No, wait, man. We can work this out."

"Forget it! You and your buddy are too fucked up on your own pills." Joe got in his car and left.

Later, Joe met with the same two guys again, only under a more controlled and monitored environment *and* with a larger caliber weapon tucked into his waistband. He knew they wouldn't try to search him again.

A deal with these two never materialized. "When you work in narcotics," Joe said later, "you meet every kind of crazy son of a bitch in the world and you need to know when to walk away."

"Joe, You Want To Do *What*?"

One night, Joe was dispatched to the Interstate 5 Border Patrol Checkpoint, 35 miles north of San Diego, where agents had arrested a guy trying to transport 300 pounds of marijuana in the trunk of his car. When the suspect was searched, the agents saw numerous blood-soaked bullet holes on his shirt. But after a closer examination, they didn't find any injuries.

Upon questioning, the subject, Timothy, told the tale.

"My buddy and I were low on money, so we came up with a plan to rob my dealer. We both worked in the movies, so we knew about special effects. We met with my dealer and right after he loaded the pot in my trunk, my buddy pulled a movie handgun and said he was robbing us. The plan was for me to act like I was resisting, then my buddy would fire the fake handgun and I'd activate the blood-spewing special-effects vest I was wearing. This all went according to plan and my dealer thought I'd been shot. He ran to his car, jumped in, and drove away — without being paid for the weed. My buddy drove home. And here I am."

After Joe interrogated him for several hours, Timothy

agreed to cooperate with a new plan in exchange for not being charged.

Timothy was unaware that Joe knew the dealer to be a Class One violator, the highest DEA ranking. The plan was for Timothy to call the dealer the following morning and tell him that his wife and son were being held at his Riverside home by a friend of his accomplice, so Timothy had no choice but to participate in the robbery. He was forced to use the special effects vest and wasn't injured by the fake gunshots. Timothy would tell the dealer that after returning home, his wife and son were freed. He could now return the marijuana to the dealer.

Joe took custody of the 300 pounds and Timothy, then drove to the NTF office. He knew he'd have to sell his supervisor on the plan. Joe anticipated the reaction and he was right. "You want to do *what*? We're in the business of *taking* dope, not giving it back!"

But his supervisor, Skip DiChercio, heard him out and as soon as he mentioned the name of the dealer, DiChercio's interest grew. He knew, with the proper plan, they could bust a Class One violator, ultimately seizing a larger amount of dope. Joe hoped for support from the higher-ups to enact this plan. Skip was one of the best supervisors Joe had ever worked for and he believed that if anyone could sell the plan to the bosses, it was Skip.

Sure enough, Skip came back with approval to proceed — within some guidelines. Even after Skip explained the rules, he and Joe agreed that the plan was risky, but the task force had the talent and resources needed for success.

After the meeting with Skip, Joe had Timothy call his dealer and tell him the story they'd rehearsed all night. He did a remarkably convincing job and the dealer agreed to meet that evening at a Denny's in Pacific Beach.

Agents from two NTF teams began planning for the exchange and surveillance of the dealer afterwards. Joe brought Timothy to a hotel to clean up and get some rest, while another agent kept an eye on him. He was given new clothes to replace what he was still wearing from the robbery. Timothy's vehicle was retrieved from the Border Patrol checkpoint and Joe transferred the marijuana from his vehicle to Timothy's.

While the agents brainstormed aspects of the plan that could go awry and what their response would be to each, a surveillance aircraft was enlisted to assist in the process.

As darkness fell, one agent drove Timothy's car, with the pot, close to the meeting spot. This ensured that if Timothy got cold feet, he couldn't flee with the dope. Then Timothy drove his car to the back of the Denny's parking lot where he met his dealer. After the exchange took place, the aircraft and seven ground vehicles began surveilling the dealer.

Soon, the dealer disappeared; even the plane lost its surveillance on the car. But after all the agents began search patterns of the area, one found the car as the dealer was getting out at a residence in a rural area.

Agents raided the residence and arrested the dealer, while Joe quickly obtained a search warrant for the house and surrounding buildings. The agents seized a Class One violator, thousands of dollars in cash, 1,000 pounds of marijuana, and many kilos of cocaine.

Inside the house, Joe stopped to reflect. *"Damn, it worked!"* Skip and Joe shook hands, both agreeing they had become a little grayer since this operation began.

Joe felt a personal satisfaction with the outcome of his plan, even though it could have ended differently, especially after losing track of the dealer's car. But he knew the agents working the case were the best at what they did and everyone involved received well-deserved accolades.

Twice Bitten

One of Joe's reliable informants contacted him about a dealer who had a U-Haul truck en route to a rural area of San Diego County. The truck was believed to contain a ton of marijuana.

Joe met with the dealer to negotiate a purchase, then sent agents to the dealer's residence to covertly gather information necessary to safely follow through with an undercover purchase. The agents immediately spotted a marijuana plant growing in the front yard, which provided the evidence needed to obtain a search warrant when necessary.

During negotiations, Joe learned that the marijuana in the truck was from Nebraska.

Soon after, Joe was informed that the marijuana was in the San Diego area and it was in fact hemp, not marijuana. Joe thought about passing on the deal because it was hemp and reconsidered when thinking about the dealer selling the hemp as good quality marijuana and the buyers coming back to the dealer seeking retribution thinking they were ripped off. Dope dealers had been killed for much less.

Joe obtained a search warrant for the house using that information and scheduled the purchase for the next day. This allowed him to make the suspects believe the bust was happening because of the plant, not from an informant.

Joe proceeded to the residence, carefully toting $39,000 in cash to purchase the hemp. He brought the dealer to his car to show him the cash. After validating the money, the dealer took him to the truck and opened the back where the hemp was kept. Joe knew the hemp was about two to five percent in THC content, though the law didn't specify any minimum amount. The product merely had to contain some level of THC.

Joe returned to his car to retrieve the money to complete the purchase. While doing so, he communicated the pre-arranged arrest signal to the surrounding surveilling agents. As the agents moved in, they arrested the dealers *and* Joe, in order not to divulge his undercover status. Further, to conceal the fact that an informant was involved, Joe and the dealers were transported to the El Cajon Police Department for processing where all suspects were separated. Joe was then escorted out the back door. The dealers were told they were going to the San Diego County Jail, but that Joe was being transported to the Chula Vista jail because of numerous outstanding felony arrest warrants.

Joe called the same dealer a few days later, knowing he had been temporarily released from jail. Remaining in his undercover role, Joe reprimanded the dealer, yelling at him for being stupid enough to have a marijuana plant growing in his front yard, causing Joe to lose all his money! "The cops seized *my* $39,000 over your plant!" While verbally receiving hell, the dealer responded that he could get some of Joe's money back. The dealer would sell Joe some kilos of methamphetamine at a good discount. The next day, the guy did sell Joe the kilos of meth, for which he was arrested *again*. This time, Joe introduced himself and did not accompany the man to jail.

A preliminary hearing was held at the San Diego Courthouse in front of the judge presiding over both cases. The court clerk read the first case number, then the second case number. The judge grew more confused as the clerk and the DA were trying to explain both cases, so he asked if the arresting officer was present. Joe came forward and explained that while undercover, he had originally purchased a ton of hemp containing THC from the defendant and was arrested alongside him to conceal his cover. Joe relayed to the judge that he later contacted the same defendant to complain about losing his money over the botched purchase, for which the dealer offered him numerous kilos of meth at a discount. The deal took place two days later, resulting in the second arrest.

The astounded judge looked Joe in the eye and said, "Either you are very, very good at what you do, or this guy is the world's biggest dumbass." Joe remembers thinking it was probably a combination of both.

Subsequently, that dealer pled guilty to both narcotic sales cases.

Karen Rose

In October 1975, Joe pulled into a parking lot of a restaurant and lounge in Chula Vista, near the Mexico border, where he was meeting a few detectives for a night out. He parked next to a car from which a young lady wearing a fancy outfit was emerging. They exchanged a few words, then went their separate ways.

Inside, Joe learned that the lady was the singer in the band that was performing there. On a break, she approached Joe's table to make small talk.

She introduced herself as Karen Rose and commented on the amount of gold jewelry one of the guys at the table was wearing.

Joe said, "Well, I'm a yacht salesman and I'm sorry to

have to leave, but we have to show this guy a yacht he's interested in buying."

Karen went home, where she lived with her parents. "Mom!" she exclaimed. "Tonight, I met a gorgeous guy who *has to be* rich, because he's a yacht salesman!"

A couple of nights passed and Joe returned to the bar and asked Karen out to lunch. While they were chatting, a cop who was friends with a member of the band approached and Karen introduced him to "Joe, the yacht salesman." After choking on his drink, the friend said, "He's no yacht salesman. He's one of us!"

Joe, looking a bit sheepish, said to Karen, "I'll tell you all about it over lunch."

That was the beginning of Joe and Karen's match made in heaven. From that first meeting, neither Joe nor Karen ever dated anyone else. They continued their relationship for three and a half years, while Karen toured with her band and Joe worked undercover for NTF. They were married on June 30, 1979, one month from Karen's 30th birthday. She'd never had any significant long-term relationships because of the time and passion she devoted to her singing career, and traveling was a big part of that. But that all changed when she met Joe.

Police Officers Association

Sickness and Distress Duties

While at NTF, Joe was encouraged to run for the open board seat at the Police Officers Association (POA), which he won. Subsequently, he became the chairman of the POA's Sickness and Distress Committee. This position usually went to the new board member. Most of the time, he was working with officers on benefits, such as medical leave and disability. The heart-breaking side was assisting families who'd lost loved ones in the line of duty. He had to help plan funerals, assist in filing claims for insurance and death benefits, and provide whatever else a family needed for many months after an officer's death. The responsibility especially weighed on Joe during pay negotiations, when city negotiators were digging in their heels right after they buried an officer.

In November 1978, he was awakened by a phone call with the news that an officer had been killed in the line of duty. The Chief of Police and other officials were on their way to notify the officer's mother. Joe was told the officer's name and the circumstances of his death.

Archie C. Buggs, a four-year veteran of the Patrol Division, had stopped a vehicle occupied by two young men for a routine traffic violation early that morning. While Officer Buggs stood at the car's window discussing the infraction with the driver, he was shot five times. Then, as he lay helpless on the street, the gunman shot him again in the head before driving off.

Within minutes, the police began receiving calls of an officer lying in the street. Fortunately, witnesses provided important details. The suspects' vehicle was soon located and officers arrested two young men, 17 and 18 years old. The two were eventually convicted of Officer Buggs' first-degree murder and sentenced to life.

The 18-year-old was sentenced to life without parole. The 17-year-old shooter received life with the possibility of parole and was up for parole by the California Parole Board three times, each denied by then-Governor Jerry Brown, most recently in July 2018. Brown was governor the year Officer Buggs was murdered in the line of duty. Perhaps this is a reason he denied parole for one of his murderers. Since it happened during his term, Governor Brown almost certainly felt a sense of duty to ensure that these cop killers would never walk free. As of this writing, the convicted murderer was granted parole, though it was rescinded by Governor Gavin Newsom. He'll be eligible for parole again in two years.

On the morning that Buggs was killed, Joe contacted the officer's mother as a representative of the POA. He met with Mrs. Buggs at her home over the next several weeks. Joe spent a lot of time with the grieving mother, helping her with insurance and benefits paperwork, including the federal paperwork for an additional policy of $100,000 for officers killed in the line of duty. While providing her with comfort and assistance, he became her trusted friend. With support from the POA staff and their leader, Alice Downs, everything was completed expeditiously.

Joe and Mrs. Buggs continued to talk a great deal in the year that followed. In May 1979, the POA sponsored their attendance at the Law Enforcement Memorial services at the Capitol in Sacramento. There, Officer Archie Buggs was added to the California Peace Officers Memorial honoring the law-enforcement officers killed in the line of duty during the previous year. Mrs. Buggs was pleased that Governor Jerry Brown was going to meet with her and honor Archie.

The following year, Mrs. Buggs often called Joe for advice or just to chat. He began to wonder about her frequent contact. He was told by Alice Downs that she had routinely worried about her son while he was a police officer, then transferred her attention to worrying about Joe. Over time, Joe assured her he was going to be safe and she shouldn't be worried.

Joe had to perform the unfortunate duties of the Chairman of the Sickness and Distress Committee again in March 1979 when a young officer who had graduated from the police academy a mere three months earlier was shot to death.

Officer Michael T. Anaya was responding to a radio call one evening about a man wielding a knife who had already attacked several family members when he was confronted by the suspect, who was high on phencyclidine (PCP), a synthetic that produces some of the most violent and dangerous effects of any drug. He attacked Officer Anaya, managed to gain control of his weapon, shot him in the neck, then turned the weapon on himself, committing suicide.

Badly wounded but alive, Officer Anaya was transported to the hospital, fighting for his life.

Joe visited him at the hospital on numerous occasions and met his wife Laura. One night, Joe visited on his way home from work. He reassured the wounded officer that his wife was being well cared for. Joe told him to use all his strength and energy to concentrate on healing and recovering.

Joe said goodbye and left, but when arriving at home 20 minutes later, he was notified that Officer Anaya had passed away. Joe believes to this day that telling the officer his wife Laura was in safe hands and with his police family allowed him to ease his worries, providing the freedom he needed to pass in peace.

Officer Anaya was a newlywed and a graduate of San Diego State College where he played baseball for the Aztecs. Later, a college baseball scholarship was established in his honor by the POA.

The period between 1976 and 1988 mark the deadliest time in the history of the San Diego Police Department.

Eleven police officers lost their lives in the line of duty, which earned the San Diego Police Department the undesirable distinction of having the highest per-capita officer mortality rate in the United States.

During that time, Alice Downs was the POA Office Manager. Joe and others involved in the organization always knew they could call on Alice to handle the needs of families who lost officers in the line of duty. She was not only an incredible friend to Joe, but also a woman he respected greatly. She's probably at the Pearly Gates today, in charge of making sure all the police officers pass through.

5

Robbery Detail
and the Plane Crash

Transfer with a Slight Hitch

In 1978, Joe realized he'd grown far too comfortable working undercover. He'd become too complacent in the job, bypassing important precautions. He knew his guard was down. This all put his safety at risk.

His insight was confirmed as he reviewed the details of a recent undercover purchase of several ounces of cocaine. When the dealer began to vacillate during the sale, Joe blurted out the word "case," used by narcotics investigators to describe undercover buys. Joe immediately realized the verbal slip and started double-talking until the cocaine was produced and the suspect arrested.

Joe met with Bob Augustine, his lieutenant, at the NTF office and requested a transfer.

Augustine was surprised. "A transfer? You? Why?"

Joe told Bob of the recent encounter and his slip of the tongue.

"Hey, that was just an accident. It happens. Even to award-winning undercover cops."

"Sure, but what would you say if I told you I was

unarmed during that purchase?"

Augustine was stunned speechless. Finally, he said, "Yeah, it might be time for you to transfer. Where do you want to be reassigned? Homicide?"

Joe shook his head no; he knew homicide involved after-hour callouts and he'd been working an average of 60 hours a week for too many years. "I'd like to go to the Robbery Detail." He knew Robbery was led by a lieutenant who had not only been his patrol sergeant, but had recommended Joe for promotion from uniform to detective.

He also knew that Robbery was the unit where he'd be dealing with the real bad guys, who would just as soon kill a victim as rob him. Robbery detectives had to be even tougher than the stone-cold killers they went after and would go to all ends to put them in prison or a coffin. Robbery detectives were the best of the best and worked hand in hand with the Major Violators Unit of the District Attorney's office.

For those reasons and more, Robbery was a highly sought-after assignment and unwritten protocol called for the unit's detectives to vote on candidates for the job. But the lieutenant approved Joe's transfer without a vote. Shortly after Joe reported to Robbery, an old partner of his in the unit told him of the protocol violation.

Joe made it a point to apologize to the lieutenant for causing him any problems. The lieutenant replied, "Joe, my policy has always been to do what I think is right and ask for forgiveness, if I have to, afterwards. I knew you were the best man for the job."

Yellow Birds and Good Men

When Joe joined Robbery, everything was running smoothly and results were consistent and impressive. On the other hand, the unit had a reputation for being a large and rowdy group. But it had such a high rate of solved cases, the higher-ups left it alone, figuring there was no need to mess up a good thing.

Joe quickly learned that the detectives had earned their reputation.

One example was when a detective found a dead sparrow on his way into the office one morning. He painted the bird yellow and wired its feet to a potted tree in the reception area. A while later, Detective Alicia Lampert of the Sex Crimes Unit was orienting a new female detective and walked into Robbery.

Alicia had been a police department secretary for many years and was accustomed to officers' pranks. She became an officer when women were finally allowed to work in uniformed patrol and held the distinction of being the first female officer dispatched on a uniformed patrol call. Alicia cautioned the new detective, "You probably won't want to come back to this office after our visit."

"Why not?"

"Well, I don't know for sure, but I'll bet you know by the time we leave."

The new detective noticed the cute yellow bird in the tree and reached over to stroke his little chest. Once touched, his head fell to the floor at her feet.

"See?" Alicia told her on their way out. "They're crazy in here!"

Hijinks aside, the unit's solved-cases rate was in the 80%-90% range and many of the criminals involved in these cases were hardcore. The unit also had joint jurisdiction with the FBI concerning bank robberies, so they worked on many cases together. Throughout his career, Joe had never worked with a better group of criminal investigators.

Dope Dealer on the Courthouse Steps

Joe was working the night Robbery shift with his partner, Kirby Wood. Driving by the county courthouse around 8 p.m., they observed a drug deal in progress. They pulled their car over and watched two men walking away from a third standing on the steps of the closed courthouse. Joe got out of the car and approached the departing men, while Kirby detained the guy on the steps.

Joe saw that the two were military. He asked them what type of drugs they'd purchased from the guy on the steps. They both denied purchasing anything. So he asked them if they'd ever played Monopoly. Puzzled, they responded that, yes, they'd played the game.

Joe let them know that their truthfulness here could result in a Get out of Jail Free card. But if he had to arrest them, the military would probably give them a Bad Conduct Discharge. Understanding the risk, the two admitted to purchasing an ounce of weed from the guy on the courthouse steps. One of the men pulled a bag of marijuana from his pocket and Joe searched him for more, but found none.

Joe asked if the two men knew the dealer and what else he sold. They said they'd seen him sell everything, including hard drugs. Joe had them empty the bag onto the street and grind the contents into the blacktop with their shoes. "Now leave!" With that, the two walked quickly toward the bay.

He approached the dealer and asked why he was selling dope, of all places, on the courthouse steps. The man replied that he wasn't selling dope, but Joe informed him that the two buyers had given him up. When Joe saw the dealer's address on his ID, he asked, "Are you familiar with a couple of brothers who live near you?"

"Yes," the dealer replied.

"So you know that they've been in and out of prison

for armed robbery, assault with a deadly weapon, and narcotics offenses?"

"Sure. Everyone knows that."

"How about a couple of murders that we haven't proved yet?"

The dealer shook his head.

"Here's the deal. If I ever see you selling dope again, I won't approach you directly. Instead, I'll call your neighbors, the ex-cons."

"Why would you do that?"

"To tell them that you'll be walking by their house shortly — carrying a lot of cash and drugs. That's why."

"You would?" the dealer asked, eyes wide.

"Sure I would. After the brothers kill you for your money and dope, I'll arrest them for murder and get all three of you off the street."

"But—"

"Listen to me. I take it personally that you're selling dope on the courthouse steps. Don't you, Kirby?"

"Yes, I do."

"To us, you're thumbing your nose at all cops. Do I make myself clear?"

The dealer gulped. "Yes sir."

When they got back into the car, Kirby asked, "Would you really call the brothers if you saw him dealing again?"

"What brothers?" Joe responded.

Wood laughed. "Ah, Community Oriented Policing at its best."

Senior Solutions

Joe was working dayshift in the Robbery Detail. He was the only detective in the office when in walked a uniformed patrol officer escorting a well-dressed man, about 75 years old, in handcuffs. Joe asked the officer, "Waddaya got?"

The old man, it turned out, marched into a bank and went straight up to the teller with nothing but a brown bag and a note in his hand. He handed her his demand note, then stood there and waited. After the teller ponied up the cash, the old man left and sat down on the curb in front of the bank.

"We answered the bank's robbery call. The bank employees said that the guy sitting on the curb was the robber. He handed over the bag to us, admitted what he'd done, and got into the patrol car with no argument."

At that point, Joe placed the obligatory call to the FBI, knowing they had mutual jurisdiction and they'd come pick up the old man. Joe then took a seat across from the man and asked him a straight question, "What the hell were you doing?"

The man's reply was unforgettable. "You won't repeat any of this, correct?"

Joe nodded, which didn't serve as a full commitment, since he wasn't completely sure what the guy was going to tell him, and said, "Well, I'm not going to admonish you of your rights or interrogate you. That'll be up to the FBI." He knew at that point from the patrolman's investigation that this gentleman hadn't threatened or harmed anyone physically and there had to be more to this story.

The old man spoke. "Let me tell you something. I know I committed a federal crime today, but I've never broken a law in my life. What I did put no one in danger."

While he was talking, Joe looked at the demand note and noted there was no threat made. The note simply read, "Give me the money."

The man continued: "I'm ready to be assigned a

court-appointed public defender and talk to the assistant U.S. attorney. I will plead guilty to bank robbery *if* they ensure that I will be sent to a minimum-security facility where I can live out my sentence. I won't cause any trouble. But there I'll get three square meals, a warm bed to sleep in, a roof over my head, and my medical bills paid. You see, I lost my wife a few months ago and, along with that, her Social Security checks. I can't afford to live on my own like this anymore and I refuse to be homeless on the streets."

Six months later, Joe received a postcard at the station, addressed to him, with a scenic picture of the sun setting over the Pacific Ocean and the return address: minimum security facility. On the back was a note handwritten from the elderly outlaw: "Safe and sound. Just sitting outside looking at the ocean …"

From that day forward, Joe dubbed this robbery investigation the "Senior Solution."

They Also Serve Who Only Sit and Wait

Waiting on others is not unusual in law enforcement.

One Sunday night, Joe and another detective were asked to check a residence for a vehicle with an Arizona license plate registered under the name of a suspect wanted for murder. The other detective was Cliff Collins, who'd been in the Robbery Unit so many years that it was sarcastically rumored he'd actually chased Billy the Kid.

The two detectives drove to the address and saw the car with Arizona plates in the driveway. The detectives called it in, were given the suspect's description, and advised they should surveille the house while a SWAT team was en route. Since Joe and Cliff were the only available detectives to respond to robbery calls that night and additional calls were coming in, they asked for SWAT's estimated time of arrival.

About 90 minutes passed and they were finally notified that SWAT was two blocks away and wanted to meet with the detectives. Frustrated by now, Cliff threw up his hands and told Joe to go to the meeting.

Joe recognized the SWAT leader, an officer he'd supervised when he was a Field Training Officer. The SWAT leader asked him, "Where are the electric power box and water shutoff located?"

Joe looked at him, baffled. "I don't live here. We were just told to watch the house and vehicle ... not to rent it."

The leader sent Joe back to Cliff's location. More time passed and more robbery calls came in, each of which Joe and Cliff were prevented from answering due to their current assignment.

"Enough of this shit!" Cliff finally huffed. "Let's go get this guy!"

Cliff had noticed that the front door of the house was open behind a closed screen door. Joe and Cliff approached and saw a man who fit the suspect's description asleep on the sofa. Joe twisted the screen-door handle. It was unlocked. They opened the screen door, entered quietly, and awoke the subject by sticking guns in his face. The house was checked and no other occupants were found. The suspect was handcuffed and taken outside.

As Joe and Cliff walked the suspect toward their car to call for a patrol unit to retrieve the man, they noticed SWAT officers quick-stepping in a line, weapons held tightly across their chests, moving down the street in formation.

As they handed over the suspect to SWAT, the leader said, "You should have waited to enter the premises. This man is considered armed and dangerous."

Trying not to roll his eyes, Joe said, "You know, when I was working at the NTF, I had occasion to kick in my share of doors. I forced entry into hundreds of locations and never had to fire a shot." He then pointed to Cliff. "And you can't count the number of times this guy has done the same." Joe surveyed the SWAT team. "Is there anything else you need from us?"

The SWAT officers were obviously perturbed.

"Listen, you can take credit for the arrest. We've missed a lot of calls while waiting on you guys."

Back in their unmarked car, Cliff turned to Joe. "Do you remember responding to crime scenes when there was no SWAT team on the way? When patrol guys and detectives were the first through a door if it was their beat?"

"Yeah, those were the good old days, huh?"

"SWAT is a valuable police resource," Cliff admitted, "but field officers are still good at getting results — often more quickly and without a lot of fire power and fanfare."

Actually, this is true of most aspects of police work. Comparing Joe's era in law enforcement to today's police force is like comparing Star Wars to the caveman. The tools they use today weren't available to Joe and his colleagues — some were too costly and others hadn't been invented yet.

In Joe's day 40 years ago, when officers left their one-man patrol cars, they were on their own. They had no bulletproof Kevlar vests; they didn't use shotguns, K-9s, or portable radios. Their police radio was a one-way system; they could hear the dispatchers, but not an officer's response. They had no tasers and no body or vehicle cameras. LED flashlights, in-vehicle computer systems, and computerized records checking were all far in the future.

Records checks had to be hand-searched and local records took up to 20 minutes. On occasion, the record would return a response such as, "This subject is wanted for murder," something a cop should know quickly. Sometimes, it took so long to get a records check, the person would have to be released, only to discover later that he or she was wanted for a felony in another jurisdiction.

Joe's "old-school" policing consisted of a six-round revolver with 12 extra rounds, handcuffs, mace, beavertail sap and night stick, flashlight — and the desire to do the best job possible with what he had.

41-Caliber Magnum Robberies

In the winter of 1979, a series of banks were robbed around San Diego. Two robbers always struck at closing time when the banks were filled with the most customers. Often, they hit on a Friday.

One bank robber carried a 41-caliber magnum revolver and was extremely dangerous, having shot one teller in the leg for not complying with his demands quickly enough. In addition, at a separate robbery during the day, they chased down a customer who entered the bank during the robbery. Seeing the crime in progress, the customer exited quickly and was running down the busy street when one of the suspects fired several rounds at him. Fortunately, no one was struck.

In another robbery, a retired detective (on disability, having been shot twice) happened to be in the bank and saw first-hand the men's brutality and blatant disregard for life. The retired detective was armed, but believed that, under the circumstances, an attempt to halt the robbery would have resulted in innocent people being injured in a gunfight. When the detective relayed his eyewitness experience to those working the case, he was told that his decision was sound and that he most likely saved lives that day.

Since they wore ski masks, identification by witnesses was impossible. They'd have to be caught in the act of robbing a bank or another business.

Eventually, a CI came forward and provided information about two locations: a bank that was about to be robbed and where the robbers were staying. Joe and other detectives, as well as FBI agents, immediately set up surveillance on the suspects' vehicle and followed them for the next couple of days. While they were being watched, the two went to the bank, pulled into the parking lot, and observed the building and its surroundings for about 10 minutes before driving off.

This targeted bank was located at the end of a shopping mall. The mall had two entrances on either side of the bank entrance, both with separate parking lots. The informant told the detectives that the robbery was planned for the following Friday at 4:30 p.m.

Early that Friday afternoon, all involved law-enforcement agencies attended a briefing in the Robbery office. Joe and his partner were assigned to guard the second mall entrance across from where they'd observed the suspects casing the place. Joe was armed with a 12-gauge shotgun loaded with double-aught buckshot.

As the briefing wound down, the captain in charge of investigations asked who was taking the shotgun.

Joe responded, "That would be me."

The captain said with emphasis, "They *don't* get into the bank. Do you understand?"

"Yes."

But after the briefing, Joe asked the captain if he could speak with him in the lieutenant's office. "Sir, I know what to do, but the federal supervisor is involved in this. Where does he stand on the matter?"

The captain called the supervisor and asked if he agreed that these suspects were far too dangerous to allow them to enter the bank. The federal supervisor agreed and it was settled.

Joe and his partner set up surveillance of the area about an hour before the robbery was to take place. The bandits had most likely chosen late afternoon, knowing that multiple customers in and around the bank at closing time would deter a gun battle with the police, who wouldn't want to endanger civilians. Also, they hoped for a smooth escape, using side streets through rush-hour traffic in the dark.

Joe and his partner were positioned outside the mall entrance while rain fell. A surveillance team also waited at the suspect's location, ready to notify detectives when the men got into their car. As he waited, Joe kept busy running various scenarios through his mind.

The robbers might enter the mall, no weapons in hands. But Joe was 99.9% sure, given their history, that weapons would be in full view. So he had to decide how best to respond once they passed the mall entrance and moved toward the bank. Only Joe and his partner were to engage the robbers in a gun battle. The other detectives and agents would only engage if the bad guys got past Joe and his partner and tried to enter the bank. Joe knew that if he had to use the shotgun, he'd have to fire from a lower position than the suspects, directing his fire up and away to keep bystanders out of the line of buckshot.

The surveillance team radioed that the suspects were on the move and were headed straight to the bank. Fortunately, the rain kept foot traffic to a minimum on Joe's side of the mall. Joe and his partner opened two of the mall doors and waited out of sight against the exterior wall.

The robbers pulled into the mall parking lot near the entrance across from Joe and his partner. Joe released the safety on the shotgun and stood prepared as surveillance reported the suspects' windows were fogging up, but they could still see them donning ski masks.

A surge of adrenaline began to flow through Joe. This operation involved very dangerous criminals, a huge threat to public safety, and risk for multiple law-enforcement personnel. Darkness and rain confounded matters. Difficult, but necessary, decisions were on Joe's mind.

The suspects sat in their vehicle for a few minutes, then abruptly drove off. Did they know how close they came to getting shot to death that day? Joe will never know. And the informant never learned why the suspects abandoned their plan.

Later, having left San Diego, the bank robbers met their demise while robbing a bank in Tennessee. Most likely, it was the same outcome that awaited them in San Diego. Same gig, different place and time.

Collision in the Air

PSA Flight 182

On September 25, 1978, Joe had just finished interviewing a witness to a robbery in east San Diego. He suddenly noticed a large plume of black smoke and drove toward it.

When he arrived at the scene, he saw total devastation. He learned later that a Pacific Southwest Airlines Boeing

727 had collided with a Cessna 172 and both planes met the ground at 300 miles per hour, noses down.

Firefighters were on site, feverishly trying to extinguish a fire on the tail section and engine of what remained of the jet. Houses were burning as patrol units rapidly evacuated the area residents.

Joe was then called to assist with an emergency nearby. Officers from a San Diego police ambulance were trying to extricate a mother and daughter from their vehicle. The mother was driving her daughter to school when the plane crashed. A flight attendant's lifeless body flew through their car's open window and crumpled against the passenger-side dashboard. Joe had never seen a case of shock so extreme. To this day, he wonders if the two were able to recover from the experience.

A while later, he took a moment to look around the area and survey the damage. Of course, he'd responded to many civilian and military aircraft crashes in the Coast Guard and he knew there would be no survivors. The deadliest aircraft disaster in California history and, at that time, the deadliest in U.S. aviation history claimed the lives of 144 people.

Five Days in Hell

Soon, Joe was ordered to return to the station.

As the horrific details became more apparent, the Chief of Police was determined not to expose the entire police department to the carnage that covered the area. He deployed half the Robbery Detail to the crash scene.

At that time, San Diego was experiencing Santa Ana weather conditions, during which the temperature could expect to rise as high as 115 degrees. As they recovered the human remains, they knew they were working against the clock as the temperatures rose.

During the initial search, they covered a three-block area and located hundreds, if not thousands, of human remains. Some body parts had impacted houses and the powerful force impaled them into walls. Others were still strapped into their seats after being propelled through the walls of homes. Joe handled two aircraft seats landing on beds that were occupied by the residents. Houses had human remains scattered across their roofs, exterior walls, and yards.

Among the worst of the recovery work was trying to remove the remains of ejected passengers that had permeated the stucco on the sides of houses, becoming stuck in the wire mesh.

The second day when work resumed at the site, temperatures exceeded 100 degrees and opportunistic flies descended on the area. The insects hindered progress so much that the City Public Works Department arrived to spray insecticide.

Joe returned home after the second day of recovery and fell into what would become an unwanted routine: a couple of stiff drinks and another restless night. The work was taking an emotional toll on him, but he knew everything he and others were going through didn't compare to what the victims had endured or the grief being experienced by their loved ones.

On day three, the search focused on finding smaller remains, some of which were suspended from trees. Air temperature was still high, resulting in the rapid decomposition of human tissue. A foul odor permeated the area. Joe and others persevered despite the constant stench of death around them, a rank and pungent smell blended with a sickening sweetness.

The day became even more difficult when Joe found out that one of the burned residences was a home day-care center. All the children were found huddled together in the basement, dead from smoke inhalation and subsequently burned beyond recognition. When Joe returned home that evening, he couldn't stop thinking of the parents and the loss and pain they were experiencing. Surely the parents didn't view the remains. At least, he hoped they hadn't.

Then Joe heard from a member of the recovery team that he had come upon two hands among the debris, detached from their arms. The description left an indelible mark in Joe's mind for 40 years; they became to him an image representing what passengers on PSA 182 were most likely feeling before 9:02 a.m. on September 25, 1978. The hands were of a man and a woman, still clasped together.

By day four, the massive efforts of all involved in the recovery were nearing conclusion. But other strangeness was afoot.

One of the uniformed officers protecting the perimeter asked Joe if he would talk to some people who wanted to enter the crash site. Joe accompanied the officer to a Salvation Army food truck where he saw numerous young women in PSA flight-attendant uniforms. One of the women told him the others were in training and that a "tour" of the site would be useful.

"Personally, I can't see how this human carnage can be used to train new flight attendants," he said. "Besides, entering the site will hinder ongoing recovery efforts. I can't let you in."

"Fine," the woman huffed. "I'll go over your head."

The security director for PSA was a former San Diego police officer and he contacted the Chief. A short time later, Joe received a call. He explained to the Chief that they were in recovery efforts and he didn't think a site visit by future flight attendants was warranted or would be beneficial to their training. The Chief agreed that their access would serve no purpose.

Everyone arrived the next morning, knowing that the fifth day would be the last. Most of the wreckage had been cleared. Some of the burned houses were demolished. Workers did final sweeps through the area and the announcement was made at 4 p.m. that the efforts were complete. The crash site would be turned over to the City Public Works Department.

Joe returned home that night and immediately threw his shoes and jumpsuits, though clean, into the trash can. Sitting in a living room chair, he relived the feelings he'd experienced over those terrible days and hoped he never had to go through anything like that again.

Alas, less than a year later, on May 25, 1979, a DC10 aircraft crashed into a Chicago neighborhood, killing more than 270 people. Joe received a call the next day from a higher-ranking officer inquiring if he'd be willing to go to Chicago to assist their police department with the recovery. Joe rarely, if ever, declined requests for help. But the five days he'd spent the previous year continued to haunt him. He couldn't go through it again. In fact, it would be 30 years before he could drive through the crash site. Even then, the horrors he witnessed flooded his mind and he vowed never to return.

In the years since the crash, Joe has thought often of the lives lost and the family and friends left to mourn the victims. The experience deeply affected him. It's an essential part of his life story.

But there's more.

Aftermath

After returning home from the crash site each evening, Joe began to drink more, attempting to cope with the horrors he'd witnessed. Even after the site was cleared and he returned to his normal duties as a robbery detective, he drank more after his shifts. He realized that he had to stop drinking so heavily, but he also knew that, though he was free of the crash site, he'd never really be free of the crash.

For months, he was constantly reminded of it. The local and national news continued to report on it. A simple thing like grocery shopping inevitably led to overhearing or engaging in conversations about the crash. He just couldn't escape it.

He eventually got control of the drinking by immersing himself in robbery investigations. As time went on, he began to feel normal again. But he was forced to relive the crash each year on the anniversary. The news reports were full of crash details. Joe began to understand that he'd never erase the haunting memories, so he had to learn to live with them on a deeper level.

Despite his experience at the crash site, Joe never hesitated to fly commercially, whether domestic or international. He attributed this to his hundreds of flight hours in the military under life-threatening conditions.

Many years later, on a trip to Tokyo, Joe turned on the TV in his hotel room and saw a news station reporting about a plane crash. The program was broadcast in Japanese, so he didn't understand the dialogue. But he certainly recognized the videos and photos of the crash site of PSA Flight 182. It was another anniversary. Joe wondered, "Oh man, am I ever going to be free of this?"

While watching the video broadcasts of the crash scene, Joe realized the viewers were only using two human senses to evaluate what they saw: sight and hearing. Joe and the other recovery workers had experienced the event through all five senses, simultaneously: sight, hearing, taste, smell, and touch. This was a rare human experience. Joe believes that the level and scope of sensory input from the crash resulted in sensory overload. And overstimulation of the senses can cause a range of emotional, cognitive, and physical symptoms similar to post-traumatic stress disorder.

After seeing the news report in another country, he realized that the world was remembering and honoring the victims of the horrific event. He was eventually able to turn his mind's eye away from the haunting images at the crash scene, focusing instead on the victims and who they were. He began to see them and know the details of their lives from the abundance of published photographs and news articles.

Beginning of the End of Police Work

A Matter of Innocence

Joe arrived at work one morning and found himself assigned to a case involving the armed robbery of a 7-Eleven. A suspect was in custody at the county jail.

The 7-Eleven was robbed during the night and witnessed by the store clerk and a customer. The robber brandished a silver revolver.

Shortly after the robbery, patrol officers stopped a black male who matched the witnesses' description. The officers drove the suspect to the 7-Eleven, where the witnesses positively identified him as having robbed the clerk at gunpoint.

Joe and his partner thanked the sergeant for giving them a slam-dunk case and proceeded to the county jail. When they met the suspect in the interview room, the detectives noticed he fit the witnesses' physical description, but his clothing was different. They kept in mind that suspects often changed clothes following a robbery.

Joe read the man his Miranda rights and he agreed to waive all rights and talk to the detectives. Over two hours, he insisted that he was stopped by police while walking to a friend's house near the 7-Eleven and consistently denied any involvement in the robbery.

No weapon or money was found when the suspect was arrested and that posed a problem. Also, Joe and his partner learned the suspect was married with two children and had a job with a good company. They told him they'd follow up on his story and get back to him. They left the interview room, took two steps outside, looked at each other, and simultaneously declared, "He didn't do it."

The detectives returned to the Robbery Unit and said the same thing to the sergeant.

"You sure? Both the black clerk and the white witness ID'd this guy." Joe knew what he was saying. Misidentification across racial groups is an unfortunate reality in law enforcement, particularly among witnesses.

On the other hand, knowing the two seasoned detectives had probably interviewed more 10,000 victims, witnesses, and suspects, the sergeant trusted their instincts. He told them, "Go out there and find the right guy!"

They had 72 hours before they had to file charges with the DA's office.

They started by verifying that what the suspect had said about his family and employment was true. They checked all criminal-record systems nationwide and found no records pertaining to him. Finally, they reached out to their CIs and requested they gather all information circulating on the street about the robbery.

The next morning, a CI called and told the detectives that a black drug addict named Sammy robbed the 7-Eleven. Joe and his partner found Sammy's last name, searched the records, and learned he was on parole. This meant he was automatically subject to search and seizure without a warrant.

Knowing addicts usually didn't wake up until around noon, the detectives headed to Sammy's residence at 9 a.m. and rousted him out of bed. Sammy was still under the influence and in a stupor. Joe and his partner began inter-rogating Sammy and his answers pertaining to an alibi were ridiculous.

The detectives noticed Sammy was similar in stature to the suspect at the county jail and the two men had the same haircut. While conducting a search of his residence, they found a nickel-plated 38-caliber pistol in a drawer under some dirty clothing.

"Sammy," Joe said, "we know this is your third offense. You're looking at some serious prison time. But we'd be willing to recommend a reduced sentence in exchange for your cooperation."

At that point, Sammy confessed to the robbery. They took him to the Robbery Unit, where he signed statements.

The sergeant told them, "I knew you two would find the right guy. Now go get that innocent man out of jail and back with his family."

The detectives returned to the county jail. After two nights behind bars, it seemed the man had aged five years and they knew he wouldn't do well in prison. When they slid his release form across the table, he picked it up with trembling hands and began to cry while reading the form, asking, "What does this mean?"

"It means that we caught the robber. You're no longer a suspect and you're being released immediately. When the deputy returns, we'll have him take you to a phone to call your wife."

"Okay, but what about my job? I was a no-call, no-show for three days and if they know why, they'll think I robbed a convenience store."

"I personally called over there," Joe told him. "I assured them that you're not guilty of any crime."

"And they believed you?"

"Not only did they believe me, but they expressed relief that you'll be returning to work."

The man thanked the detectives from the bottom of his heart. He'd felt certain he would be charged with the robbery after the witnesses identified him.

Of all the cases Joe investigated and all the awards bestowed on him, no career experience brought him as much pride as the look on that innocent man's face when he was cleared of a crime — not by his lawyer, but by two cops who understood they had a responsibility not only to investigate and prove guilt, but also to prove someone's innocence.

A Well-Deserved Vacation

Cops are on duty 24/7. If a situation arises and they fail to take action, they can be suspended without pay. Also, they can be suspended for not carrying their firearm while off-duty ... even on vacation.

A group of San Diego's finest went on a ski vacation for a week, every year for 25 years, never telling anyone that they were cops. Early one evening, he and Gary Gleason were having a drink at a restaurant in the ski area. They couldn't help but notice two guys being loud and rowdy. The men were more than the bartender could handle, so he called the sheriff. A young deputy arrived and soon after he confronted the boisterous men, the fight began. Within seconds, Joe and Gary jumped into the middle of the melee to aid the deputy, who was on the floor.

Gary and Joe had to utilize sleeper holds on both of the suspects to render them unconscious, a standard police procedure at the time. Then they secured the two with the deputy's handcuffs. As they brushed the floor's sawdust from his uniform, the deputy asked, "Who the hell are you guys?"

They identified themselves as detectives from San Diego and the deputy profusely thanked them for their much-needed assistance.

As they were giving the deputy their information for his report, one of the suspects woke up and asked, "What happened?"

Joe said, "This deputy cleaned your clocks."

"Man, he was fast!"

The deputy left with the two prisoners.

Shortly thereafter, the cocktail waitress came on duty. Joe and Gary were sitting next to her station and Gary struck up a conversation. Joe overheard Gary telling her he was on parole for bank robbery. When she left to take an order at a table, Joe turned to Gary. "Are you nuts?"

Gary answered with a grin, "Yeah. I found out she loves bad boys."

Joe left Gary at the bar. He returned to their condo and didn't see Gary until the next morning. After skiing the next afternoon, Joe found a message on his condo door to call the sheriff.

Joe began going over the previous night's scene. Did they choke the guys too long and they dropped dead?

The sheriff got on the phone. "Thank you for helping my young deputy."

Joe was waiting for the sheriff to say, "But ... one of the suspects died." Finally, he asked, "Is everyone okay?"

"Yes, the deputy and the two bar brawlers survived the ordeal." Then he added, "And if you ever need anything, don't hesitate to call."

Gary eventually showed up—and Joe didn't have to call back the sheriff to see if he had a list of ladies who liked bad boys.

Time to Leave

In early 1980, an agent from the Nevada Gaming Control Board (GCB) contacted Joe concerning an investigation into a gaming-license application that the GCB's Investigative Division was conducting. The agent was in San Diego and needed Joe's help checking some records about a junket representative from the Bahamas, who also had some business in southern California. While working together, the GCB agent mentioned that he'd been trying to establish contact with law-enforcement personnel in a country in which Joe had connections from his days with the NTF. Joe connected the agent with the country's national police.

When the agent returned to Las Vegas, he informed his deputy chief of Joe's assistance and apparent network of international contacts. The deputy chief, a retired captain from the Intelligence Unit of the Texas Department of Public Safety, was impressed. He asked the agent to return to San Diego to explore the possibilities of recruiting the cop.

The agent and Joe met for lunch.

"Foreign nationals are becoming increasingly interested in the casino business," the agent explained. "So are major international companies. More and more, we need qualified agents, people such as yourself, to conduct investigations in offshore jurisdictions. Are you at all interested?"

Joe smiled. "It just so happens that my wife, Karen, is a singer and she's currently negotiating a contract to perform at MGM Grand hotels in Las Vegas and Reno for an extended duration." Obviously, a reassignment to Nevada would benefit Joe's marriage greatly.

"My deputy chief, Howard Smith, would like to talk to you about a position within the Control Board."

Joe said, "I appreciate that. I'll think about it."

It didn't take long for Joe to call the GCB. The deputy chief asked him to come to Las Vegas for an informal interview. Joe flew in and met with Howard Smith, who informed him of the duties and responsibilities of a law-enforcement position that would be opening within the next couple of months.

"You'll have to complete an employment application and the San Diego Police Department will be contacted as part of the application process. Is that acceptable to you?"

"Yes, sir. It's perfectly acceptable."

The salary for the position was $5,000 more annually than Joe was earning in San Diego, even after 12 years with the police department and having moved through the ranks to his current position of detective. He had a fair amount of seniority and was devoted to his work, but the Nevada opportunity was intriguing and the salary increase and no state income tax were icing on the cake.

When Howard Smith contacted Joe and officially offered him the position, the next step was to contact the San Diego Police Department. Joe asked Smith to please wait one week.

He wanted the chance to meet with the board of the Police Officers Association and inform them that he was leaving.

He got together with the board and together they strategized. The members suggested that Joe play the trump card of his new employment offer during the upcoming salary negotiations between the POA and the city.

As expected, the city negotiators made a pathetic offer for police pay increases.

Joe was incensed. "That's your final offer?" he said, obviously disgusted. "You should be ashamed of yourselves. It's not only insulting to all the loyal officers of the San Diego Police Department, but it's also disrespectful to the citizens of your city."

"Our city?" the negotiators scoffed. "It's your city too."

"Not anymore it isn't!" Joe slammed his formal resignation papers onto the table. "If you continue down this path of offending your police officers, pretty soon there won't be any left. What do you suppose will happen then, gentlemen? I'll tell you! Pencil-necked geeks like you will have to fill in to serve and protect!" With that, Joe shouted, "Good luck!" and walked out of the City Hall conference room.

Joe believes that if he hadn't been a board member of the POA, he probably wouldn't have left the police department. Having to negotiate with oblivious and ungrateful city administrators left a bitter taste in his mouth. In the same year that Joe resigned, more than 250 officers also left, the majority for other law-enforcement agencies. And if they'd known of the city administration's true attitudes toward them, many of the officers who remained would have quit in disgust as well.

Nevada Gaming
Control Board

A New Life in Las Vegas

Joe left the San Diego Police Department in May 1980 and began work with the Nevada Gaming Control Board as an agent in the Investigations Division in the Las Vegas office. He could have gone to the other office in Carson City/Reno, but Karen was starting an engagement in Vegas at the same time.

Control Board agents were designated law-enforcement officers with authority to regulate and enforce gaming laws and regulations. Joe started work there as a "background agent," which required five years' experience in the investigation of felonies. Background investigators were primarily responsible for delving into the histories and qualifications of individuals and companies seeking gaming licenses, as required by Nevada law. He reported to the GCB with more than 11½ years of experience—four in uniform and 7½ as a detective. He was assigned to the Las Vegas office the same day Karen opened with her band at the MGM Grand (now Bally's).

The Gaming Control Board isn't just a law-enforcement agency, it's also an administrative agency of the state government's gambling apparatus. The Nevada Gaming Commission acts in a judicial capacity. If, after investigation, the Control Board determines that an applicant is unfit for a gaming license, the Commission as the adjudicator denies the application. Likewise, if the GCB finds that some disciplinary action should be taken against a gaming licensee (casino), it prosecutes the case before the Commission, the final authority when it comes to approving, restricting, suspending, or revoking any gaming license.

In addition to investigations, enforcement, and administration, the Gaming Control Board has audit, tax and licensing, and technology divisions. The Board is composed of three members appointed by the governor who serve four-year full-time terms, while the Commission has five members, also appointed by the governor, who serve four-year part-time terms. (There's also a Gaming Policy Committee that meets from time to time at the governor's request. Its recommendations are advisory only and are not binding on the Board or Commission. It consists of 12 members from government, casinos, academia, and the general public.)

It didn't take long for Joe to realize the enormous power the GCB and Gaming Commission wielded over those applying for a gaming license. An individual or company seeking a license had to apply through the Board's applicant services and pay an initial investigation fee of $25,000. The application was then assigned an investigative account number.

The applicant was required to fully disclose personal and professional history as far back as 25 years and to sign releases for financial, criminal, and education records, IRS tax returns, and investment information concerning stocks, bonds, associated partnerships, and other business dealings. To facilitate the financial part of the investigations, background agents were paired with GCB financial agents.

Joe found that the financial agents were not only invaluable in investigating gaming-license applicants, but helped him lift his investigative skills to a level he'd never been exposed to. The investigative and financial agents became very close, functioning essentially as a single unit, garnering and evaluating background information on the potential licensees.

Investigators gathered and reviewed all the paperwork, then met with their supervisor to plan the investigation, estimating hours and travel expenses. The applicant's lawyer was then notified of any fees over and above the initial $25,000 deposit, which needed to be paid to cover additional time and expenses. Investigations never began until all the funds were in the investigative account. There was no guarantee that further funds wouldn't be necessary, depending on what agents uncovered during their investigations.

Circa 1980, front-line employees (dealers, floor supervisors) in the gaming areas were issued a work card by the Las Vegas Metropolitan Police Work Card Unit; today, the Gaming Control Board issues gaming work cards. The cost was minimal and the card was good for five years. Higher level gaming employees with a certain amount of authority were reported annually as "key" employees and could be called forward for licensing at any time. In that case, the casino picked up the cost of the investigations. But as a background investigator, Joe was assigned the job of looking into the past and present of casino board members, owners and potential owners, junket representatives, and companies applying to do business in the casino industry, such as manufacturers.

A local Las Vegas applicant with minimal financial holdings and a simple history could be investigated quickly and Joe could conduct several key-employee investigations at the same time. An investigation that required more extensive travel took longer and was more complicated — and those were plentiful. Agents spent an average of six months a year on the road conducting investigations.

For example, one investigation required eight agents to delve into a manufacturer of gaming devices in Australia that wanted to sell its machines to Las Vegas casinos. By this time Joe was a senior investigative agent; along with a senior financial supervisor, he accompanied the agents as they traveled all over the country. The first trip kept them in Australia for eight weeks. A return trip uncovered unfavorable information. The investigation took more than a year and cost the applicant upwards of $365,000. Due to what Joe and his agents learned, the application was withdrawn and, of course, there was no refund of fees.

The longest and most complicated investigations involved casinos being bought and sold. If a casino was being purchased by an individual or corporation that had never held a Nevada gaming license, it could take many months to complete the background and financial investigations.

Having the licensees pay for the investigations made total sense to Joe. Why should the taxpayers subsidize the licensing of an individual who would more than likely benefit financially? This was also true of applicants who were denied licenses, having taken the financial risk when their applications failed. The investigation fees also ensured that applications would come from serious individuals and companies only.

The stakes were different than when Joe was a city cop.

Generally speaking, in San Diego, his "clientele" had their freedom to lose, while in Nevada, applicants were at risk for substantial sums of money. But as a GCB investigator, Joe was dealing with a higher level of clientele. Initially, he missed the excitement of being an active cop, but that passed after a few investigative trips.

Joe's job was made easier by his extensive network of domestic and international law-enforcement contacts, but his outreach didn't stop there. He also began to recruit seasoned detectives from the San Diego PD. One was Keith Copher, a highly experienced Robbery detective who eventually became Chief of the Enforcement Division at the GCB. Another, Elton "Beetle" Bailey, was an experienced supervisor from both the Narcotics Task Force and Robbery. Gordon Dickie, one of San Diego's top street cops, had retired with a back and neck injury from a beating he took while working uniformed patrol, but Joe convinced him to unretire and move to the GCB to go to work at the Enforcement Division.

Last but not least was John Murray, known as "JP," a legendary undercover officer in the late '60s and early '70s. JP went deep undercover — no badge, no police ID, no cover unit — for many months and mailed taped reports back to his handler in the Intelligence Unit at the SDPD. JP infiltrated radical anti-war and leftist organizations and rose to a level of inclusion during the protests against the Vietnam War when these groups were planning and scheduling actions against military installations. He was eventually outed as a police officer and subsequently received numerous threats on his life. Radicals even put a hit on him, offering a reward to anyone who killed him. Ultimately, he was instrumental in indicting numerous members of these groups, testifying for many days about their criminal activities.

Tools of the Trade

In the first two weeks of his employment in the Investigations Division, Joe received an ID card, a badge, and an American Express credit card — but no handgun.

Background and financial investigators for the Gaming Control Board didn't carry weapons. They traveled too often in and out of various jurisdictions and at the time, reciprocity among states and cities for officer handgun privileges was too involved. Also, there was really no need, as they weren't in any danger. The applicants weren't only seeking a gaming license, they also weren't made aware of what an investigation had uncovered until it was concluded. No one, including the investigators, would know the outcome of a licensing hearing until the Gaming Control Board and Gaming Commission voted on it. Some applicants attempted to cozy up to the agents to determine if they'd found anything derogatory, but investigators were well-trained on how to conduct themselves. The only GCB agents who carried weapons worked in the Enforcement Division. They were responsible for responding to licensees for jackpot verifications and reports of cheating and they made arrests for violations of Gaming regulations.

As for other tools of the trade, in the days before cell phones and GPS-equipped cars, roadmaps and the ability to read them were essential. Agents traveled to the biggest cities and the smallest towns on their investigations.

Agents also needed the ability to make cold calls to police departments and to get information well beyond what they found in simple records checks. They had to obtain information from ongoing investigations regarding the applicants, if any were in progress. Once they made contact with local law enforcement, agents often had to describe their own police careers; many locals had never heard of the Nevada Gaming Control Board. In most cases, once they were aware of Joe's extensive police background, local police and officials opened all their files to him.

Personal credibility with other law-enforcement agencies, however, didn't always do the trick. In some investigations, Joe was told he couldn't see certain reports if a local investigation was under way. He might be directed where to investigate in order to find his own information, but on occasion, local detectives and investigators couldn't risk their information being placed in a public report or revealed in a public hearing, which would cause them big problems in their agencies.

It didn't happen too often, but on occasion, Joe's search turned up completely empty.

For example, right after receiving his American Express card, he set out on the road for the better part of the next six months, mainly in Chicago, investigating some connections gaming-license applicants had to the Mob. As part of that inquiry, he drove from the Windy City to a town so small that it had a four-way red-flashing traffic signal at its one intersection. On the door of the police department was a note: "In the diner." Joe walked down the street to the eatery, where he found the chief of police, one of two officers in the town's police department.

"My name is Joe Dorsey. I'm from the Nevada Gaming Control Board and I'm here to do a records check." Joe showed the chief his badge, then gave him the applicant's name, Frank K, along with information that connected him to the town.

The chief began pulling loose papers from his jacket pockets—from napkins with pencil scrawlings to official documents with the town's criminal records. After looking through the pile of scrap paper for a few moments, the chief replied, "Nope. Don't have anything on Frank K."

Joe was kept very busy in his first year with the Board and traveled as much as he wanted to. He stayed at much nicer hotels and received a per-diem for meals at a much better rate than traveling for the San Diego Police Department. He was making a little more money and basically supervised himself, but was responsible for completing investigations within a reasonable amount of time. He really liked the work and travel, but especially appreciated the opportunity to make new law-enforcement contacts.

Conducting investigations for the GCB also provided Joe the opportunity to travel worldwide. His work connected him to local, state, federal, and international law-enforcement agencies, as well as organized-crime units in countries ranging from Australia to Italy.

The GCB agents used outside travel agents who were well-versed in the accommodation and air-travel parameters for investigators. When traveling domestically, if the trip exceeded 2,000 miles, agents could fly first class and all international travel was first class. Hotels were of the Marriott tier. The per-diem for meals was about $65 domestically and higher abroad. Receipts for all out-of-pocket expenses were submitted for reimbursement. Entertainment, such as dinner with law-enforcement contacts, was receipted and reimbursed.

And then there were the infamous RUMP sessions. Joe was briefed early on by his senior agent about RUMP, which was not so much an acronym as a code word. To Joe, RUMP was a lot like a criminal pre-trial conference with the prosecutor in the office of the District Attorney. At the GCB, the senior agent and his investigative agents met with the Gaming Control Board members to go over the completed reports for applications being considered on the agenda of the next public meeting.

The senior agent told Joe, "This is, basically, the time you'll get your ass chewed over an investigation and report. That's why we call them the RUMP sessions."

Joe smiled and nodded as the senior agent continued. "It's your job to know each Board member's likes and dislikes when it comes to presenting the investigations and to be sure you cover them all." The senior agent paused, then asked Joe, "Why are you smiling like that?"

He said, "With all due respect to the Board members, I doubt that a RUMP will bother me much. When it comes to ass chewing, all they'll get is scar tissue."

"What do you mean?"

"What I mean is, a San Diego Police patrol sergeant has already been there on occasion. Nobody, not even an Army drill sergeant, can chew ass better than a uniformed police sergeant."

Joe recalls that he served under a GCB deputy chief once who made it his life's work to find one thing wrong with every report ever submitted to him. So Joe placed a glaring error—an obviously misspelled name, wrong date, or number that made no sense—on the first couple of pages, rendering it a simple matter for the deputy chief to find his one error. That was all he was ultimately looking for, so he could one-up the agents. Then he left the rest of the report alone.

How Investigations Worked

Typically, Joe was assigned an investigation, then met with his supervisor, a senior agent with the Investigations Division, to discuss the scope of the investigation and travel. He then started making all the necessary arrangements—

flights, hotels, and rental cars. A typical trip within the U.S. lasted up to two weeks; Joe didn't plan on traveling for more than that.

Next, he checked his law-enforcement contacts at the destinations to seek assistance, then scheduled appointments with his contacts and the applicant. He submitted written requests to the Internal Revenue Service, banks and other lending institutions, and national law-enforcement databases for financial and criminal-record information. He also contacted personal references supplied by the applicant and made informal requests for information through federal law-enforcement agencies prior to travel.

Once he arrived in the applicant's city, he made his connections, kept his appointments, and began his records searches via local, state, and federal law-enforcement agencies, along with county, state, and federal courts.

The agents had authority to inventory safety-deposit boxes, as well as personal safes and lock boxes. Search warrants weren't required during investigations and applicants had no automatic right to the presence of an attorney during interviews. In fact, the applicant himself or herself was required to answer all questions.

In one investigation, Joe wanted to look in a safety-deposit box belonging to Harry R at a local bank. He and the financial agent, Gregg Schatzman, accompanied Harry to the bank, where the gaming-license applicant filled out the proper documents to access his box. As Joe and Gregg started walking with Harry into the safety-deposit-box vault to inspect the box's contents, the bank employee said, "I'm sorry, gentlemen, but you can't enter that area."

Schatzman said, "Ma'am, we're investigators from the Nevada Gaming Control Board." He and Joe presented their badges. "The reason that the three of us are here is to inspect the contents of Mr. R's box."

"Be that as it may, I can't give you permission."

Schatzman, a fairly new agent at the time, looked at Joe.

Now Joe wasn't sure if Harry had contacted the employee, telling her not to grant them access. She might have even been part of his criminal organization. The press at the time had been reporting that some local banks were involved in money-laundering activities with international drug traffickers. But he also knew that he had to get a look inside the box and Harry was fully prepared to allow it, even if the bank wasn't.

"Ma'am, does Mr. R pay a monthly fee for his box?"

"Yes."

"Then does Mr. R in essence own the box — to do what he wants with it?"

"Yes."

"That being the case, if Mr. R wanted to allow us to accompany him to examine the contents of the box, would that be permitted?"

"Yes."

Joe turned to Harry. "You want us to see what's in the box, right?"

Harry said, "Right."

Though the employee showed distinct signs of displeasure, Joe and Schatzman proceeded to inventory the contents of the safety-deposit box. As they (and Harry) expected, nothing in the box hadn't already been furnished by the applicant (will, property deeds, and personal papers). It was well-known that GCB background agents inventoried deposit boxes and safes, so Joe never found anything derogatory — during an initial search. But the GCB didn't advertise that the first inventory was procedural and agents conducted follow-up searches; the second and third inventories proved fruitful on occasion, when applicants returned things to their boxes that they didn't want the gaming authorities to see.

After traveling to the various parts of the country and world and collecting all the information and copying documents, Joe did a preliminary evaluation, then returned to Las Vegas for in-depth reviews and a determination of whether or not any of the information might open other areas that needed to be investigated. Often, one thing led to another.

Once he'd completed his investigation, Joe wrote a report, providing all the information the investigation had turned up. He highlighted any derogatory information in "Areas of Concern" fields in the report template. Joe's senior agent reviewed the report, then documented questions, concerns, and recommendations, and sent the package up the chain of command to the division's assistant chief for review and on to the division chief, who placed it on the agenda for the licensing hearing in front of the Gaming Control Board members and the Gaming Commission.

Joe conducted dozens of investigations during his five years at the Gaming Control Board, many concurrently. Even as late in the game as the early and mid-1980s, Joe frequently found himself up against organized-crime organizations still trying to infiltrate the casino business in Las Vegas and outlying areas.

One of his background checks led to the removal of organized crime from a new-casino construction operation.

The Edgewater Investigation

Early in 1981, Joe and two other agents were assigned the licensing investigation of the Edgewater Hotel and

Casino, which was completing construction along the banks of the Colorado River in Laughlin, Nevada. It didn't take long for them to start receiving information that the Detroit organized-crime family was placing investors in the project, but hiding their ownership involvement. Trusting the information, they began to focus on finding the route that Detroit's investments were taking into the Edgewater. But after three weeks, they'd had no luck.

The financial agent assigned to the case returned from Cleveland, Ohio, after interviewing an applicant for Edgewater ownership by the name of Ron Glazer.

"Glazer insisted that his investment funds, all in cash, came from an inheritance from his father, who was a physician in Cleveland. Glazer said that his father didn't trust banks, due to living through the Great Depression, which is why his father had four hundred thousand dollars in cash hidden in a shoebox in the basement of his house."

This was exactly the break Joe and his team needed.

Starting their investigation of Glazer, they discovered he'd threatened the life of a Salt Lake City man, a potential investor in the Edgewater. As for his father not trusting banks, they found more than 10 bank accounts he'd had through his life, along with active accounts at his time of death.

Glazer proved to be the center of a hub that started growing quickly. The investigators learned that one of the spokes connected up with Emmett Munley. Early in the investigation, agents had learned that Munley had been detained by Caribbean authorities for removing cash assets from a casino. Curiously, when Joe contacted those authorities in Aruba, they told him that they wouldn't discuss Munley's detention. Joe escalated the call to the Aruban commissioner of police, who refused to disclose any information or help in any way.

Then Joe contacted a friend with whom he'd worked at the Narcotics Task Force in San Diego, now assigned to DEA Miami.

"Well, Joe, you're in luck," the friend said. "It just so happens that I'm now in charge of the whole Caribbean. Let me see what I can do for you."

When he called back, he said, "I vouched for you, Joe. Give the commissioner another call and if he doesn't cooperate, let me know."

When Joe spoke again to the commissioner, he was still standoffish, but was willing to meet Joe and his team in neighboring Curaçao.

At the meeting, at first it seemed to Joe that the commissioner was trying to obtain more information about Munley than divulge it. After a little more back and forth, the commissioner said, "Look, the only reason I'm talking to you is because of the DEA." Then he placed a file on his desk. But when Joe reached for it, he pulled it back and said, "I'll read it to you."

By now, Joe had figured out what was going on.

In as friendly a voice as he could muster, he said, "We're not here to judge anyone or their actions. We know Munley was attempting to leave your jurisdiction with financial records and a lot of cash from a casino. We also know that after being detained for a while, Munley was allowed to board a private plane and leave the area with no charges being filed." He paused to let that information sink in. "Commissioner, we're simply trying to prevent the same type of theft from our casinos. Knowing the particulars of Munley's activities and detention might give us insight into his operations, in the event he's granted a license in Nevada."

"Okay," the commissioner replied, pushing the file back to Joe. "You can't copy the reports, but you can take notes."

The information the agents gained from the reports led them to various areas of the country, where they slowly but surely uncovered the ways that the Detroit Mob was able to infiltrate the Edgewater Company.

In Detroit, for example, they interviewed Jimmy Tamer, who was involved with the Teamsters Pension Fund that had provided financing for most of the newer casinos in Las Vegas. Tamer was surprised that they knew so much about the Edgewater operation and its investors.

While in Detroit, Joe also met with local FBI officials who, believing the agents were in possession of all the information about the Detroit's move into the Edgewater, talked freely with the agents from Nevada. The officials didn't know that the agents were unaware of some of the information they'd revealed.

As soon as Joe returned to Las Vegas from Detroit, he was hastily summoned to a meeting with the Las Vegas FBI agent who'd set up the FBI meeting in Detroit. "Damn, Joe. The Detroit office gave you some pretty sensitive information they thought you were already aware of. So now we need to know how much of that you'll be putting into your report that could become public."

"I have absolutely no intention of including anything you and the Detroit office deem critical to your investigations," Joe assured him. "Actually, if you want to read the report regarding my contact with your Detroit office prior to my submitting it, I'll make it available to you."

Next, Joe and his partner paid a visit to the Edgewater in Laughlin, where they were startled to find William Pompili working as the so-called food and beverage manager. Pompili had been investigated for improprieties at other casinos thought to be Mob-related; in Laughlin, he was directing the placement of gaming tables and slot machines.

Pompili knew that as the food and beverage manager, he wasn't required to submit to licensing as a key employee.

The plot was thickening, so Joe took a longer look around.

What he found was astonishing. The Edgewater was set up in such a way that even a blind person could see the skim. The count room was located on a lower floor within 30 feet of the loading dock, perfect for hiding cash and coin in boxes on the way to being shipped out. Not only that, but it was totally enclosed, with no windows to observe the count activity. The Enforcement Division hadn't inspected the property as yet and with the information the background agents gave them, Joe was sure it would be a very thorough inspection.

Meanwhile, the Gaming Commission granted a six-month conditional license for 16 table games and 300 slot machines. In addition, because of licensing problems, the legitimate investors were forced to buy out five banned investors at a rate of $70,000 per percentage point of ownership, a substantial markup over their buy-ins. One questionable investor had bought in for $60,000 and received $664,000; another put in $110,000 and got back $375,000; and for his $80,000, a third sold out for $140,000. Munley himself had invested $146,000 and received $1.7 million. The Commission's conditional approval put a significant financial burden on the legitimate investors who had to abide by the Commission's conditions.

However, the Enforcement Division, responsible for the surveillance of and control in the count room, ordered significant changes before the Edgewater could be licensed.

About that same time, Joe was in Montreal conducting another licensing investigation. Karen called him all excited. "We just landed a gig at a fairly new casino in Laughlin called the Edgewater!"

"That's great, honey, but don't let them know you're married to me!" Someone there might have been nursing a grudge.

The next morning, Joe called his Deputy Chief, Howard Smith, and informed him of the situation. Smith didn't see any conflict and Karen's show remained at the Edgewater, problem free, for another two years.

But the Edgewater investigation had far-reaching ramifications. The report that the background agents prepared was used more than 20 years later to help convict organized-crime figures from the east coast on racketeering charges. The guilty individuals all received sentences of life in prison.

Bad Junket Reps

Junket-rep applications required even more travel than usual; these applicants often resided all over the U.S. and the world.

Junkets were, and still are to a certain extent, trips taken by a group of known gamblers who put up front money, then travel to and play at a particular casino. In exchange for a guaranteed minimum bet and number of hours at the tables, the casino picks up the players' travel, accommodations, and often food expenses. The junket representative serves as an independent liaison between the casino and the high rollers, helping to organize the trip and often guaranteeing the cash up front.

In the days when Joe was working for the GCB, Atlantic City had only recently legalized casino gambling, so Nevada was still the promised land for gamblers all over the world. And the junket reps had to fill planeloads of gamblers who could put up stacks of cash to qualify for the trips, many of whom were of questionable character — owners of cash businesses, bookmakers, loan sharks, drug dealers, robber barons, organized-crime types. As such, the reps had to run in similar circles and Joe discovered, to his surprise, that upwards of half the junket-rep applicants had such questionable pasts that, as investigators dug deeper and deeper into them, they ended up withdrawing their applications.

Why did junket reps with shady backgrounds go to all the trouble of applying — opening themselves up to being investigated back 25 years and paying tens of thousands for the privilege?

The answer is that in those days, junkets brought in planeload after planeload of heavy gamblers, among the casinos' most lucrative customers. And so many junket reps were waiting to be investigated that they were allowed to bring in players and be compensated for their play without being licensed. As Las Vegas grew, so did the number of Gaming Control Board personnel, who started to catch up on the backlog of investigations. But even then, every other gaming investigation came before a junket-rep investigation — and some junket reps worked for many years while their applications were pending.

Still, many did go through the procedure. Joe and financial agent Gregg Schatzman were assigned one and, when they interviewed Michael G, they learned that he'd previously been a law-enforcement officer for some years.

After the interview, Schatzman began looking into his financial details, while Joe proceeded to the law-enforcement agency where the applicant had reportedly been employed. He made initial contact with a police officer who directed him to a location where he could conduct a criminal-history inquiry of Michael G. After the inquiry, he was leaving the building when a ranking officer approached him.

"Excuse me, Joe, if I may call you that."

"Yes, sir. What can I do for you?"

"Can I ask where you're staying?"

Joe gave him the name of the hotel and handed him a business card.

"Listen, do yourself a favor and don't believe anything anyone here at the PD tells you about G. I'll call you at seven this evening at your hotel to explain."

Even in Joe's line of work, that was a strange thing for him to hear and he made sure to be back in his room by seven to take the call.

Over the phone, the ranking officer told him, "When he was a narcotics detective, Michael G was investigated by the police department for assisting drug dealers. He was conducting counter-surveillance for the dealers, informing them of law-enforcement activity in the areas where the drug deals would take place."

With all his years working in the Narcotics Task Force, Joe knew that Michael G would have knowledge of all the surveillance being conducted by narcotics units.

"Your guy caught a big break when he was allowed to resign rather than being terminated, which would have brought scrutiny from the press."

"Ah," Joe said. "So that's why my inquiry at your PD hadn't revealed any criminal history or derogatory information."

"That's correct. I recommend you contact the federal authorities to corroborate this information."

Joe thanked the officer and did just that. Digging deep, Joe discovered that after his release from the police department, Michael G had started paying his mortgage with cash. Further information revealed that he began by leasing small aircraft through a newly formed company; as time went on, he moved up to full-size cargo planes, which were lost to crashes in the Caribbean due to mechanical issues. The losses were covered by insurance.

Finally, at a later interview, Michael G understood that, by Joe's line of questioning, the investigators had uncovered all they needed for the Gaming Control Board to deny his application, which he withdrew. He knew he would never qualify for a gaming license in the state of Nevada.

Skimming at the Stardust

In 1983, Joe and other agents of the Investigations Division went undercover as gamblers at the Stardust. The reported owner was a company called Trans Sterling and the GCB and FBI had information that the casino was running a skimming operation from the blackjack tables, transferring unreported funds from the casino to organized-crime members. The GCB's Enforcement Division agents were unworkable in an undercover capacity, because the casino operators and employees knew their identities.

Casinos use chips from the chip vault to replenish high-stakes blackjack tables as they're depleted paying out the winnings of high rollers. The new chips, known in the business as "fills," are brought to the blackjack pit, where the pit boss and dealer count them, then add them to the game. They both sign a fill slip. The dealer places the chips in the table tray, then drops the fill slip into the table's drop box.

For the skimming operation, an employee transported $2,500 in chips from the vault to the table. But the pit boss and dealer signed the fill slip for $25,000 in chips, then placed the slip in the drop box. The blackjack table immediately booked a paper loss of $22,500. That amount in cash was removed from the cashier's cage and diverted to well-known eastern organized-crime bosses.

During the Stardust investigation, Joe, Gregg Schatzman, and other agents entered the casino at various times to observe casino operations and look for the false fills. They soon identified the guilty dealer. On the final night of their investigation, Joe and Gregg sat down at that dealer's table as players and waited for the false fill to take place.

Soon, the employee brought the fill to the game table and the slip was falsified right in front of them. GCB and FBI agents immediately entered the casino and secured the area to protect the evidence.

As word spread through the casino, the pit boss approached the skimming dealer and told him that GCB agents were everywhere. The dealer looked around the blackjack table and said to Joe, "Are you with Gaming?"

Joe responded, "No, I don't like to hunt or fish." Joe could tell by the man's facial expression that the dealer was thinking, "This guy's just a dumbass."

Agents from the GCB Enforcement Division approached the table, then Joe and the others stood up to inform the dealer he was under arrest. He was handcuffed and led away, while the agents guarded the evidence in the drop box until it could be removed.

Investigators believed that $14 million had been skimmed from the casino over a 10-year period. In the days that followed, federal indictments were handed down for skimming and hidden ownership of the casino. Allan D. Sachs and Herb Tobman, owners of Trans Sterling and the Stardust, Fremont, and Sundance (now the D) hotel-casinos, were pressured by Nevada regulators into selling their holdings to the Boyd Group, a reputable gaming company headed by Sam Boyd and his son, Bill. They also agreed to pay a $3 million fine, the highest ever imposed up until that time.

Joe was given the job of supervising the Boyd Group's licensing investigation, with a request to expedite it. He did so, finishing the report in record time and giving the Gaming Control Board and Gaming Commission a comfort level in approving the Boyd Group's purchase from Trans Sterling.

Sachs and Tobman later filed suit in federal court, accusing the gaming authorities of coercion in forcing them to sell to Boyd. The Ninth Circuit Court of Appeals dismissed the case in September 1986, around a year after Joe left the GCB.

A Good Day—Followed by a Bad Day— in Guadalajara

In early 1985, Joe was sent to Guadalajara, Mexico, to investigate a junket rep.

Joe contacted a DEA friend, with whom he'd worked on smuggling cases when he was with NTF. His friend assisted Joe in an investigation of a Mexican junket rep, doing all the criminal-background checks in Guadalajara and briefing Joe on the results.

Joe and his friend went to a long lunch and talked over old times. Then they drove to a house on the outskirts of Guadalajara to look at a classic car his friend hoped to buy and fix up with his sons. An older man sitting on his front porch met them there.

The agent and the man spoke in Spanish, then the three of them walked to a barn behind the house where Joe saw a Mercedes-Benz 300SL Gullwing. The two-seat sports car had doors that were hinged at the roof and opened up, rather than out, to resemble the wingspan of a seagull. The 300 SL had been manufactured sometime between 1954 and 1957 and had been stored for a long time. The agent admitted that it would take some work to restore the vehicle, but it would be a great project for him. The owner wasn't ready to sell, but told the agent he'd have first dibs when he was.

Joe was in Guadalajara for only two days before returning to Las Vegas. Shortly thereafter, he learned that the agent, Enrique "Kiki" Camarena, had been kidnapped by five corrupt police officers while headed to lunch with his wife. The police officers had learned that Kiki was about to expose their multi-million-dollar drug operation.

Camarena's lifeless body was discovered on March 5, 1985, a month after he disappeared, in a rural area in the state of Michoacán. He'd suffered extensive injuries, including his skull, jaw, nose, cheek bones, and windpipe being crushed and his ribs broken. In addition, his kidnappers had bored a hole in his head with a power drill. He'd been injected with amphetamines and other drugs to keep him alive during his torture, which went on for more than 30 hours.

Kiki's death provoked a swift response from the DEA. The agency launched Operation Leyenda, a massive homicide investigation in which numerous government officials were implicated in the kidnapping and murder. Due to the extraordinary efforts of the DEA's special unit, Kiki's killers were arrested and convicted.

The chilling part was that Camarena was kidnapped on his way to lunch. If it hadn't been for good luck and timing, Joe might have been mistaken for another DEA agent and been abducted with him on *their* way to lunch a couple weeks earlier.

Enrique Camarena posthumously received a number of citations and multiple organizations have established

awards in his memory. The Enrique S. Camarena Foundation was established in 2004 to honor Kiki's memory and
promote drug and violence prevention.

Any time Joe sees or hears of a Mercedes-Benz Gullwing,
he thinks back to the great day he spent with his friend
"Kiki" in Guadalajara.

"The war on drugs has resulted in numerous casualties.
Those involved in that war know those casualties personally,
because they stood shoulder to shoulder fighting that war
and feel the personal weight of the losses."

Rest in peace, Kiki.

The Reluctant Applicant from Zimbabwe

One of Joe's international investigations for the GCB
involved a U.S.-based gambling company with a principal
owner who lived in Europe. Joe and his colleagues reviewed
the application and found the owner, Andrew T, also had
a business in Zimbabwe, where he'd previously lived,
working as a CPA and financial adviser.

Joe and Gregg Schatzman met with Andrew T's lawyer.

"The way it works," Joe told the attorney, "is that we
require a deposit in order to begin the application process."

"How much is the deposit?"

"It's twenty-five thousand, plus ten thousand in travel
expenses."

"Ten thousand in travel expenses? Where are you
going? The moon?"

"No," Joe said. "Just to Zimbabwe."

"Zimbabwe!" the lawyer exclaimed. "You shouldn't
go to Zimbabwe! It's extremely dangerous for Americans
and Europeans to travel there now."

Joe informed the lawyer that he had spoken to the superintendent of the Zimbabwe federal police, to whom he had been introduced by a friend at the State Department. "The superintendent has assured me that he and his agency will assist with the investigation during our visit."

Zimbabwe, a country in southern Africa, was formerly known as Rhodesia. Similar to other previously colonized nations, Zimbabwe experienced political unrest and power struggles after gaining independence from Britain in 1980. But the superintendent with whom Joe was in contact was well-entrenched; he'd held the same position prior to independence and the change in the country's name.

"Listen, my client had to flee Rhodesia just prior to it becoming Zimbabwe. If the government finds out where he lives now, his life will be in danger."

That sent up a red flag. Why did Mr. T have to flee and what did he do in the process that would put his life in danger? "Let me ask you this," Joe said. "If you had business in Zimbabwe, would you travel there?"

"Certainly not!"

When Joe reiterated to the lawyer that he and Gregg had been approved to travel and pursue the investigation in Zimbabwe, the lawyer ran out of the conference room and went directly to a Board member's office, proclaiming again that it was too dangerous for the agents to travel to southern Africa.

The board member called Joe and Gregg into his office. "What did you say to that guy to make him so hysterical?"

Joe explained the situation and their intention of proceeding with the investigation. At first, the board member agreed with the lawyer—it was too dangerous to go and not worth the risk. But when he learned about the contact with the Zimbabwe federal police and the superintendent's assurance of assistance and cooperation, he reluctantly agreed with the travel plan.

As fate would have it, shortly after the incident with the lawyer, Andrew T withdrew his application for licensing, without any explanation.

Joe now knew that something was definitely wrong, so he contacted a friend, who got in touch with the Zimbabwe federal police to request a criminal-background check. Joe learned that the Zimbabwe government held an arrest warrant for Andrew T for absconding with all of his clients' funds when he fled Rhodesia. The lawyer's alarm about GCB investigators traveling to Zimbabwe to look into his client's affairs now made perfect sense.

Promotion to Senior Agent

After about 2½ years as a background investigating agent, Joe was promoted to senior agent at the GCB. This put him in a position of supervising a team of two background and two financial agents. As a supervisor, Joe often oversaw as many as six background investigations at a time.

The deputy chief assigned Joe the jobs and he delegated them. Of course, he examined all the applications and signed releases, then determined how in-depth the investigation would be, how much travel was involved, and an estimated cost. It was also his responsibility to request funding for the investigation from the applicant. An investigation never began until funding was received.

As a senior agent, Joe was also a backstop for the agents when an applicant had issues or was noncompliant. Occasionally, he had to travel to a city where an investigation was being conducted in order to explain to an applicant that his cooperation was extremely important; without it, he'd send his agents back to Las Vegas and reassign them. This meant his application went to the bottom of the pile.

He also explained the definition of a "privileged license."

The legal status of gambling isn't the same as most types of businesses, which have a "right" to be conducted. It's a well-established principle in business and law that a regular business, meaning harmless and legitimate, cannot be regulated out of existence. The gambling business, on the other hand, is a "privileged" business. There is no right to open a casino and a town, city, county, or state can—and often does—deny applications for a gaming license from undesirable applicants.

This scenario was played out during an investigation of yet another junket rep, Tony A, from an eastern city. After arriving at Tony's office, the background agent called Joe and said, "This guy isn't cooperating."

"Should I give him a call?" Joe asked.

The agent laughed. "Actually, a personal visit from you might shake his tree." He knew how well Joe played the good-cop bad-cop role.

The very next day, Joe flew east for a scheduled meeting with the agents and applicant.

"I'm a very busy man," Tony informed Joe, "and I'll furnish the documents your agents want when I'm good and ready."

"Okay, Mr. A, but before we go any further, let me tell you how a Nevada Gaming Control Board investigation works," Joe began. "First, you applied for a license to do business in the casino industry in our state. Second, you or someone else also paid good money for us to conduct this investigation. I flew all the way out here, on your dime, to tell you that either you cooperate in your own licensing investigation or these two agents here will accompany me on my return trip to Las Vegas tomorrow."

"So?" Tony A said. "They can come back some other time when I'm not so tied up."

"Well, sir, if they fly back to Las Vegas tomorrow, your application will be placed at the back of a long line. And since I'm the one who assigns the agents to their cases, I can tell you in no uncertain terms that it could months, maybe years, before your application reaches the top of the pile again."

Tony's expression changed as he considered what he was hearing.

"Also, you can't work in Nevada until you're approved. And your application won't be put on any agendas without a completed background and financial investigation."

Tony began furnishing the documents to the agents that same day.

In the meantime, Joe had received back-channel intelligence that this Mr. A had an association with organized crime. When he returned to Las Vegas, he met with the GCB chairman, handing him a memo from a law-enforcement source attesting to the association. Joe was explicit that the source was extremely reliable, but the memo should *not* be included in the investigative report or divulged in the Gaming Control Board hearing, which was a public proceeding.

During Mr. A's hearing, the chairman read out loud the confidential memo, burning Joe with his source. Joe immediately contacted his source to explain the situation and apologize. The source was livid over what had happened, but he didn't hold Joe responsible. "I *will* contact the chairman," he added, "and hold *his* ass responsible."

The Gaming Board denied the application and it was forwarded to the Gaming Commission for a hearing and vote.

Normally, at the Gaming Control Board hearings, the chief of the Investigations Division presented the investigative report and answered any questions pertaining to its Areas of Concern. In all Joe's time at the GCB, he never saw or even heard of agents being present at a Gaming Commission hearing. The GCB and the NGC hearings are public, so interested parties, media, and citizens are always present for the proceedings.

A Commission hearing regarding the east coast applicant was held two weeks later and Joe was told by the GCB chairman, who'd already blown his source, to have his agents attend.

During the hearing, Joe ran into his division chief as he was using the restroom and asked how it was going.

"Bad," the chief responded. "Very bad."

When Joe entered the hearing room, he saw that the newest investigative agent, who had no experience ever testifying anywhere, was being grilled and struggling out of nervousness. Although the agent was highly educated, he'd never been put in a situation like this and he looked like the proverbial deer in the headlights. Worse, he couldn't answer the questions that didn't pertain to his portion of the investigation.

After his testimony, he and Joe left the hearing and returned to their office.

"Damn, I'm sorry, Joe," the agent apologized, embarrassed.

"Listen," Joe said, "none of this is your fault. You shouldn't have been put in such a tough spot."

The Gaming Commission overturned the Control

Board's denial of the junket rep's application, even after learning of his mob connections, and granted him a license.

Joe happened to be going back to the restroom when the GCB chairman exited the Commission hearing and he started yelling at Joe. "Your agent screwed this whole thing up!"

Joe kept his cool, responding, "Why did you put a brand-new agent with no experience on the stand?"

"I don't answer to you! But you'll be answering to me for this!"

"Why didn't you put me up there? You know how much experience I have testifying from my time as a detective in San Diego."

"I'm your boss' boss, remember? You better watch your step!" he kept yelling as he headed down the hall toward the back stairway to the Board members' offices. By now, he'd drawn a crowd of people who came into the hall to see what all the yelling was about and, at the same time, Joe had had enough.

"*My* agent isn't to blame. *You* are — for putting him in a position that he couldn't handle!"

Joe returned to his office, where he found the other agents wide-eyed and speechless for about a minute. Then they began asking questions and he explained the situation, covering for the agent. He was concerned for a while about an insubordination charge and the potential fallout, but the two other Board members had his back. This particular chairman didn't last long. He left for greener pastures, which was probably good for his health; the pressure of the chairman's position was — and is — intense.

In cases such as this one, Joe was often asked if he disagreed with the Board's or Commission's approvals or denials. But he never took the bait. He always understood his job—whether as an investigator, detective, or street cop. In this job, he knew he was simply a tool for gathering reliable and credible information for an authority that could use the information to make an informed decision on an issue, whether criminal or civil.

He always told his agents, "Until we're given the authority in the decision-making process and the pay to go with it, it's not our job to judge. They have their jobs and we have ours. We're all ultimately responsible for our decisions."

The Way It's Done Today

The process for acquiring a Nevada gaming license is time-consuming, expensive, and nothing if not thorough. However, it's not shrouded in mystery or secretive in any way. Each step is prescribed, either by statute or precedent or both, and follows a logical and internally consistent order.

A highly detailed description of the process was published in 2011. It was written by two of the most prominent gaming attorneys in Nevada history. One of them, Robert Faiss, practiced gaming law in Nevada for nearly 50 years and helped shape much of the regulatory structure under which Joe Dorsey labored at the GCB and remains in place today; the other, Gregory Gemignani, is also a long-time and highly respected lawyer for the gaming industry.

After reading the 32-page paper, "Nevada Gaming Licensing—Qualifications, Standards, and Procedures," Joe found little difference in the investigative procedures that he used from those that current GCB agents employ in their investigations, except of course for their access to web-based information and sources that Joe could only dream about a decade or so before the Internet became widely accessible.

"Other than a little less leg work, thanks to all the information that can now be found online, agents in 2020 conduct their investigations the same way my fellow agents and I did forty years ago," he says. "It's still the most exhaustive, intensive, and painstaking experience a prospective Nevada gaming licensee will ever go through — next to a colonoscopy."

Going to the Dark Side

Welcome to the
Hilton Corporation

In 1985, Joe had just returned from supervising the gaming-licensing investigation in Australia when he was asked by representatives of the Hilton Corporation if he had any interest in working as the director of security at the Las Vegas Hilton. At the time, the Las Vegas Hilton was the world's largest hotel, with just under 3,000 rooms.

The Hilton's security department was staffed by 150 armed personnel; as such, it was among the largest armed organizations in the state.

Again, Joe's connections opened the front door to the Hilton.

Gordon Dickie had retired from the San Diego Police Department on a disability and Joe got him a job with the Gaming Control Board. After about four years working in the Enforcement Division, Dickie was hired as one of three investigators for the Hilton Corporate Security Department. About a year later, Joe happened to be having lunch with Dickie, who told him the company was looking for an experienced director of security for the Las Vegas Hilton.

Joe was intrigued, so Dickie explained why the previous director had been terminated. He also mentioned that the Hilton president, Henri Lewin, was a tough executive to work for. Joe had interacted with Lewin while he was with the GCB and knew he could handle him.

Dickie's boss set up an interview with Lewin's right-hand man. The next interview was with Lewin himself. When Joe was ushered into the executive conference room, none other than Barron Hilton was there. Both men went over Joe's resumé, then questioned him for about 20 minutes.

When it came time to discuss compensation, Lewin threw out an obviously lowball offer.

"Well," Joe responded, "that won't work for me. Unless you double my salary, I won't leave the Gaming Control Board."

"All right, Joe," Lewin said. "You got it. But you better be worth all that money. I'm holding you to it."

Barron Hilton chimed in, "You better watch out for Joe taking your job as president, Henri."

All three laughed and shook hands and the deal was done.

Joe submitted his resignation to the Gaming Control Board and provided the standard two-week notice. One week before his departure, he attended a meeting with the chiefs of the Investigation and Enforcement divisions, where he was offered the position of chief of the Intelligence Division. He was also guaranteed attendance at three months of training at the FBI Academy in Quantico, Virginia.

Joe was flattered. However, chiefs were hired as "at-will" employees, governed by the Board member to whom that chief reported. Joe had been with the GCB in the Investigations Division for five years and had worked for five different Investigations Division chiefs. He knew that when a new governor was elected, he usually appointed new Gaming Control Board members. They, in turn, appointed new chiefs. Thus, longevity wasn't a benefit of a chief's position. He declined the GCB offer.

Joe left the GCB in September 1985 and assumed his new position at the Las Vegas Hilton, arriving one week after the annual Tailhook Association Symposium. Tailhook is a name that lives in a certain amount of infamy in Las Vegas. The Tailhook Association is a non-profit fraternal organization that supports the interests of sea-based aviation with emphasis on aircraft carriers. The association had held its annual convention at the Hilton for many years and Joe would oversee the next two Tailhook events. But in 1991, a scandal erupted following allegations of sexual assault and other improper conduct by naval officers in attendance at the symposium. The subsequent investigations led to sweeping changes regarding the role of women in the military.

Director of Security Reports for Duty

In his new role as director of security, Joe reported to the hotel president, Henri Lewin, the vice president, and the president of the casino, Dennis Gomes. Dennis had been chief of the Audit/Intelligence Division at the Gaming Control Board prior to becoming a casino executive at the Hilton, but the two hadn't met; Dennis left the GCB prior to Joe's employment there.

In 1977, Dennis had been responsible for exposing the skimming operation at the Stardust. Numerous organized-crime figures were eventually convicted for their involvement in the illegal activities. The scandal was chronicled in a 1995 non-fiction book written by crime reporter, Nicholas Pileggi. The book subsequently served as the basis for the 1995 Martin Scorcese film *Casino*, which starred Robert De Niro, Joe Pesci, and Sharon Stone. Dennis Gomes features prominently in this chapter of Joe's career.

It didn't take long for Joe to learn the details of the story behind the firing of the previous director of security: A number of other directors and managers were interfering with the operations of the security department. This was a familiar scenario; everyone, the saying goes, thinks they're an expert in security and law enforcement. But it's similar to Monday-morning quarterbacking, which is a world apart from looking to pass a football with two or three 250-pound linebackers gunning for your blood on the field and only seconds to react.

Joe quickly determined that a certain number of his management counterparts not only didn't understand the chain of command, but had actively undermined the former director. Part of the reason, he learned, was the fear that Henri Lewin had instilled in the ranks of executives and managers, which often led to mistakes in judgment and authority due to the intimidation they felt when dealing with the hotel president.

Joe experienced it first-hand one morning early in his tenure when the Hilton received a bomb threat and he was overseeing the operational procedures in dealing with the situation. Joe's secretary entered his office, visibly shaken, to inform him that Lewin was on the phone from San Francisco, demanding to know what Joe was doing about the threat.

Joe picked up the phone and starting taking Lewin through the procedures. But before he got very far, Lewin said, "You've obviously been through this before. Good work."

As time went on, Joe realized that the former director had performed his duties responsibly, but Lewin believed all the outsiders concerning his performance. Joe dealt with all the problem managers efficiently, but one; that problem was solved when Joe threatened to demonstrate for him — and *on* him — the principles of the police choke hold. After that, his interference in Joe's job and department suddenly stopped.

When Joe reported for work at the Hilton, the security department was operating with a temporary director. Joe had investigated the department's performance before he assumed the director position and learned that the acting chief, Dave Austin, had been a shift lieutenant prior to being promoted to acting director. Austin not only held the department together while the company searched for a new director, but for someone who had never been a law-enforcement officer, he was the most knowledgeable security professional Joe had ever met. He was also a licensed EMT and had set up all the Hilton's emergency procedures. (Several years later when the new MGM Grand was in its planning stages, Austin was hired as the vice president of security with a staff of 300 and was involved in all aspects of construction-site surveillance at the mammoth hotel-casino.)

Joe quickly learned that Austin had experienced — as did most of the security officers still at the Hilton — the terrible fire at the hotel in 1981, only four years earlier. That fire killed eight people, injured 200, and forced the evacuation of 4,000 guests.

The night of the fire, Joe was flying back to Las Vegas from Chicago after completing a GCB investigation. He saw the blaze from the plane on the approach to McCarran Airport and could relate to the trauma those employees and guests were going through. He knew it would be a long time before they got over the disaster.

As incoming director, Joe quickly concluded he needed a right-hand man and Dave Austin fit the bill. He could educate Joe on the workings of the department and its personnel, so he requested that Dave be promoted to permanent assistant director. He and Austin bonded quickly.

While touring the property together for the first time, Austin showed Joe an outbuilding containing a new $37 million fire-control-system monitor room. After the disastrous 1981 fire, the Hilton corporation was determined to never let that type of tragedy occur again and installed the giant high-tech monitoring system. After the fire system was completed, the Las Vegas Hilton was voted the safest hotel in the world by the International Association of Firefighters.

Joe entered the room, thinking he'd walked into NASA's Mission Control Center. He asked, "Who controls this system?"

Austin said, "You do."

"I do?" Joe replied, surprised. "I didn't realize I was also applying for a position as the fire chief." As Joe gazed at all the computers, monitors, and printers recording the system's activity, Austin began chuckling.

Time went by and various Hilton staff members who experienced the 1981 fire began to visit Joe. One by one, they heard that Joe went through a similar tragedy, the PSA plane crash, and they sought a sympathetic ear. Employees wanted to talk about the fire and express their feelings to someone who understood the trauma of such an event. Joe believes those conversations, particularly among the security personnel, helped bring them together and enabled them to function as an effective professional team.

That team was tested sooner than Joe expected.

Joe's daughter and son, Kelly (6) and Bobby (9)

Kelly and Bobby today

Joe and his sister Mary Jo, who rescued him as a teenager

Lt. Robert A. Perchard Memorial Trophy

Whereas LT. Robert A. Perchard, while serving aboard Coast Guard aircraft HU-16E 7233 on July 3rd 1964 engaged in a rescue mission in Alaska did give his life in company with his fellow crewmembers for the highest motives known to man, and because during his life he persevered for the growth of professionalism in military aviation and the highest standards for aircrewmen, this award is granted to

AD3 JOSEPH P. DORSEY 252 953
U. S. COAST GUARD

Who, having been considered by the officers of this Air Station to exemplify the high standards of character, professionalism, ability and leadership, which is in the highest traditions of Coast Guard Aviation.

This certificate is awarded this 31ST day of MARCH 1967 and the perpetual trophy displayed at this Air Station, will be so inscribed.

just a few awards, commendations,
and recognitions Joe has received
throughout his career

UNITED STATES DEPARTMENT OF JUSTICE
DRUG ENFORCEMENT ADMINISTRATION
1340 WEST 6TH STREET
LOS ANGELES, CALIFORNIA 90017

November 20, 1975

Officer J. P. Dorsey
San Diego Police Department
801 W. Market, P. O. Box 1431
San Diego, California 92112

Dear Officer Dorsey:

On behalf of the Drug Enforcement Administration I would like to commend you for your outstanding contribution to the San Diego Narcotic Integrated Task Force.

Your performance exhibited a high degree of professionalism and was a major factor in the successful conclusion to several important cases.

It is this example of dedication and cooperation which symbolizes what task forces contribute to overall narcotics enforcement. Please accept this certificate as a token of our appreciation for a job well done.

Sincerely yours,

John E. Van Diver
Regional Director

The Winged "S" symbol is awarded for a lifesaving rescue using a

Sikorsky Helicopter

"I personally would like to express my deepest respect and admiration for these gallant pilots and helicopter crews who performed these flights. Their action, representing considerable skill and courage, equals the most heroic battlefield achievements. It would be right to say that the helicopter's role in saving lives represents one of the most glorious pages in the history of human flight."

-Igor I. Sikor
Inventor of the Helicop

HELICOPTER RESCUE AWARD

THE "WINGED S" AIR RESCUE EMBLEM

has been awarded to

AD3 J. P. Dorsey USCG

for his skill and courage while participating as

a crew member on 28 March 1965

in a lifesaving mission with a Sikorsky helicopter

PRESENTED ON BEHALF OF THE
MANAGEMENT AND EMPLOYEES OF
Sikorsky Aircraft

UNITED STATES DEPARTMENT OF JUSTICE
DRUG ENFORCEMENT ADMINISTRATION
LOS ANGELES WORLD TRADE CENTER, SUITE 800
350 SOUTH FIGUEROA STREET
LOS ANGELES, CALIFORNIA 90071
(213) 688-2650

April 7, 1977

Detective J. P. Dorsey
San Diego County Integrated
 Narcotic Task Force
San Diego District Office
San Diego, California

Dear Detective Dorsey:

In 1976, our Nation in cooperation with the Republic of Mexico, mounted a concentrated effort to stem the deluge of brown heroin into our country. DEA manifested this effort with the Special Action Office/Mexico, better known as SAO/Mex. This effort included all regions of DEA along with the fine assistance of local law enforcement.

You have been recognized as a major contributor to this effort. For your fine work in DEA's SAO/Mex Program, DEA Administrator Peter B. Bensinger has approved a Certificate of Appreciation Award. Please accept my personal thanks and appreciation for the outstanding job which earned you this recognition.

Sincerely yours,

Jerry N. Jenson
Regional Director

Karen Rose wearing fatigue jacket given to her by the military, with patches where she performed during a USO Tour of Southeast Asia in 1969

above: photo that made a major San Diego heroin bust famous (Joe is bottom row, fourth from left)

Joe in front of the same photo at the DEA Museum in Washington, D.C.

below: Joe and Dale Kitts counting the seized cash

Team III Narcotics Task Force (1974)

Some of the Team III Narcotics Task Force at their 38th reunion (2012)

below and facing page: It took years for Joe to recover from the devastation he witnessed after the crash of PSA Flight 182 in San Diego in September 1978.

J.P. Murray, deep undercover in the late '60s/early '70s to infiltrate radical political groups

J.P. Murray after leaving undercover operations, with wife Betty

Kirby Wayne Wood, one of Joe's partners in the Robbery Unit (June 29, 1934–October 3, 2018)

Joe and Karen touring their new hometown (1980)

Joe and Karen, Las Vegas Hilton, 1985

Joe (far left) and Gregg Schatzman (seated second from left, toasting) and their Nevada Gaming Control Board investigative team with the Chief Superintendent and his team, New South Wales, Australia

Las Vegas Hilton, Joe's
first job as casino
security director

To Joe Dorsey
With best wishes, Ronald Reagan

Joe meeting President
Ronald Reagan at the
Hilton

Joe and "Miami Vice" star
Don Johnson at a Heavy-
weight Championship
fight held at the Hilton

From the Hilton to the Aladdin, working again for Dennis Gomes—
and a clueless owner

Joe's fourth casino where he worked for the hard-driving Steve Wynn.
There, he enlisted Metro Police and the county District Attorney to collect
domestic casino debt and began traveling the world to personally collect
international debt.

following page: Joe's
third casino, working on
the executive team for an
absentee owner

Joe couldn't believe how contaminated the company culture at the Tropicana was when he first arrived (1995); his international collection travels were a respite from the corruption.

Jim Mydlach worked security with Joe at the Hilton, Aladdin, Dunes, and Golden Nugget; he knew everyone, could get anything done, had been employed by Elvis and even looked like him (with his wife Wendy).

Frank and Mary Jo Ellis (no relation to the author),
founders of the original Village Pub

Ron Lyle, who went 11 rounds in a championship fight
against Mohammed Ali in 1975 and was later hired by Joe
to work security at the Dunes

Joe and Karen Rose celebrating their 25th and 40th wedding anniversaries

Karen's restored 1938 International Harvester pickup

Small but mighty Ellis Island Casino & Brewery has expanded over the years as a favorite among Las Vegas locals. Gary Ellis welcomed Karen and Joe into their extended family in 1990; in 2001, Gary promoted Karen to president.

Marilyn Hilton and the Elvis Suite Fire

Even with a state-of-the-art fire-control system, Joe had to deal with small fires in and around the Las Vegas Hilton. The new system couldn't prevent fires, but it handled them perfectly when they broke out.

One such fire was in the famous Elvis Suite, a 3,000-square-foot penthouse on the top floor of the hotel. Security received an alarm notifying them of an active fire in the huge suite.

Only Hilton family members used the Elvis Presley Suite and Marilyn Hilton — Barron's wife who was bound to a wheelchair — was in the suite at the time of the fire. Security officers and Joe immediately responded to the alarm, but arriving at the suite, they learned that security had no entry key. The suite was off limits to everyone.

The suite had two very large front entrance doors. Joe had forced his way through his share of doors and he knew these couldn't be knocked down. The suite also had a rear door used for room-service access. It was locked, but the security team managed to knock it off its hinges. Mrs. Hilton was quickly rescued from the smoke-filled suite.

A sterno can, used to keep food warm, was the source of the fire. The can was somehow overturned on the breakfast buffet table, causing the tablecloth to burst into flames. The responders extinguished the flames and attended to Mrs. Hilton. Thankfully, other family members had left the suite after breakfast. No one was injured and the fire caused minimal damage. Mrs. Hilton was extremely grateful to Joe, the security officers, and the fire-control system for containing a possibly disastrous situation.

Following the incident, Joe hightailed it to the hotel locksmith and had keys made for security to use in the event of another emergency in the Elvis Presley Suite.

The Hilton Security Staff

When he first got to the Hilton, Joe reviewed the personnel files of all 150 of his security staff to get a personal view of each of them. Then he met with them one at a time. He was extremely impressed with what he saw.

Among his team were retired military who had held high ranks and secret clearances, retired New York City cops and firemen, and a number of licensed emergency medical technicians. Several of his officers had been designated report writers and the quality of their work was as good as might be found in any high-level law-enforcement agency. But one attribute that stood out immediately was their customer service; the accounts of the departments' interactions with the guests of the hotel and even the casino were uniformly glowing.

The one concern that almost all of them expressed was that Joe would disarm them; they carried sidearms and desperately wanted to keep them. Even in those days, the trend for casino security was toward unarmed guards.

The main reason for the disarming of security, as can easily be imagined, is money — money saved from the cost of the training required for each and every guard, money saved from having to shell out in settlements for shootings, and money saved from the high premiums charged by insurance companies to allow private security to carry heat. Today, with casinos proliferating throughout the country and more security officers receiving less training and having to handle more issues, officers have been known to misplace their weapons, drop them in the casino pool, pull them in beefs with fellow officers, have them stolen, and discharge them negligently — all of which is why insurance premiums are so high. In addition, the guns are usually the property of the casino and the weapons are stored on site (this raises the insurance cost even higher).

Another element involving the casino's money is, necessarily, the casino's money: It's insured for max value. Factoring in insurance settlements, a casino has rarely if ever lost a dollar to a robbery. So given the potential for harm and lawsuits, the casino has little incentive to arm its guards to prevent getting ripped off.

Finally, the whole purpose of carrying a sidearm is negated when, as started happening toward the end of the armed-guard era when Joe was in charge at the Hilton, the security officers were warned never to use or even present their weapon. Should they unholster a gun, they were completely on their own. For example, if a security officer tried to help an elderly woman being attacked by using deadly force, he could be sued (civil) and prosecuted (criminal) as a private citizen.

In his capacity as director of casino security, Joe believed there were two types of security employees: officers and guards. Officers were hired based on their military and/or law-enforcement experience; their salaries reflected their qualifications. Not only were they highly trained coming in, they also continued their training in service. If they were armed, they attended rigorous state-certified training classes and qualified with their weapons three times a year at a certified gun range with certified instructors.

Guards were employees of licensed security companies who received very little training. They were, essentially, warm bodies. Las Vegas and the casino industry are well-known for security operations and staff, but the various levels of competency depend on the companies' willingness to allot security budgets that reflect professionalism.

In addition, Joe later learned the hard way that an unarmed security department left out one consideration: officer safety. At the start of Joe's tenure at the Tropicana in the 1990s, security officers there were unarmed, so he left the policy in place.

One evening, an officer was assigned to the convention center, which was unattached to the rest of the resort. He had a verbal altercation with a young man attending the event and had to remove him. The man went to his car and returned holding a handgun. The officer retreated, but the armed man kept charging. The officer fled outside the convention center trying to reach the resort buildings when he was chased and gunned down. The shooter fled to Mexico, but was eventually arrested and convicted of murder.

Joe assured his charges at the Hilton that he was their strongest advocate for remaining armed. Once the officers believed that he wouldn't allow anyone, including executives and managers, to disarm or demean them or their efforts or work ethics, they trusted that changes for the better were imminent. And they were. The operational responses of the Hilton's security staff with both emergency and non-emergency situations were on a par with major law-enforcement agencies.

While reading one file, Joe learned something interesting about a particular officer, Dave Bertrand, and requested they meet the next afternoon. When Dave arrived at Joe's office at 2 p.m. as instructed, he appeared quite nervous.

"I read in your personnel file that you graduated from Ohio University with a bachelor's degree in marketing," Joe said, watching Dave closely. "Are you hiding from the law?"

"No sir, I'm not," Dave replied, now even more on edge.

"That probably seemed like an odd question," Joe admitted, "but there's a reason for it." He then went on to explain that his wife was a professional singer and at one time sang at a casino in Winnemucca, Nevada. When Joe went to see Karen there, he met a bartender, a former Notre Dame football player once featured on the cover of *Sports Illustrated*. Notre Dame had played the University of Southern California and the future bartender gained a reputation for facing O.J. Simpson and holding him to a few abysmal yards.

Joe met others at the Winnemucca casino, including a table-game dealer with a doctorate in psychology. He made friends with a pit boss, who at one time was a well-established mechanic (card cheat) and couldn't work anywhere else, but was a boss in Winnemucca. The man dealt Joe four blackjacks in a row to demonstrate his card skills.

"At the time, I was still working in San Diego for the Narcotics Task Force," Joe explained, "so my cop antenna was quivering, right? These guys all had to be on the lam."

"Were they?" Dave asked.

"Nah. I learned later that they were just burned out and looking for a simpler life in a small Nevada town. But it leads me to ask you, why are you working as a security officer with a degree in marketing?"

"Well, sir, it's just that I eventually want to go into law enforcement, but I'm not quite ready."

"Good enough."

After hesitating, then hemming and hawing for bit, Bertrand asked Joe, "You mean … I'm not getting fired?"

Right at that moment, Dave Austin happened to step into the office.

"I've called in Bertrand here for a two o'clock meeting," he told Austin, "and for some reason he assumed that he was about to get canned."

"When your predecessor, the former security director,

called an employee to a two o'clock meeting, it meant he was getting fired. Everyone dreaded a two o'clock meeting request," Austin explained, laughing.

Joe monitored Bertrand's job performance over time and realized that he was perfect for a law-enforcement career. He reached out to some of his DEA contacts about a suitable position for Bertrand, but was told that the agency was hiring mostly minorities and females. He then called Clark County Sheriff John Moran, whom he'd come to know. After some preliminary testing, Bertrand was hired by Metro.

While settling into his new career, Bertrand kept Joe apprised of his activities and promotions. Dave actually mirrored Joe's career by working patrol, then narcotics. Dave often called Joe to discuss his selection of possible upcoming detective openings. He fondly called Joe "Dad." Dave Bertrand retired after a distinguished 22-year law-enforcement career. He eventually returned to Ohio and spends warm winters playing golf in Florida.

Textbook Response

Joe found the Hilton security officers to be professional and highly competent. They proved that one night after the front-desk staff inadvertently checked a couple into a room that was already occupied by a high roller with $35,000 cash in the room safe. When the arriving couple opened the door with their key, the high roller pointed a handgun at them. The situation grew more complicated, as the man checking in happened to be a Los Angeles police officer.

The guest/officer backed out of the room and called security. Personnel quickly responded and secured the entire floor. The officers had been informed by the front desk that the room was unoccupied. Thus, the on-duty supervisor believed an armed and unauthorized suspect was now holed up in a room that should have been vacant. Security evacuated guests from adjacent rooms while calling the police.

Meanwhile, they cordoned off the area. They kept their weapons drawn in the event that the suspect attempted to leave. The suspect shouted insistently through the door that the room was his, while the front desk was equally adamant that no one should be in the room. The situation was a recipe for disaster.

The shift supervisor called Joe at home and explained what was happening. Joe assured him he was doing everything correctly, but instructed him to inform the suspect to remain in the room and not attempt to leave with the handgun. "Let the suspect know the police will be showing up shortly to sort out the situation." Joe hoped that keeping the suspect well apprised would contain him and prevent him from foolishly emerging from the room with a weapon in his hand.

Metro quickly removed the suspect from the hotel room and everyone soon learned that he was, in fact, an authorized guest of the hotel and the rightful occupant of the room. Somehow, the hotel record was missing.

Joe met with the Los Angeles cop the next morning and apologized for the situation. The man was very understanding; he knew full well that the situation could have ended in a deadly confrontation. He commended the security officers on the scene and asked if they were former law-enforcement officers. Joe explained that though some on his staff were, those handling the situation the night before weren't, but they were well trained. One of the LAPD's finest agreed and described their response as "textbook."

After reading the incident reports the next morning,

Joe met with the hotel president, John Fitzgerald, who had replaced Henri Lewin, to critique the events of the previous night. Fitzgerald seemed fixated on the fact that the officers drew their weapons during the incident, but didn't mention anything about the error that occurred at the front desk. He grumbled and complained about the drawn weapons, ignoring Joe's attempts to turn his attention to the front-desk screw-up. He simply refused to acknowledge the catalyst of the entire incident.

Finally, Joe said, "I'm sorry, but I have another meeting to attend in a few minutes, so I'll have to excuse myself."

But Fitzgerald wouldn't let the drawn weapons drop. By this time, Joe was irked, thinking: Here's a top hotel executive who knows nothing of security procedures or how to deal with a situation such as this. He's wasting all this time beating a dead horse. At that point, Joe remembered his predecessor and all the interference that cost him his job.

"I wasn't on the scene last night, but I was in radio contact with the security team throughout the event. And I can tell you that you didn't *want* me there, because if the suspect had come out of the room brandishing a firearm, I'm afraid I would have responded with lethal force. So I'm not going to second-guess what by all accounts was a perfect response on the part of your officers." Finally, he stated, "Don't forget that the screw-up occurred at your front desk." With that, Joe got up and walked out. He didn't look back, but to this day, he swears he heard Fitzgerald's jaw hit the floor.

The Casino

"Think of a casino-resort as a small city, with a population that fluctuates between ten thousand and twenty-five thousand — and it was my security department's job to please them all," Joe says about his philosophy of running the police force at the immense Las Vegas Hilton in the 1980s.

At the Gaming Control Board, Joe and the other investigative agents received training in the various games and the governing rules of play, but they didn't spend much time in the casinos. The investigations kept them on the road most of the time and the only circumstances that necessitated their presence on the gaming floor was when they had to go undercover as players for one reason or another. So Joe wasn't unfamiliar with the casino environment, but he also wasn't responsible for surveillance from the eye in the sky or game protection on the floor. Other than an armed officer at the cage and armed officers making their rounds among the tables and machines, along with the rest of the property, the gaming areas were mostly the responsibility of surveillance, which reported to Hilton corporate security, the casino and shift managers, and the front-line pit bosses, floormen, and dealers.

Of course, security was summoned frequently to assist surveillance. Officers went to the eye in the sky, which in those days still consisted of catwalks above the one-way mirrors overlooking the tables and slots, to observe a suspicious player or players on a game. The officers reported back to surveillance, whose agents made the final determination. If cheating was suspected, security removed the player from the floor and took him to a holding room in the security office, where he was interviewed by surveillance or corporate security employees.

When crimes were committed or criminals were spotted in the area around the Hilton, the police department contacted Joe and his supervisors to be on alert. One such notification led to the arrest of a bank robber on the property.

Hilton security spent a good part of their time protecting the customers and players from themselves and one another. Officers watched for rail thieves who operated on and around the crap tables. They also kept a close eye on the high-limit slot areas for theft from players or slot machine cheating.

In those days when a big convention was in town, the working girls arrived en masse from California and Arizona and flooded the place. One officer who worked for Joe knew every hooker in Las Vegas and had a photo file that was better than the one maintained by the police. When he spotted one, he read her the Trespass Act, 86'ing her from the property for good.

The Hilton especially looked out for trick-rollers, prostitutes who robbed their johns, often drugging them in the process. The victim usually thought he was picking up a visitor or local in a casino bar and taking her to his room, where she spiked his drink with knockout drops, usually from a Visine bottle. The victim woke up 12 hours later to find his money and valuables gone. These robberies weren't limited to unsuspecting rubes; even street-wise johns were susceptible to being victimized. The welterweight boxing champ "Sugar" Ray Leonard allegedly once lost $40,000 to a trick-roller. But when some victims started dying of overdoses of drugs like Rohypnol, the notorious "date-rape" drug, the police and casino security cracked down hard on prostitution in the hotel.

Joe, Dennis Gomes, and Barron Hilton met to discuss the policy regarding prostitutes, some of whom were no doubt trick-rollers. To Joe, it was a no-brainer. "A husband and wife come to Las Vegas for the weekend, stay at the Hilton, and see hookers hanging around the casino and bars," he told his bosses. "Later, the husband has to attend a convention in Las Vegas. Naturally, his wife remembers all the sex for sale at the Hilton and doesn't let her husband stay here on his own. Every way you look at it, it's bad for business."

Gomes and Hilton agreed. The hotel subsequently enforced a strict no-hooker policy and the trick-rolls stopped, at least at the Las Vegas Hilton.

High Rollers, Lost and Found

Not infrequently, Joe provided security for big bettors. His department was notified when a high roller was due and every security officer working the casino was familiar with the bios of most of them.

On one occasion, a whale from the Middle East spent 30 days at the Hilton. In order to show his appreciation for all the protection he received, just before he left, he tipped the security staff $35,000.

"This became my problem," Joe recalls. "The casino officers felt the toke should be split only among them, since they were the ones directly involved with the sheik. That, of course, created bad feelings among the rest of the staff, who would be left out of the windfall. I gathered the casino officers and explained that I was splitting the money among all the officers, because while they were dealing with the high roller during his stay, the rest of security was filling in, covering the casino officers' duties. They weren't happy that they had to share, but I was. And so was the rest of my staff."

Another policy of which Joe was proud was how his department handled lost cash, or anything of value, found by an employee. If the owner didn't contact the casino looking for the property or the casino was unable to contact him or her, after 120 days, the property could be claimed by the employee who found it. This policy encouraged employees to turn in valuable property left behind or lost, so that it could be returned to the owner, at the same time that it gave the employees the possibility of winding up with it if it was never claimed.

Asian Food and Trespassing Allen Glick

Joe worked at the Hilton when Benihana was making a splash on the casino-restaurant scene. The Japanese exhibition-style teppanyaki eatery, with its action hibachi tables, lush Japanese gardens, flowing ponds, and an authentic torii arch, was quite exotic for Las Vegas at the time (it's still at the Westgate after more than 40 years). Later in Joe's career, when he traveled extensively throughout Asia on trips to collect markers (casino IOUs) from international players, he had to go to great lengths to avoid the indigenous cuisine, which he just couldn't stomach. Even long before that, he didn't like Japanese food, though he did eat at Benihana on occasion, sticking strictly with the steak and shrimp.

The Hilton had a steakhouse and an Italian restaurant across from Benihana where Joe ate more frequently. But he says, "I mostly went to the coffee shop. If it was good enough for Elvis, it was good enough for me."

Shortly before he moved on from his job as Hilton's security director, he visited Benihana one last time, though it wasn't for food.

One afternoon, he received a call from Dennis Gomes. "Joe," Gomes said, and Joe could already hear the excitement in his voice, "you're not gonna believe this. Allen Glick is in the Benihana lounge having drinks with someone."

Gomes and Glick had a history from back when Dennis

was the chief of the Audit Division of the Gaming Control Board and he uncovered the skimming operation at the Stardust, where Glick was the nominal owner. It led to the suspension of Glick's gaming license.

"I want you to go down to Benihana, throw Glick's butt out of the hotel, and trespass him while you're at it!"

"Okay —"

"And let him know," Gomes interrupted, "exactly who knew he was here and is initiating his removal from the property."

Joe proceeded to the Benihana lounge. On the way, he considered the fact that Glick wasn't in the Nevada Gaming Control Board's List of Excluded Persons, more popularly known as the Black Book, which contains the names of all the people who've been banned for life from entering any casino in the state. So he had to come up with another reason for his being removed.

"Mr. Glick, I'm sorry, but I have to ask you to leave the Las Vegas Hilton," Joe said with authority.

"What? Why? I have just as much right to be here as —"

"I'll tell you why. Because I was a detective with the San Diego PD when your partner Tamara Rand was murdered in San Diego. And without going into a lot of unnecessary details, I can tell you that Tony Spilotro was the suspect in the case and Homicide believes you were aware of the intent to murder Rand."

Joe didn't bother telling Glick that he'd been a detective in Narcotics and not Homicide. He didn't think he needed to. The murder of Tamara Rand had all the markings of a mob hit and he knew that mentioning Spilotro and Rand would impel Glick to leave without further ado.

Glick paid his tab, then Joe escorted him to the front door and read him the Trespass Law: "If you ever step foot on this property again, you can and will be arrested for trespassing, so you and your friend won't ever be returning to the Las Vegas Hilton." Just before Glick walked through the door, Joe said, "Oh, and Dennis Gomes sends his regards."

Backrooming

In all his years at Gaming Control and Las Vegas casinos, Joe never participated in or saw any backrooming of card counters. If he had a prima facie case and evidence of cheating, he didn't worry about lawyers. But as far detaining card counters, he says, "Even in those days, when other casinos were using their security departments to intimidate card counters and worse, I wouldn't have allowed it. The Hilton was highly reputable; the way the casino dealt with card counters was simply to inform them that their play wasn't welcome and they had to leave."

"Today," he continues, "the GCB has regulations dictating video and audio surveillance of cheating suspects or anyone else being detained in holding facilities."

The Fights

Hilton Hotels obtained the rights to host the heavyweight unification-series matches to determine one undisputed heavyweight-boxing champion. The unification series, known as the Heavyweight World Series, was produced by HBO Sports and promoted by Butch Lewis and the infamous Don King.

Prior to the scheduled fights, Joe was required to attend pre-event conferences with the promoters, fight managers, and Hilton executives, including the Chairman of the Board, Barron Hilton. During one pre-event conference, Don King stood up and asked for some additional services by the Hilton staff after the contract had already been finalized, as the blustery King often did. After hearing King's request, Barron Hilton looked to Joe and asked, "Joe, all three accommodations concern security. What do you think?"

"I can assist with one request, but the other two will raise the costs. Plus, the contracts are already in place."

Barron Hilton looked at Don King and said, "We can accommodate the first request. That's all we can do."

After the meeting, King walked over to Joe and jokingly said, "You drive a wicked bargain!"

Joe retorted, "Don, when you were learning your street smarts in the projects on the east side of Cleveland, I was learning mine in the projects on the west side of Cleveland." They shared a laugh and later discussed their days in the projects.

During this time, a young fighter named Mike Tyson rose to fame. His first few fights were held in the 8,000-seat Las Vegas Hilton Convention Center. But since the unification series drew large numbers of people, an outside 18,000-seat venue was constructed. Fight weekends at the hotel yielded more profit than New Year's Eve, attracting heavy action in the casino from all the high rollers the Hilton bosses invited in for these special sporting events.

Then, on April 4, 1986, President Ronald Reagan ordered an attack on five military targets and terrorist centers in Libya in retaliation for Libyan sponsorship of terrorism against American military forces and civilians abroad. A family member of Libya's leader, Muammar Gaddafi, was allegedly killed in the U.S. military strike. Eventually, Libya was found responsible for the 1988 in-flight bombing of a Pan Am flight over Lockerbie, Scotland, a heinous act that killed all 259 passengers onboard and 11 people on the ground.

Due to the global unrest, the unification series posed numerous security concerns and risks; Joe had his hands full as director of security, given multiple events and the influx of fight fans, without having to take international politics into account. But the upcoming unification series was the first large event since the U.S. attack on Libya and Joe had to plan for possible revenge by Libyan terrorists in Las Vegas.

Joe and his supervisors created a plan to secure and control the 18,000-seat outdoor arena, as well as the 3,000-room hotel. They shared their plan with the FBI, the Federal Bureau of Alcohol, Tobacco, and Firearms (ATF), and the Las Vegas Metropolitan Police Department, from which an additional 175 off-duty officers were hired.

Joe submitted a request to the ATF for a sweep of the stadium by explosive-sniffing dogs just prior to allowing the public access, but the Bureau replied that the Hilton was a private company and a dog search for a private venue was against policy. Having worked with the White House's Secret Service advance teams on other occasions, Joe knew how to get the dog search approved. He told the ATF that a certain congressman was planning to attend the event. The sweep was instantly approved and a search plan executed on schedule.

At the time, the Department of Homeland Security, Joint Terrorism Task Forces, and terror-alert systems didn't exist; the 1993 bombing of the World Trade Center and September 11, 2001, were years away. So Joe had local-level responsibility for the safekeeping of 25,000 Las Vegas Hilton guests, all without alarming them or even causing undue concern. Joe stationed armed security officers on the rooftops of buildings surrounding the outdoor stadium and implemented other preventive measures commonly used today.

Starstruck

Host of numerous prize fights, the Hilton expected all kinds of movie and TV stars to attend the fights. To control the movements of the celebrities in and out of the arena, Joe suggested a cocktail party for the luminaries, so they could be escorted by security officers to and from a ballroom near the venue.

On one occasion, Don Johnson arrived at the hotel. At the time, "Miami Vice" was one of the hottest shows on television and Johnson was its star. Joe met him at the front door and was walking him to his suite when Johnson asked him, "What's your position here at the Hilton?"

"I'm the director of security."

"Well," Johnson responded in his laconic and perpetually amused fashion, "I should let you know that when I drink too much, I sometimes remove my clothes."

"I can believe that, Don. In a previous life, I was a real-live narc for a long time and I've seen it all."

They both laughed and a connection was established.

When the two reached the suite, Johnson invited Joe in and they swapped undercover stories for a while. Later, Johnson attended the pre-fight cocktail party. He asked Joe to escort him into the arena early, so he could take in some of the preliminary fights.

Joe led him through a side door where his security command post was located. Halfway through the door, Joe said, "Don, you see the woman over there in the polka-dot dress talking on the phone?"

"Sure."

"Well, she's your biggest fan. She's one of my staff and she's working tonight only because she hopes she might get glimpse of you. Could you do me a big favor and say hello to her?"

Johnson walked right up to her, called her by name, took her in his arms, gave her a big kiss on the lips, and told her he was very happy to meet her.

After the kiss, Joe's employee was completely speechless as she clutched the phone in her hand, knuckles turning bright white.

Joe finished escorting Johnson into the arena, then returned to his command post to check on his star-struck staff member. She was no longer in the room, so he asked a nearby lieutenant about her. The lieutenant replied that she had to be helped to the restroom and when she returned, she was so flustered, he had to send her home. To this day, no one knows who was on the phone with her when Johnson swept her off her feet. She couldn't remember.

The security procedure was repeated in reverse after the bout that evening, with the celebrities ushered to an after-fight party. Responsibility for the logistics also rested with Joe, with the help of his staff and some Metro police officers on detail. Joe recalls that at the end of these evenings, his heart rate dropped about 30 beats a minute, back down to normal. He always felt a bit like the woman in the polka-dot dress, but for very different reasons!

Joe invited some of his former fellow detectives to one of the fights. His old partner Kirby Wood, plus colleagues Frank St. John and Benny Byrd, flew to Las Vegas for the weekend. Joe provided them with comped accommodations and tickets to the fight and stocked their rooms with everything he knew they liked to drink.

The night before the fight, the Hilton hosted the pre-fight cocktail party on the 30th floor adjacent to the Elvis Presley Suite. Joe invited his detective friends to attend, but didn't tell them about all the stars who would be there. He accompanied them to the party and couldn't stop laughing when his three sidekicks began to recognize the celebrities throughout the room.

"Is that so and so?"

"It sure is. Come on; I'll introduce you."

A minute later, there it was again. "Is that such and such?"

"It is. Let's go."

After another minute, "Is that who I think it is?"

"Yep."

Joe had the greatest time standing back and watching the guys fit right in with the stars, chatting them all up. Needless to say, they loved the party and would remember that night forever.

Later, when Joe attended a retirement function in San Diego for his friends, the Las Vegas Hilton cocktail party was a major topic of discussion among Kirby, Frank, and Benny. They'd been just as starstruck as Joe's polka-dot employee.

Heavyweights in All Corners

In his prime, Mike Tyson was not only unbeatable, but most of his fights didn't last long. During one of them, Bob Hope and Barron Hilton were seated in the front row. Mr. Hilton called Joe over and asked that he assist with getting him and Hope out quickly when the fight concluded. Joe agreed, of course, and stood off to the side, but close enough to make a move as soon as Tyson knocked out his opponent.

It didn't take long for the other fighter to go down for the count. Joe rushed over to Hilton and Hope to lead them out. While exiting, two other front-row guests stood and crossed in front of Joe and his VIPs. Joe heard one of the men say, "I don't want to fight that guy." Joe recognized the man as the next boxer in line to challenge Tyson in Atlantic City.

As soon as Joe escorted Barron Hilton and Bob Hope safely into the hotel, he rushed to the sports book to make a healthy bet that the fighter he overheard wouldn't make it through the first round of the bout in New Jersey. Sure enough, Tyson knocked him out within seconds of the start of the match.

At another fight, the brother of one of the contenders showed up at the arena in his bathrobe; he'd obviously been drinking. Suddenly, in the middle of a later round, he jumped up and attempted to enter the ring. Members of Joe's security staff stopped him, then dragged him back to his seat. Joe went over and asked, "What the hell do you think you're doing?"

"I was just trying to help out my brother who's losing the fight."

Joe just stared at the guy in disbelief. He could just imagine a surprise two-on-one in an arena of 8,000 people. A riot would result!

"Please, man, let me stay," he begged Joe. "I won't cause no more trouble. That's my little brother up there."

"All right. I'm trusting you. But if you even try to enter that ring again, my men have permission to shoot your ass. Understand?"

"Yes sir, I surely do."

Just to play it safe, Joe relocated him to a seat farther

away from the ring and assigned three officers to watch him. Luckily, he didn't cause any more trouble and Joe's staff didn't have to use lethal force.

The last unification fight was Tyson vs. James "Bone-crusher" Smith. Joe was absolutely certain that this event was going to be trouble; the Hilton was receiving phoned-in death threats against Tyson. Complicating matters, the fight was scheduled for the outside arena. Joe beefed up security as much as was physically possible, then had one of his assistants notify Tyson's managers of the threats and assure them that everything was under control. Which it was.

Smith was the only fighter ever to go the distance, 12 long rounds, with Tyson. Rumors buzzed that Smith had placed a very large bet that he would make it through the last round with Tyson. After observing Smith's strategy of hugging Tyson like a long-lost friend, then running away the rest of the time — what the tabloids dubbed "the Bone-crusher Smith Waltz" — Joe started to believe the rumors.

Stadium Security

These fights posed seemingly endless problems for Joe. Among his myriad other concerns and responsibilities, he oversaw the credentialing process, managing who received access to the arena. This involved issuing categorized passes to such groups as the press, fight officials, and an alphabet soup of law enforcement. In addition to celebrities, the media, boxing-industry bigwigs, and thousands of fans, professional fights draw criminal elements such as pickpockets, prostitutes, trick-rollers, organized-crime figures, drug-cartel leaders, and drug distributers. This drew the involvement of surveillance teams from the FBI, DEA, ATF, IRS, Nevada GCB, U.S. Customs, the Metropolitan PD

Intelligence Unit, and others. All were there to gather intel on who met with whom, gaining a better understanding of how various groups were connected to criminal activities.

Joe received hundreds of calls for tickets to the fights from these agencies. Bogus requests from personnel who just wanted free tickets to a big fight had to be culled from the genuine work-related solicitations.

But mostly, Joe wanted to assist the law-enforcement agencies. He was, after all, a former cop. He met with the hotel president to try to coordinate the Hilton's response to these requests. But the president didn't see it as a priority.

One afternoon, Joe was dealing with security aspects of the stadium layout. He met with the convention manager responsible for designing both the indoor and outdoor arenas. During their conversation, Joe mentioned that the president refused to give up any tickets for the government agencies. The convention manager shook his head and said, "That's too bad." They made plans to meet again as the date of the fight got closer.

A few weeks before fight night, Joe got together again with the convention manager at the stadium to inspect seating for safety and security purposes. The two men walked along the floor risers and agreed that everything looked in order.

The manager then said, "Joe, look more closely at the risers. Notice anything different?"

"Nope. Can't say as I do."

He walked Joe to the top row of seats on the riser, eye level with the ring, which had been added and didn't appear on the seating schematic. "These are yours."

"Really? All of them? For me?"

"That's right."

"Can you mark the seats as reserved?

The manager explained. "Unnecessary. The whole top row, on four sides, all hundred and twenty seats, are for your use."

Joe could barely believe his ears and did his best to express his gratitude. He could now offer seats to law-enforcement agencies from all over the country. Better yet, since Joe issued credentials, his guests wouldn't require a physical ticket with an assigned row and seat number, circumventing the hotel president. Best of all, providing the agencies these seats was a worthy cause due to the value of the information that would be garnered by the law-enforcement personnel. Joe also knew that the additional 120 pair of police eyes would greatly assist in keeping the venue safe.

After the fight, Joe informed Dennis Gomes of the additional row for law enforcement and Dennis was curious as to who used the seats. Joe told him and Dennis responded that he wasn't sure it was a good idea. But when Joe added, "There was an extra seat available and I gave it to your son," Dennis thought that adding seats via the top riser was a *fantastic* idea.

Joe later learned that by clustering all the officers and agents together in one general space in the arena, they became familiar with one another. Their cooperation and collaboration extended far beyond fight night. For Joe, that was icing on the cake. Given who he was, there was nothing better than helping out his brothers in peace-keeping.

Only in Vegas

Secret Service

Joe also worked with the U.S. Secret Service assigned to

protect dignitaries visiting the Las Vegas Hilton. The most important of these included the president (Ronald Reagan at the time), the president's family, and royalty from abroad.

Once during Joe's tenure there, the president was scheduled to visit Las Vegas and stay at the Hilton. A White House advance team arrived about 30 days prior to the trip to coordinate security. Joe got to know the agents well. Before their security visits, the team contacted Joe, who reserved hotel and conference rooms where they stayed and worked, conducting their detailed planning.

On one such visit, the team supervisor requested a room with a ceiling mirror over the bed to play a joke on a "new guy" in the crew. When the team arrived, Joe learned that the new "guy" was a female agent. Being familiar with law-enforcement's rites-of-passage pranks, Joe played along.

The team of agents arrived and Joe took them directly to the special hotel room, which the supervisor showcased to all the agents. The female agent was slightly embarrassed and jokingly called her boss an asshole. Joe leaned toward the female agent and whispered, "You're about to get even."

The team then proceeded to the supervisor's room. Everyone, including the supervisor, laughed out loud when they entered the room and saw not only a round bed and a mirrored ceiling, but also a life-sized porn-shop blow-up doll propped on the bed wearing a large sign welcoming the supervisor by name back to the Las Vegas Hilton.

The female agent approached Joe, shook his hand, and thanked him. Joe whispered to her, "I have four sisters and payback's a bitch!" It was a different era, no one was offended, and all involved had a good laugh.

Prior to President Reagan's visit, a Secret Service agent approached Joe and said, "We want you to meet the president when he arrives." Joe was flattered and honored and he joined the vice president of hotel operations in welcoming President Reagan to the Las Vegas Hilton. Of course, Joe had a photo taken while shaking the president's hand.

As he started to let go of Joe's hand, President Reagan asked, "Young man, have we met before?"

"Yes, Mr. President, we have."

"I thought I recognized you. When and where did we meet?"

Joe said, "When you were governor of California and I was assigned to a security detail while I was with the San Diego Police Department."

"Well, it's nice to see you again," the president said.

The meeting with President Reagan was one Joe would never forget. Before leaving, the Secret Service agents presented Joe with a pair of cufflinks displaying the presidential seal, signed by President Reagan, as a gift for his assistance.

Leave It to the Shriners

One Saturday, Joe walked through the Las Vegas Hilton Convention Center to check on a Shriner's Convention. While heading from the casino to the convention area, he noticed an unusual sight, even for Vegas. Several men were sitting against the wall in a hallway, wearing baby bonnets and diapers. They also had pacifiers in their mouths. Joe figured it was some sort of initiation.

However, when he passed the group, he recognized one of the men, even though he was sporting a diaper and bonnet. The man was a retired chief of police from the San Diego PD.

Joe greeted him. "Hello, Chief. Something you weren't telling us?"

"Jeez, Joe, of all the places to run into one of my former

officers!"

Joe waited for an explanation.

"I'm sure you won't be surprised to hear that we're participating in an initiation event for the Shriners."

Joe responded, "Great cause!" He then noticed the chief nervously eyeing one of the hundreds of cameras in use by the Hilton.

Joe immediately eased the chief's mind. "I promise, Chief, no photos. I'll see to it personally."

As Joe walked off, he was more than amused by the thought that only in Vegas was it possible to see a man who once held Joe's career in his hands sitting against a wall in a diaper and bonnet. Too bad he wasn't still with the San Diego Police Department. He could have used what he saw to get any assignment he wanted!

Las Vegas … What a city!

8

Don't Ever Hang Anything on the Walls or Order Too Many Business Cards

A Brief Stint at the Aladdin

In 1987, Dennis Gomes told Joe that he was leaving the Las Vegas Hilton; he'd accepted a position at the Aladdin on the south Strip. Dennis offered Joe the position of vice president of security, surveillance, and corporate security at the Aladdin.

The Aladdin had an extremely checkered past and had been closed for a year. It started out in 1963 as a large motel, the Tally-Ho, that billed itself as the first non-gaming resort on the Strip. It was an idea whose time had not yet arrived and it folded after eight months. When it reopened in 1964, it was called the King's Crown, which lasted six months. In fall 1965, the property was sold for $16 million. The rooms were completely renovated and a casino, 500-

seat showroom, and gourmet restaurant were added, all in a three-month span in order to open on New Year's Day 1966 as the Aladdin.

It changed hands again in 1968 and 1972, was investigated for hidden Mob ownership in '74, and was closed by the Gaming Control Board in 1979. Wayne Newton owned it for a short time, but the Aladdin went bankrupt in 1984. It was purchased by a Japanese investor and a well-known high roller in Las Vegas, Ginji Yasuda, in 1985.

Gomes filled Joe in on the new owner. "Yasuda has a two-year gaming license and you know what that means."

Joe certainly did. "Sure. He needs reputable people to run the casino if he wants to get his license renewed when it expires."

"It also means a pretty nice salary increase for you."

"I need a day to think about the offer," Joe responded.

Joe was well aware of the history of the Aladdin and its seemingly non-stop inability to show a profit. In addition, it was tied to the Teamster Pension Fund and its run-ins with the gambling regulators meant that organized crime probably still had some fingers in the pot. Finally, Yasuda had closed the Aladdin for a year while he renovated the property and applied for his gaming license, which didn't bode well for the profit situation in the short-term after reopening the hotel.

In addition, Joe had some memories of the Aladdin from when he worked at Gaming Control.

For one, just before the meeting at which the Gaming Commission was expected to order the Aladdin closed down for its many transgressions, passions were running high and Joe and a fellow agent were dispatched to the Clark County School Board building where the Commission hearing was being held with orders to protect Gaming

Commission Chairman Harry Reid, who went on to serve as a U.S. Senator for 30 years.

On their way to the hearing, Joe asked the other agent, a former deputy sheriff from California, "How do we protect Reid when we're not armed?"

"Good question, Joe. Got any ideas?"

"Well, I suggest we don't get too close to him, just close enough to respond to a physical threat."

"Do you think we should talk to Reid and tell him what to do—for instance, if he hears a gunshot, he should haul ass to try to catch up to us?"

Joe grimaced. "That doesn't sound so good. Probably better not to alarm him about his safety."

Though the hearing was attended by a large contingent of hostile Aladdin employees who were about to lose their jobs, no violence erupted. Even so, after the order was issued to close the Aladdin, Joe and his colleague scurried Reid out of the building to his car, making sure he got out of the parking lot without being followed. When he was safely gone, they were off to their next task, closing the casino.

Joe was assigned to the slot machine area, where after the announcement that the Aladdin Casino was closed, he and the other GCB agents walked down the slot aisles, telling players they had to leave. Things went relatively smoothly until Joe was confronted by a woman in her late sixties. She had her cup of nickels resting in the payout tray with her right leg raised and her foot resting in the tray. She was still putting one nickel at a time into the machine while reading the bars through her cheater glasses. She had a lit cigarette between her lips with an inch-long ash waiting to fall on her blouse or slacks.

"I'm sorry, ma'am," Joe told her as he moved to place tape over the coin slot, "but the casino has been closed by the gaming authorities and you're going to have to leave."

The woman stood up. When she turned toward him, Joe noticed numerous small brown spots on her blouse from where the falling ashes had burned it. Squinting against the cigarette smoke and looking over her cheaters, she cried, "The Mob is going to get you for this!"

"Thank you for the warning," Joe responded, trying not to smile. "But in return, I should tell you that your cigarette ash is burning your blouse."

She looked down. "This?" She pointed. "Shit. Happens all the time."

"Well, ma'am. Try not to catch on fire."

She gave Joe a shit-eating grin and left to conquer other slot machines.

A little later, Joe was assigned the licensing investigation of Wayne Newton's purchase of the Aladdin, along with Newton's partner Ed Torres, who'd been Newton's boss when he broke into show business by performing with his brother Jerry at the Fremont downtown, in which Torres had points. Torres had also just sold his stake in the Riviera, so he had cash to invest. But Torres was connected, which led to all kinds of problems for Newton, who ultimately sued NBC for defamation after the network accused Newton of being a front man for organized crime at the Aladdin.

Joe testified in the defamation lawsuit; the trial was held at Las Vegas federal court.

"Did he know organized-crime people?" Joe asks. "Sure he did—as did most entertainers during the period. But NBC's top investigative reporter was full of shit about Wayne's connections. As I stated in my testimony, I investigated Newton three times and basically found him to be gullible, but nothing more. When I contacted the feds regarding his ties, I was informed that Newton was a victim and had cooperated with law enforcement, which was recorded on a wiretap."

Newton won a $19 million judgment, but never collected; he couldn't prove damages, so the judgment didn't stand on appeal.

Even with all the bad memories and lack of potential for success, Joe accepted the position. The casino was still closed, so it had no history with Ginji Yasuda, and it was another opportunity for Joe to work closely with Dennis Gomes, who involved him at every level in the business and was a great boss. He also received a substantial raise in pay. The Hilton not only wouldn't consider matching the raise, but there, he was destined to remain a director of security, while with Gomes, he was promoted to vice president. So Joe submitted his resignation to the Las Vegas Hilton.

Shortly thereafter, he was called in to meet with John Fitzgerald, the Hilton's president, who asked him to stay and offered him a raise. But Joe declined, saying he'd already given his word to Dennis Gomes. Joe did, however, recommend Dave Austin for the position of director of security, due to his tremendous service record at the Hilton. Sure enough, Dave was promoted to the position after Joe left and he eventually became the vice president of security at the MGM Grand. (He served in this role for many years until his untimely death.)

Joe met with Gomes the next day and accepted the offer at the Aladdin.

"That's great, Joe, but John Fitzgerald will be talking to you about staying at the Hilton."

"Actually, he already has."

"Really? That was fast. When?"

"Yesterday."

"What did he offer you to stay?"

"Not anywhere near what you offered me to leave!"

"Was he mad?"

"No," Joe said. "He was just sorry to see me go."

"Well, it's a good thing for you that you already met with him."

"Why?

"Because today, he's going to learn that I'm also taking the casino manager, the slot manager, the marketing manager, and a finance guy."

When Joe started to laugh, Gomes cut him off. "Oh, and we have forty-five days to complete background investigations for fifteen hundred new employees."

"Forty-five days? As in six and a half *weeks*?"

"Correct. Can we do it?"

"Not without help."

"Get all you need. Don't worry about how much it costs," Gomes told him.

As Joe was getting up to leave the meeting, Gomes dropped another bomb. "By the way, Joe, I'm planning on offering Karen the job of director of VIP Services."

"Karen—"

"Yes, that Karen. Karen Dorsey."

"Okay, but what's the Aladdin's employee-fraternization policy?"

Gomes laughed. "Whatever it is, it doesn't apply to you. You're already married."

Gomes had met Karen socially and believed she would fit in, thanks to her ability to interact with customers, as she did as an entertainer. After getting tired of all the traveling with her band, a gig at Cleopatra's Barge at Caesars Palace provided her with the perfect swan song to her singing career. She'd been working at the Hilton, but she left during the mass exodus from there to the Aladdin with Gomes.

Joe went to work. He quickly realized that since the Aladdin had been closed for a year, he could offer positions to outside people without terminating any existing employees. He immediately met with Jim Mydlach, a senior security officer and EMT at the Hilton. Mydlach was a perfect choice for security director. He was like Radar O'Reilly from "M*A*S*H." He knew everyone in Las Vegas and could get anything anyone needed and any job done. Jim also had the gift of gab and even worked for Elvis Presley.

He then approached Dick Armandi, a retired New York City cop and firefighter, to take on a security lieutenant's position, which he accepted.

Joe also hired some other former law-enforcement people to assist with background investigations and filled the positions of surveillance director and corporate security manager.

As for investigating the 1,500 prospective employees, since the vast majority were only receiving work cards, the investigations were cursory. Joe and his staff followed up on any that they determined needed a closer look; some of them weren't hired. Others had to be terminated during the probationary period. But all in all, rehiring and reopening the Aladdin proved to be drama-free.

Less than seven weeks after Joe waved goodbye to the Las Vegas Hilton, the grand-opening day arrived and the Aladdin, incredibly, was ready.

The problems with owner Ginji Yasuda, however, started immediately. Joe quickly realized that Yasuda knew how to be a casino customer, but not an operator; he knew nothing about a hotel-casino's organizational flow chart or departmental responsibilities. Right off the bat, he wasn't happy that the casino didn't make millions the first day of operation and as the days and weeks went by, he got more and more frustrated with the slow pace of profits. He didn't understand that the casino had opened so quickly, it was going to take time for marketing and player development to kick in.

Exacerbating the situation, Yasuda and his wife were living in the penthouse with access to the surveillance system. He called Joe in the middle of the night to report a fire alarm; he disturbed Joe at home to tell him that the lounge lighting was too low. During one meeting, he insisted on putting metal detectors at all the entrances to the property. After a suicide jump from the upper floor of the hotel, he wanted to lock all the windows. Joe explained they couldn't do that; it would drive away guests who preferred fresh air over air-conditioning.

One weekend early on, Gomes and marketing were expecting a group of high rollers to arrive with a total of $12 million to play in the casino. Some of the players were from Japan and since Yasuda knew them, he met them to pay his respects. He was well aware that under gaming regulations, an owner was prohibited from gambling in his own casino. What did Yasuda, an avid baccarat player, do? He took all the players and their $12 million out of the Aladdin and up the Strip to the Dunes, so he could play with them. Gomes was furious and let him know about it.

Someone had convinced Yasuda to install a state-of-the-art surveillance system, which was overkill. But he stayed up late every night, watching the monitors like a hawk and going crazy looking for people stealing from him. The system was installed prior to Joe's arrival, but one of Yasuda's men who oversaw the installation approached him with an invoice for the second half of the completed work — for $500,000. Joe started asking questions and Yasuda's guy went into his "no-speak-English" mode.

Joe said, "Since I had nothing to do with the system and you oversaw the Japanese company's installation, you should sign the invoice."

Now he went into the "I-don't-understand" phase of the conversation.

Joe had conversed with Yasuda's guy in the past, so he knew two things: 1) He spoke perfect English; and 2) he was trying to run a game. He said, "Okay, I know you understand me, so you're just trying to play me. But now I'm going into my 'fuck-you' mode."

That was when Joe started to learn that "fuck you" is understood everywhere around the world.

Yasuda and his cronies weren't screwing with just Joe and Gomes. One night, the security shift supervisor called Joe to tell him that the casino manager had been called to Yasuda's suite, where the owner insinuated that the reason the casino was losing was because the casino manager was short. The casino manager was about 5'4" and resented anyone who called attention to his stature.

"The casino manager left the property really pissed off," the shift supervisor told Joe, "and returned after he'd had a few drinks. We found him at the porte-cochere, kicking the door of Yasuda's Rolls Royce."

"How bad is the damage?" Joe inquired.

"Just scuff marks that can be rubbed out. But there's more."

"Uh-oh. What?"

"The casino manager's office has six surveillance monitors ripped from their shelving and destroyed."

"Jeez. Put him on the phone."

When the casino manager was on the other end of the line, Joe said, "I'm going to have you taken home by security. If you're seen on the property before ten tomorrow morning, I'll have you thrown in jail. Understand?"

"Yes, I do. I really fucked up," the casino manager admitted. "But Yasuda kept beefing me for being unlucky because of my height." He paused, then asked, "Do you think I'll get termed?"

"Well, let's wait and see what it all looks like in the light of day. But don't take any calls from Yasuda. If the phone rings, have your wife answer."

Then Joe instructed the security supervisor not to let anyone into the casino manager's office, except for a tech to change out the monitors, until he arrived in the morning.

Truth was that everyone from Gomes down, including Joe, was aware that their days were numbered and they were destined to follow the casino manager into the ranks of unemployed. But they also knew that Gaming Control wouldn't look kindly on Yasuda running the joint after hearing from the Aladdin's ex-casino managers about his paranoia.

Barely five months into their tenure at the Aladdin, everyone who came in with Gomes went out with him again.

Gomes and his minions coordinated their departure with Gaming Control and a planned move across the Strip to the Dunes, which needed an influx of fresh casino management. At the time, the Dunes was the only other Las Vegas casino owned by a Japanese businessman, Masao Nangaku.

One day just before starting work at the Dunes, Joe asked Gomes, "With Nangaku in charge, are we going to go through this all over again?"

Gomes replied, "I sure hope not."

A Brief Stint at The Dunes

In early 1988, Gomes formed Clark Management, a one-stop casino-operations company. Within the company were highly regarded senior executives: vice presidents of finance, casino and slot operations, marketing, human resources, and security (Joe), along with a director of entertainment and VIP services (Karen). Dunes owner Masao Nangaku, another wealthy Japanese businessman from Tokyo, had recently purchased the Dunes and was in the beginning stages of being investigated for his gaming license. Nangaku had recently been reported as the world's number-two-wealthiest man. Nangaku hired Clark Management to run the property.

Gomes opened an office away from the Dunes and prepared for the transition. Like the Aladdin when Gomes and Joe went to work for Yasuda, the casino wasn't operating, because there was no gaming license. So getting the casino open and generating revenue were the top priority. Regulators licensed Clark Management and Gomes until Nangaku was licensed.

Upon arrival at the Dunes, Joe could easily see that the property was not only showing its age (33 years old, it opened originally in 1955), but it had also been neglected. He wondered if the Dunes was good enough to get Gomes' big players from the Hilton and Aladdin to come to the property. But that wasn't his bailiwick, which rested with casino and hotel operations, marketing, and the host department. Joe had other concerns.

He immediately brought Jim Mydlach over from the Aladdin as director of security and Dick Armandi as captain, as well as Al Spriggs to head up corporate security. Spriggs was a former Metro officer who had many contacts at the police department. Joe brought him on as an investigator to assist with the 1,500 background checks they had to conduct at the Aladdin. He was eventually let go from the Aladdin after Joe went to the Dunes. The surveillance director in place was well-known and a retired police officer who wanted to stay on. A surveillance supervisor was also brought in from the Aladdin.

Joe and Jim Mydlach began a search for friendly employees in every department to help get them up to speed as to what was going on in all areas of the operation. Within the first few weeks, they heard that money was being pilfered from the soft-count room by a count-room employee and a custodian. The cash was placed into a small trash bag out of view of the surveillance cameras, then into a larger trash bag. The janitor removed the large trash bag from the count room as garbage. Meanwhile, the security officer outside the count room never checked the contents of the bag, a clear violation of gaming rules. The large trash bag went out the maintenance door to the Flamingo Road side of the property, then was discarded; the small bag was hidden in the shrubs alongside the building for pickup by unknown accomplices. After Joe was alerted to the scam, he caught the janitor in the act. The interview concerning how many times this type of theft and others had been perpetrated was unsuccessful, so the janitor was fired and all new procedures were put into place.

A short time later, Gomes informed Joe that Nangaku's gaming attorneys had requested that he assist them in arranging meetings and acquiring the necessary documents for Nangaku's gaming-license investigation in Japan. Joe knew the lawyers, who had represented gaming clients when he worked for Gaming Control; they believed that with his experience, Joe would know what the agents required, which might speed up the investigation. Off he went to Tokyo, where he conferred with the GCB's supervising agent, who indicated the documents that needed to be obtained in Japan, brought back, and interpreted. He also scheduled a meeting among Nangaku's staff and attorneys and the Gaming agents.

Joe was accompanied by a Japanese intermediary on Nangaku's Dunes staff, Nick, who spoke fluent English and had the authority to supervise and direct the staff in Tokyo. Nick had graduated from a university in Japan and earned a master's degree in the U.S. He'd also traveled extensively throughout the country and was very happy to be assigned to the Nangaku's Las Vegas subsidiary so he could return to the States. Nick and Joe became close friends and Nick educated him on the many cultural issues that he might encounter in Japan. The enculturation proved to be extremely helpful, not only at the time, but also in Joe's future as an international casino-debt collector. Since Nangaku visited the Dunes only when he was traveling, Nick was his go-between.

In the meantime, even though Nangaku wasn't yet licensed, he still owned the Dunes and Dennis Gomes transmitted frequent requests to him concerning funding — bills that needed paying, casino transactions that needed approval, and the like. Just like at the Aladdin, the Japanese owner had no experience in the gaming business by which to make a quick decision. Many times, Gomes heard a variation on, "He'll get back to you." The problem was that, in the casino business, decisions need to be evaluated and made quickly and if they aren't, millions of dollars are on the line. Gomes later learned that the decisions were ultimately made by staff in Japan who had never been in the U.S., let alone a casino.

The logistical challenges with the owner notwithstanding, after a few months, Clark Management had made a lot of headway in cleaning up the Dunes, which began to show an increase in business. To some degree, Karen, as the director of entertainment and VIP services, helped that cause. With her experience as an entertainer and her contacts in the industry, she knew what the casino needed to draw people. For example, she found talented but unknown groups outside of Las Vegas, such as Earl Turner, who attracted a following. She also re-opened the Top of the Dunes showroom with Bob Anderson, a perennial Las Vegas favorite.

The Dunes' Roulette Wheel

On a Saturday night, Joe received a call at home from Gomes about suspicious play on a roulette table. He headed back to the casino, where Dennis told him that he'd agreed to a specific play and betting limits brought to him by a casino host. Joe didn't like or trust this host, whose customers seemed shady.

"What terms did you agree to?" Joe asked.

"I raised the betting limits when the player bet on four specific numbers."

"What happened?"

"I don't know, but the player is up seven hundred grand. At friggin' roulette!"

Joe knew that Gomes was always open to taking risks on non-normal play. At the Hilton, he allowed a gambler to place a $50,000 field bet at a crap table for one roll of the dice. Of course, Dennis realized it was a great way to generate publicity and had a local television news station film the event. Joe watched it on TV and when he showed up for work the next day, Dennis asked him if he saw it.

"Sure I did," Joe said. "But I couldn't hear anything."

"Why not?" Dennis took the bait.

"Because when the player rolled a twelve, all I could hear was your ass slamming shut and sucking for air as the dealers slid over the double payout."

Gomes laughed and said, "Yeah, a hundred grand. Better luck to us next time."

Joe liked a lot about Dennis, but this might have been what he loved the most: He didn't get upset. His attitude was always, "Well, another great day is coming." And it was.

Or was it?

A few weeks later, Gomes convinced the lucky crap player to come back to the Dunes with another $50K and damned if he didn't hit boxcars again! Joe doesn't recall whether the player returned again with another fifty-grand bet, but if he did, Gomes certainly would have taken the action.

Back to the $700,000 beating the Dunes was taking on the roulette wheel. Joe met with the director of surveillance while the player went to the Sultan's Table gourmet room for dinner. Knowing he would be awhile in the restaurant, they rolled through the videotapes of the play and quickly realized the four numbers being bet per the agreement were coming up way too often. They deduced that the wheel was not only biased (it favored certain numbers due to an imperfection in the mechanics), but that the problem had been discovered by an employee or others who look to exploit weaknesses in casinos. When discovered, they either make the play themselves or sell the information to professionals willing to risk big money to take advantage of the juicy situation.

Examining the wheel, Joe and the surveillance director

found that a loose fret on the wheel was causing the bias. They quickly switched out the wheel for one from a closed roulette game. The player returned and played for a few hours more, but his lucky streak was over. He lost back a half-million and left with only $200,000 in winnings.

Kashiwagi Part One

Dennis and Joe had known Akio Kashiwagi since the 1980s. He was a Tokyo-based real estate investor and a big *big* gambler at the Hilton, Aladdin, Dunes, and Golden Nugget in Las Vegas and later in Atlantic City. Kashiwagi brought millions in cash, then had credit extended in the same amount. He often played for days on end, never sleeping.

The casino's baccarat pit was required to have his preference of food available and two unoccupied tables available for him to play, so that when one dealer needed to reshuffle the cards, the second table could open immediately. This "revolving-table" scenario repeated many times during his play. In addition, his deal with the casinos dictated the minimum amounts of cash required and win/loss amounts had to be met before play could be stopped by him or the casino.

Joe recalls one Las Vegas visit when Kashiwagi came to the Dunes and requested a betting limit of $175,000 per hand. He'd brought $4 million in cashier's checks and was extended another $4 million in credit. The Dunes had a new $25,000 chip manufactured for him due to the amount of his bets.

On a Saturday night of one of Kashiwagi's early visits, Joe met with Gomes, who told him Kashiwagi was up nearly $4 million. Dennis was calm; he knew from experience that either the Japanese whale or the casino could be up or down a million dollars every five minutes, given his style of play.

On this particular trip, Kashiwagi abruptly stopped his play when his winnings reached the $4 million and informed his host that he was leaving. The host went right to Dennis, who exhibited a rare display of emotion. Dennis and Joe had been at the Dunes for only a short time and Dennis had convinced Masao Nangaku that big players were the way to go. Now, one of the first big players had just beaten the casino out of seven figures. Not an impressive way to start.

Kashiwagi received his winnings in a check and left the property with his host. They headed toward a hastily arranged chartered flight to San Francisco. But about 90 minutes later, they returned to the Dunes.

It turned out that the host had accompanied Kashiwagi to the plane and bid him farewell. He started to leave, which wasn't the norm; he usually flew with Kashiwagi to San Francisco to meet his flight back to Japan. When Kashiwagi questioned the host about not going to San Francisco with him, he replied that he didn't feel good about this flight.

The host told him that the flight could be bad luck, because Kashiwagi was leaving early, according to his agreement with Gomes, and he'd never done that in the past. He also pointed out that the pilots looked exhausted, or at least haggard, possibly from too much fun in their Vegas layover. Kashiwagi looked at the pilots and contemplated his options. He agreed that this could be a sign of bad luck and returned to the Dunes—and eventually lost back all his winnings and then some.

Ron Lyle

Joe was asked once if he thought his relationship with his mother's boyfriend, the drunken ex-con, had influenced his law-enforcement duties. Did he harbor any prejudice against felons and convicts?

"Actually," he said, "I was often willing to give deserving convicts a chance."

One day at the Dunes, Joe received a phone call from a non-law-enforcement advisor to the Metropolitan Police Department. He asked Joe to help him find a position for an ex-felon, adding that the request had come directly from the sheriff. "This guy did time in Colorado, but since his release, he's turned his life around and is now working with disadvantaged youth."

"What was he convicted of?" Joe wanted to know.

"Homicide."

Joe was taken aback that the Clark County sheriff was requesting that he hire a convicted murderer.

"But he was pardoned by the governor of Colorado," the advisor explained.

"Well, since the sheriff is asking, I'll interview him. But I'm not making any promises."

"Good enough," the advisor said.

"What's his name?"

"Ron Lyle."

"Ron Lyle? The Ron Lyle who fought Mohammed Ali in a championship fight?"

"The very same."

Before Joe met with Lyle, he investigated and learned that he'd been involved in a large street fight as a teenager, during which he shot another teenager who was reportedly attacking him with a lead pipe. That teen died and Ron was convicted of second-degree murder, then sent to state prison.

Joe was fortunate, because the lawyer for the Dunes, Peter Alpert, was a former judge in Fort Morgan, Colorado. Alpert was familiar with the case and filled Joe in on the details, explaining that Lyle had served his time in an exemplary manner. He learned to box while in prison, continued boxing after his release, and ultimately challenged Muhammad Ali for the heavyweight title on May 16, 1975, in a nationally televised bout from the Tropicana in Las Vegas. Lyle went toe-to-toe with Ali for 11 rounds and was actually ahead in the scoring — until Ali pounced, knocking the 33-year-old Lyle across the ring with a straight right that left him loopy and defenseless against the Champ's juggernaut.

Joe met Ron Lyle, now 46 and a little down on his luck, for an interview the day after the police advisor's initial phone call. He remembers that when Ron entered his office, he seemed to fill the entire doorway. He was so big, as Joe puts it, "Each of his hands was as big as my head." Lyle was just under six-four, weighed 220, and had an arm span of six and a half feet.

Lyle thanked Joe for giving him an interview, but Joe could sense the man was very nervous. He asked Lyle why he was so tense. He responded that he was concerned that Joe might pre-judge him because of his law-enforcement background. Apparently, Lyle had done his homework too.

Joe spent two hours with Lyle and, during that time, he grew more comfortable with the man. He could certainly relate to Lyle's background as a member of a family with 19 kids from the projects in Denver with very little formal education.

In order to ease Lyles' anxiety, Joe shared the story of his own youth, growing up in the projects of Cleveland. Lyle then opened up more, explaining his conviction, his time in prison, and what he'd done to redeem himself for the crime he'd committed. He also explained how his boxing career had ultimately brought him to a bout with Muhammad Ali.

Joe realized that here sat a man who, but for the grace of God, could have been himself. By this time in his career, Joe had talked to hundreds of felons, but he'd never encountered one as remorseful or who had tried harder to make amends to rectify the errors of his past. He was never more impressed with an ex-convict.

"Ron," Joe said, "I'm going to talk to my boss about you and I'll call you tomorrow."

As Joe said goodbye and shook Ron's enormous hand, Ron said, "No matter what happens, Mr. Dorsey, I'll always be grateful that you told me about Cleveland. We have some struggles in common and that put me at ease in your presence."

Joe met with Gomes and explained the situation, relating the details of his interview with Ron Lyle. Joe told Dennis, "I think he's earned a break."

Dennis agreed. "But what about the potential difficulty in obtaining a work card for Lyle?"

Joe smiled. "Not a problem."

"How do you figure?"

"Well, work cards are approved by the sheriff. He recommended Lyle!"

"Well then ... it's a done deal. But what about arming him?"

"I say no. No sense in creating any potential problems."

As he promised, Joe called Ron the next day and requested that he meet at Joe's office. When Ron arrived, Joe said, "Ron, you're hired."

"I am?" Lyle breathed a huge sigh of relief.

"Yes, you are. You'll be a security officer with one restriction. No firearm."

"That's all right with me, sir."

Joe remembers that to Ron, it seemed like Christmas — a

steady paycheck, medical insurance, and a position of respect and responsibility.

In the years that followed, Joe worked at many different casinos with Lyle and he was always a great asset, especially when a heavyweight fight was scheduled in Las Vegas. Joe always made sure that Ron was out of uniform, working instead in a suit and tie on the casino floor. Every well-known fighter coming to Las Vegas stopped by to pay his respects to Ron Lyle.

One day Lyle came into Joe's office. After a little small talk, Joe realized that Ron wanted to ask him something.

"What is it, Ron? Whatever it is, you know you can ask me."

"Well," Ron started, then paused, gathering himself. "You know, I've been receiving fan mail —"

"No, I didn't know that. But that's really cool."

"Yes, but …"

"But what? Out with it."

"I … I need … I need help answering the mail."

Ron showed Joe letters from fans, both children and adults, as far away as England.

Joe told Ron he would help him write the responses and Ron could sign the letters. Joe then called the marketing department to tell them Ron was coming down; he needed 50 copies of a head shot. Over the next few years, Ron met with Joe and together they answered the letters he'd received, including signed photos. Joe came to realize this meant a great deal to Ron, being able to respond to his fans, many of whom thought he'd won the Ali fight.

One day much later at the Tropicana where Ron had followed Gomes and Joe, Ron and another security officer responded to a medical emergency involving a guest of the hotel. The guest was having a heart attack and losing consciousness, so they performed CPR until emergency services arrived. Thanks to the efforts of Ron and the other officer, the man's life was saved. However, the life-saving procedure did come with some risks: They were informed later by the hospital staff that the patient had tested positive for tuberculosis. Ron and others with whom this man had contact were tested and, fortunately, found to be free of the disease. Ron Lyle, who in his youth took a life, had now saved the life of a complete stranger.

Joe eventually left the casinos and later, Lyle went to work for Karen Dorsey at the famous locals casino, Ellis Island. The casino on Koval Lane was near Lyle's apartment. Ron loved working at Ellis Island. It was a small family-owned operation and had, and still has, some of the best food and drink deals in Las Vegas, which attract locals in droves. Having Ron there gave Joe peace of mind. He never had to worry about his wife working late into the night, because he knew Lyle hovered around her like a guardian angel.

Ron eventually returned to Denver to run a Salvation Army-sponsored boxing program for underprivileged children. He was later charged with shooting a former Colorado State Penitentiary inmate who had come to Lyle's home. He claimed self-defense and was found not guilty by a jury.

On the evening of November 26, 2011, Joe was notified by Ron Lyle's wife that Ron had passed away at the age of 70 due to a sepsis infection. Ron may have been troubled in his youth, but he died with the reputation of being a productive man who was helping those in desperate need.

Joe feels privileged that he got to know Ron and witness his transformation to a man of good character and a life of dignity. He was thankful he and Karen had taken the opportunity to share their lives with Ron over the years.

Leaving the Dunes Behind

Masao Nangaku's licensing investigation cost $730,000 and took almost a year, due to his wealth and worldwide holdings. But in December 1988, Nangaku was approved for a two-year license and told he could begin to share in the gaming revenue. This meant Nangaku and Gomes had to negotiate over whether Gomes would continue to run the Dunes and share its profits with Nangaku or Nangaku would purchase the Gomes company, whereby all of his hotel-casino employees would be absorbed onto the payroll. The chairman of the Gaming Commission stressed that Nangaku had to deal with Gomes directly and not through his intermediaries or lawyers who weren't licensed in Nevada. They struck a deal and the casino was turned over to Nangaku. At the stroke of midnight on the day the new deal began, the old chips were taken out of circulation and new ones were brought in.

Gomes and company had lasted seven months at the Dunes, two months longer than they had at the Aladdin under Ginji Yasuda.

Gomes tendered his resignation to Masao Nangaku at the Dunes and took all of Clark Management with him to the Golden Nugget. It was 1989 and Gomes had been contacted by Steve Wynn, who wanted to hire Clark Management to take over the Golden Nugget prior to the Mirage opening in November of that year. Wynn had opened up the doors of the Mirage to all Golden Nugget employees; they had the option of staying at the Nugget or moving to the bright shiny new casino on the Strip. Ninety percent of the employees chose to transfer to the Mirage.

Joe stayed on at the Dunes until Gomes had everything set up at the Nugget downtown. Karen, too, remained at the Dunes for the duration. Joe lasted another month, until a replacement for Gomes arrived: Jack Speilman.

One of Speilman's first duties was to call Joe in and let him know he was being let go due to the change in management. It came as no surprise to Joe. Everyone in the casino business, even to this day, knows this as a fact of life. But in Nangaku's case, it was a bit extreme. For some reason, he had a scorched-earth policy when it came to anyone loyal to Dennis Gomes and Speilman informed Joe that the terminations of all those employees came directly from the top.

Joe said, "I understand your position, certainly, but this is kind of sudden. I'm leaving for San Diego tonight for the weekend and I was planning on using my company car."

Speilman was gracious. "Go ahead, Joe. Just call me when you get back and I'll have the car picked up."

"Thank you, Jack. I really appreciate that." As Joe got up to leave, he had one last question. "What about my wife, Karen? Is she being termed too?"

"Actually, no, she isn't." Speilman smiled. "She's not on the list I received from the owner's people."

Karen, in fact, was asked to stay at the Dunes after Jack Speilman arrived. She remained at the Dunes for another 18 months until Bert Cohen replaced Speilman.

Joe's friend Nick, the translator and intermediary for Nangaku, was recalled to Tokyo. He'd been put in the position of agreeing with Gomes on various issues of casino management, which set him on a collision course with Nangaku, who demanded loyalty over all else, even sound business practices in his far-flung empire. Nick soon left Nangaku's employ.

Masao Nangaku paid $155 million when he purchased the Dunes in 1987, but essentially ran it into the ground. By 1992, he was shopping the property and the first stop for his real estate brokers was Caesars Palace. The price was $78 million, roughly half of what it he'd paid five years earlier. Caesars turned down the opportunity; they had no idea what they would or could do with 85 acres of prime center Strip property — and that didn't include the 162-acre Dunes Golf Course. Instead, Steve Wynn swooped in and scooped up the Dunes for $75 million, a bit more than $300,000 per acre. Today, Bellagio stands where the Dunes once stood and parts of the Cosmopolitan, City Center, Park MGM, New York-New York, and T-Mobile Arena occupy what used to be the golf course.

A Longer Stint at The Golden Nugget

From the Frying Pan into the Fire?

Steve Wynn was well-known as a tyrannical boss and casino owner. Joe had conducted the licensing investigation of Bobby Baldwin, a professional poker player whom Wynn hired to run the Golden Nugget, and had many contacts and discussions with Wynn when he was a supervising agent at the GCB. He knew what he was getting into. But Wynn was extremely preoccupied with opening the most expensive hotel-casino ever built up until that time. So he left a lot of the day-to-day operational details to Gomes and company, though he still kept his finger on the pulse of the casino of which he'd been the majority owner since he was in his early 30s.

One Saturday night while at home, Joe received a call from Wynn, summoning him to the Golden Nugget executive offices floor at midnight. Joe cleaned up and met Wynn at the witching hour.

Wynn told Joe that he had information from a source that an active scam was going on in the slot department concerning the 24 Karat Club. The forerunner of slot and players clubs, 24 Karat was a program in which enrolled players automatically received a physical ticket each time the last dollar of a total of $75 was played in designated slot machines. After the player wagered the 75th dollar, the slot machine dispensed a ticket, similar to a skee-ball machine, worth 50 cents toward the purchase of a Gold Certificate. Gold Certificates could be redeemed for gaming chips, cash, and Golden Nugget comps.

"Listen, Joe, you can't share any of the information I'm about to give you with anyone."

"Yes, sir."

"My source tells me the 24 Karat Club is losing thousands in ticket redemptions for cash. I know the first name of one of the people involved — Bruce. This guy did time in a state penitentiary in Walla Walla, Washington. The only other information I have on this Bruce is the phone number of his grandmother."

His grandmother's phone number? Joe stifled a laugh. The whole cloak-and-dagger midnight meeting was starting to seem funny, but he knew better than to show any amusement; Wynn was deadly serious.

"I have no idea how the theft is taking place, but I can tell you this, Joe: I believe my source.

"You say I can't tell anyone, but should I inform Dennis Gomes of my investigation?"

"Let's just keep this between you and me for the time being. We can always tell Gomes later, after we have more information."

The next day, Joe cold called Grandma. He pretended to be a fellow convict who served time with Bruce and heard he was in Las Vegas. He needed to contact him regarding a job that Bruce would be perfect for. The grandmother gave it all up, telling Joe that Bruce was living in Las Vegas with his mother and stepfather. She even supplied his address and phone number.

So now, Joe was supervising the Golden Nugget's security, surveillance, and safety directors and conducting a one-man surveillance on this Bruce character. Joe recalls, "I was surveilling a moving vehicle and trying not to get made, just like on the unrealistic cop shows on television — you know, when their vehicle is so close behind the subject that they can tell if the guy needs a shave. Thank God Bruce smoked a lot of dope. I could've been in his back seat and I don't think he would have thought anything of it."

Joe followed Bruce around for a month, but he never went near the Golden Nugget. He took photos of Bruce and gave them to surveillance to notify him if he was seen on the property, but he never was.

Finally, Joe showed up at the 24 Karat booth and approached the attendant. "Hi," he said. "I'm a new security guy. Can you please explain to me how this club works?"

After a little back and forth, Joe asked, "What happens when the tickets from the slot machines are redeemed? How do you cancel them?"

"Cancel them?" the girl asked. "I don't understand."

Oh shit, Joe thought, getting an inkling of how the scam might work. "You know, marking them so they can't be redeemed again."

"Well, we count up the tickets, pay the customer, and put them in a big trash bag."

"And where does the trash bag go?"

She responded, "I don't know."

From there, Joe approached the 24 Karat shift supervisor and, pointing at the big black bags behind the counter, said, "You sure get a lot of trash."

"That's not trash," she told Joe. "Those are redeemed slot tickets."

"So do the custodians pick them up?"

"No. The shift supervisors deliver them to the accounting office."

Next stop: the accounting office. Joe was told that clerks randomly checked the bags, then placed them in the hallway to be disposed of by a custodian.

"And how does the ticket-canceling process work?"

"With so many tickets, we don't have time to cancel them."

A further check revealed that the husband of a 24 Karat slot club employee was the janitor for accounting.

Joe now knew how the uncanceled tickets got into the scammers' hands, but he still had to figure out who they all were and how they redeemed them for cash.

Then, on a Sunday night, Wynn called again; he was angry that Joe hadn't solved the case yet.

"I'm just a one-man show on this case and I still have to run three departments at the same time."

Wynn didn't want to hear excuses and Joe wasn't taking any more pressure. "My office. Tomorrow morning. Ten o'clock." Wynn hung up.

Karen asked, "That wasn't Steve Wynn, was it?"

"Yes it was."

"You were kind of gruff with him."

"He was kind of gruff with me," Joe responded. "So now I guess we're even. Oh, and by the way, I might get fired tomorrow."

The next morning, Joe called Gomes and told him what happened.

"Should I call Wynn?" Gomes asked,

"Hell no! You're not supposed to know what I'm working on. Let me go to the meeting first."

At 10 on the dot, Joe was there, not knowing what to expect. He walked in, sat down, and calmly explained that Wynn had come to him with a first name, the name of a prison, and a phone number. He revealed what he'd uncovered so far and that he knew the employees involved.

Wynn asked what he needed to finish the job.

Joe replied, "I need a four-man surveillance team, rental cars, radios, two of my security investigators, and the freedom to do what I believe is necessary."

Wynn approved everything and that was that.

On his way out, Joe said, "By the way, your source is highly reliable. Speaking as an ex-cop, I'd keep him or her close."

A few days later, with the team set up and ready to go, Joe and his men went to the employee's apartment and recovered numerous trash bags with thousands of redeemable 24 Karat club tickets. He interviewed the club employee and her custodian husband and ascertained that they had eight people, Bruce among them, coming to the casino from all over the country, acting as registered slot club players and redeeming the tickets.

Knowing the game was up, the employees cooperated, calling all their cohorts from as far away as Chicago and Texas, who had no knowledge of one another's identities, to come in for token redemptions. They were arrested and charged with grand theft. The employees and the participants were convicted or pled guilty and received jail time.

New slot-ticket redemption procedures were adopted

immediately. Joe even got an "attaboy" from the D.A. for the case presentation, but of course, it wasn't his first rodeo. Gomes asked why Joe interviewed the subjects before turning them over to the cops. He said that he didn't have to Mirandize them before the interviews and anything they confessed was admissible. Metro interviewed them afterwards, armed with the interview statements given to Joe.

Wynn treated Joe differently after he solved the case.

Turning the District Attorney's Office into the Casinos' Collection Agency

One day, Joe stopped by a convenience store for some coffee. There, he noticed a picture on the cash register of the Clark County District Attorney with a written statement that it was a crime to intentionally write a bad check in Nevada. Something clicked.

Though he didn't realize it at the time, Joe Dorsey was on the cusp of revolutionizing the casino debt collection business.

An industry platitude says that a casino has to earn its money twice. First, it has to win it at the tables. Second, it has to collect it from the gamblers. This is especially true if the gamblers are borrowing their bankrolls from the casino by signing what are known in the business as "markers."

Casinos extend credit to their gambling customers and any gambler in the world can request credit to play. To check the gambler's ability to repay the credit, casinos request bank statements showing that the gambler has the funds to cover the credit. The casino also checks with a company called Central Credit, a repository for gambling-related credit data for casinos worldwide. Central Credit tracks casino play, unpaid gambling debts, and marker activity. Casinos have used the services of "Central" since 1956. Rarely is credit granted to a customer who has an outstanding balance with another casino, as indicated on his casino credit report.

When casinos do issue credit, the gambler takes chips in the form of a marker. A marker looks exactly like a bank check. It's issued by the casino in the amount of money, via chips, that the player is given. For example, if a player has $100,000 in a checking account, the casino might issue credit of $50,000. When the player shows up at the cage and asks for $25,000, a cashier prints out the marker, which the player signs, and is then handed $25K in casino chips.

Now, say the gambler loses the $25,000. He can request the remaining $25,000 in credit, either at the table or from the cage. What if he then wins $50,000 and decides to cash out? He redeems the two markers for $25,000 each and is even with the house. If he wins $100,000, he redeems both markers and walks away after doubling his money. But if he loses the entire $50,000 in chips he took from the casino on credit, he still has to repay it at the end of his trip or according to his credit terms, usually within 30 days. What if 30 days roll around and he hasn't paid? Then the marker is run through his bank account like any check that he writes. If it bounces? Well, that's where the casino has to go to some lengths to earn its money a second time.

Big gamblers, a.k.a. "high rollers" and "whales," often sign an agreement that dictates rules of play, such as betting limits, length of daily duration at the tables, accommodation and food comps, and airfare reimbursement for the gambler and those traveling with him. These agreements always include a timeline for repayment, which provides a failsafe for the casino if the gambler goes home, or to another casino, without settling his debt.

But even the credit agreements between casinos and gamblers don't ensure that whales will pay their debts.

In the old days, a mish-mash of regulations governed the legality of casinos collecting their debts in other states. When Nevada was the only state with legalized casino gambling, many states' laws didn't recognize gambling debts as collectable. So a player might take chips on credit, then sneak away without paying off his markers. If his state of residence disallowed collection, he was in the clear. Of course, no casino would ever extend him credit again, thanks to a derogatory note in his Central Credit file; he became what's called "pay and play" — in other words, the casino required cash up front. In the Mob days, such a player would be wise not so show his face anywhere near a casino to which he owed money. But in general, marker collecting was a major conundrum for Nevada casinos.

Then Joe bought a fateful cup of coffee.

A Visit to the Sheriff

Joe returned to his office and looked up the relevant Nevada statutes. Clearly, the bad-check law had implications for casino collection efforts.

Armed with this legal information, Joe prepared a crime report, witness list, and copies of bounced checks (known in the financial business as "non-sufficient funds" or "NSF") for a Golden Nugget gambler who'd written NSF checks to redeem his markers, then left town.

Joe scheduled a meeting with his friend, Sheriff John

Moran. He'd known Moran for about five years and had the highest respect for him. He'd served as a Marine in WW II and was the chief of police in Las Vegas prior to the merger of the Sheriff's Office and the Las Vegas Police Department into the Metropolitan Police Department, or Metro.

Joe explained to Moran that the DA's photograph and notice about bad checks at the convenience store had prompted him to request assistance from law enforcement in collecting casino debts. Joe handed him the crime report and evidence and witness lists on the casino debtor and asked if a detective in the Fraud Unit could take the details to the DA's office and get a complaint filed. This would lead to the issuance of an arrest warrant, giving Joe some leverage and enhancing the casino's efforts in collecting future debts. The customer resided in the U.S. and Joe didn't feel the need to divulge that he planned to request warrants for international non-paying customers as well, should this strategy prove successful.

John read Joe's reports and said, "I believe you might be onto something here." Then he looked up and smiled. "You've never forgotten how to think like a cop. Always one step ahead."

Sheriff Moran assigned one of his detectives the task of filing the complaint, which wasn't difficult, since Joe had already completed all the paperwork. In a short time, an arrest warrant was issued for the bad-check customer.

Joe contacted the customer, faxed him the arrest warrant, and informed him that the warrant was enforceable in all 50 states. He didn't mention that after arrest, extradition required approval from the court in the jurisdiction where he was taken into custody. In addition, since the NSF crime law was new, the DA wouldn't approve the cost of any extradition. But again, Joe was thinking one step ahead.

When the Golden Nugget received a wire-transfer payment from the debtor within four hours, Joe knew this was the start of something big in debt collection.

An Industry Game Changer

Over the next few years, Metro detectives took over filing the NSF complaints and writing the requisite reports.

Joe's approach yielded such great results that the DA's office soon imposed a 10% administrative fee to handle their insufficient-funds filings. Through the use of these warrants, the DA's office received 10% of the debt collected by casinos. This amounted to hundreds of thousands of dollars in revenue, just for doing their job and enforcing the law.

These procedures that Joe put into place, using the NSF warrants, proved to be a game changer for the collection of casino markers. After all, most gamblers couldn't wait to return to Las Vegas – in those days the world's largest casino destination – and outstanding warrants not only prevented them for doing so, but could also mean a stint in jail.

Next, Joe turned his attention to the collection of other casino debts, in particular those that were simply overdue, like any late payment on a credit account. Once again, he was thinking a step ahead, believing he'd be asked to collect on delinquent markers. But as he researched the laws covering debt collections in the U.S., he found that the mish-mash of laws among states ranged from casino collections being enforceable to unenforceable all the way to illegal. Thus, he concluded that all the different laws and policies state to state would hinder collection efforts, so he decided to leave U.S. collections to the casino collection departments.

Initially, the Golden Nugget was the only casino to use the NFS approach. Other casinos were slow to catch onto the idea of employing a designated law-enforcement expert to collect debts. They continued to use traditional collection-agency personnel with no experience in identifying an enforceable crime to fit the scenario.

By the late 1990s, however, the rest of the Clark County casinos had fallen in line and a regular collections system was put into place by the District Attorney. Today all casinos are now part of this system, for which they compensate the DA. Now, if a gambler has a delinquent marker and doesn't respond to a casino's efforts to collect on it or fails to negotiate a reasonable payment plan, the file is submitted to the Bad Check Unit (BCU). The gambler must deal with the agent assigned by the prosecutor's office to take over the collection responsibilities. Once the account is submitted to the BCU, any opportunity the gambler might have had to negotiate a discount on the marker is forfeited; the BCU collects 100% of the marker. The money is deposited directly into the BCU's account; it takes 10% of the total amount for services rendered, then forwards the rest to the casino.

Finally, now that commercial and tribal casino gambling is legal in 30 states, casino debt collections are enforceable in all 50. What Joe had done, in simple terms, was turn the Clark County District Attorney into the official collection agent for the Las Vegas casinos. The innovation is regarded as being among the most significant ever in the collection component of the casino industry — and it all started with a cup of coffee.

Collecting Casino
Debts All Around
the World

While managing the Golden Nugget casino, Dennis Gomes, as he usually did, extended a hefty amount of credit to international gamblers. When too many of them were slow to pay, Steve Wynn started questioning Gomes' ability to collect the debt.

Up until that time, the casinos hired lawyers in the debtor's country, which was expensive. In some cases, payment to the lawyers could be as much as 50% of the debt collected. Gomes needed a better method. Knowing Joe had a significant number of international law-enforcement contacts and having witnessed first-hand his ability to collect domestic debt by using the NSF law and arrest warrants, Gomes asked Joe to help collect on the outstanding offshore markers.

Thus, Joe turned his attention to foreigners who'd walked away from markers owed to the Nugget. He knew the learning curve would be steep, but he had an advantage: international contacts made mostly during his days as a narc for the San Diego Narcotics Task Force, as well as an investigator for the Gaming Control Board. They helped him in his crash course of familiarizing himself with the different gambling-debt collection laws around the world.

Joe was aware that the NSF laws and arrest warrants could work in some international collections, but by no means all. He traveled to a number of countries, met his contacts, and began to organize his collection procedures based on the specific local laws.

Through his connections, Joe learned everything he could about the debtors — addresses, marital status, financial details. The gamblers were surprised that an executive from the Golden Nugget had come to their home country to request payment. They were accustomed to dealing with their junket rep or casino host, neither of whom was in any hurry to approach them concerning outstanding markers. That, and Joe's knowledge of their situations, gave him a big leg up.

Initially, most of Joe's collections were in Japan, where many of the foreign gamblers who owed the Golden Nugget money lived. Once again, as he had for the domestic NSF collections, Joe found himself breaking new ground — as the personal emissary from a casino the Japanese debtors were hoping never to hear from again. By trial and error, Joe began to pioneer numerous methods, some standard and straightforward, others indirect and creative, for persuading indebted gamblers to pay what they owed.

Payments began to arrive at the Nugget cage and Gomes assigned Joe debt collections all over Asia.

While conducting background investigations, Joe also focused on the country's organized-crime situation and their known and suspected members. He knew that in some countries, illegal gambling was controlled by criminal organizations, such as the Yakuza in Japan, the Triads in China and Chinese-affiliated countries, and the Premans in Indonesia.

And at least in one case, the way organized crime collected its debts was driven home to him quite graphically.

The Yakuza Collects One Way or Another

On one debt-collecting trip to Tokyo, Joe was watching TV one night when a report aired on the local English-speaking station. A member of the Yakuza had been sent to collect a gambling debt. The story was televised live as events unfolded, with the TV crew filming activity outside of an apartment.

Joe watched as a Yakuza debt collector pounded on the front door. After no one answered, the man moved to a front window. He turned briefly toward the camera, then broke the window to enter the residence.

As the man climbed through the window, the cameraman moved closer and filmed the Yakuza stabbing the occupant to death. He exited the residence and ran down the narrow street.

The next day, Joe discussed the incident with his contacts at the Tokyo Metropolitan Police Department. He learned that the victim did, in fact, owe an unpaid gambling debt to the Yakuza. One of their members was sent to kill him to set an example for other debtors. The message was clear: Gamblers will be forced to repay their obligation, in one way or another, even if the other is with their lives.

Joe found it morbidly intriguing that even though the Yakuza member was fully aware he was being filmed, he still could not leave without fulfilling his orders. Joe believes the unmitigated violence of organized-crime syndicates in Asia makes the modern-day American Mafia look like amateurs.

Tokyo Collections and Matsuo

Matsuo was a good friend of Joe's and Joe often employed his interpreting skills. One time, Joe had a customer who owed $50,000. Matsuo called the guy to set up an appointment. Matsuo was nervous about the collection, because the customer made a reference to the Yakuza. Matsuo wasn't sure whether he was insinuating that he was a member or that he knew some members.

The meeting was in two days, which gave Joe plenty of time to check with his law-enforcement contacts in the Japan organized-crime unit. The results came back that the subject was not a member of the Yakuza and had no known ties to them.

At the meeting, Matsuo began to explain why they were there and the gambler's reply obviously startled Matsuo. Joe asked him what was wrong.

"He just threatened to have us both killed."

Finally at the end of his rope, Joe asked Matsuo to translate exactly what he was about to say. "Buddy, I've already investigated you through my contacts in Japanese law enforcement. I know you're not a member of the Yakuza and have no affiliation with them. And how's this? If you insist on implying an affiliation with organized crime, I'll let my Japanese friends know who you're claiming to be and I'm sure they'll open an investigation immediately, which will also involve investigating your business activities."

Joe waited for Matsuo to finish, then added, "And by the way, my law-enforcement friends are aware of where I am and who I'm meeting with."

Joe always made a point to wear lapel pins given him by law-enforcement agencies throughout Asia. Joe could tell the customer noticed it and said, "As for the matter of killing us, my friend Matsuo here is just an interpreter and threatening him is extremely disrespectful. As for me, there's a very long line of people waiting to do that same thing and at your advanced age, I don't think you'll live that long."

Joe realized he'd hit the right buttons when Mr. M began to laugh. He said something to Matsuo, who translated to Joe that he was not going to have them killed. He also told Matsuo that he must have misunderstood about the threat. Mr. M then wrote a check for the full amount, which Matsuo and Joe took directly to the nearest bank to cash.

In a taxi on the way back to the hotel, Matsuo had a grim look on his face and with his head cocked to the side said, "Joe, I can't do this anymore. That guy scared the shit out of me."

Joe told him he knew the guy wasn't Yakuza, but he completely understood. They agreed to just meet when Joe was in Tokyo and Joe would only hire Matsuo to interpret documents.

Jim Mydlach

When Joe returned to Japan for his next collection trip, he was accompanied again by Jim Mydlach, the "Radar O'Reilly" of southern Nevada who could get anything done, day or night. The two had worked together in the casino business for many years. Jimmy, a large man of six-five and 270 pounds, had worked for Elvis Presley and now sported similar Elvis sideburns and his hair style.

The Japanese were huge fans of Elvis and Jimmy brought photos of himself together with the King. Once word spread that Jimmy was a pal of Elvis Presley, the customers who wouldn't meet with Joe about their debts were now coming forward to meet Elvis' good friend. They proudly posed for photos taken with Jimmy and that helped Joe get some of the customers on payment schedules.

One customer, Mr. H, had an outstanding debt of around $35,000. A translator called him and asked him to pay his debt. Mr. H became angry and told him to go to hell; he wasn't going to pay. Joe asked the translator to transcribe into very large Japanese symbols a statement Joe had written down: "Mr. H does not pay his debts. Details will follow."

Joe and Jimmy went to Mr. H's office building the next day and placed copies of the translated statement on his office door before he was scheduled to open for business. About 30 minutes passed, then Joe received a call from someone shouting loudly in Japanese. Joe knew it was the customer, of course, so he had the translator deliver a message. After a while, the translator called back, saying Mr. H would meet Joe and Jimmy at noon at the Imperial Hotel to settle his debt. He was there and paid what he owed, then they all enjoyed tea together and parted on friendly terms.

Jimmy Mydlach passed away in 2017 after a nearly five-year battle with cancer. Joe describes his friend as a "fingerprint," because no one on the entire planet was like him. Jimmy was well-established and highly regarded in Las Vegas. He was always the first person to offer a helping hand to anyone in need. Jim is missed by many.

Japanese Honor

An unpleasant collection experience involved a Japanese customer in debt to the tune of a half-million dollars.

When Joe discovered that he could easily pay it off, he flew to Tokyo and met with the man, who blamed his losses on Joe, even though they'd never met. It was all *Joe's* fault that he'd lost all that money gambling.

Joe had done his homework. He knew that Japanese law allowed a gambler to sit in jail for up to *two years* before going to trial and he found a Japanese gambler who was in jail for evading Japanese taxes. He'd also taken the inflight magazine from the plane to Tokyo; the cover had a photo of a Japanese man and the headline "Japanese Honor." Finally, he had with him an IRS 1099 form with the debtor's name and information listed on it, filled in for the amount of US$100,000.

While talking to the debtor, Joe cited the Japanese law and the gambler sitting in jail; he also threw the magazine on the table, pointed to the cover, and asked, "Where do I find *that* in this office?" Then he explained that the Tropicana would forgive $100,000 of his $500,000 debt and he'd be given the 1099 for his records. Copies of the 1099 would also be filed with the IRS and the Japanese National Tax Agency. If he accepted the offer of the $100,000 discount, he would be required to declare it as income. Joe further clarified that the debtor should probably be prepared to explain where he got the $500,000 to place on deposit to gamble before receiving an equal amount of credit.

Joe could see the man thinking long and hard about everything he'd just heard. He said, "Can I repay the four hundred thousand and we'll just forget about the extra hundred grand, with no tax form?"

Joe replied, "Sorry, we can't do that. You've already cost us a lot attempting to collect this debt."

Within 24 hours, the entire $500,000 was wire transferred.

After the Tropicana received the transfer, Joe revisited the man, gave him his markers, and told him: "Now *that's* the Japanese honor I read about in the magazine."

A Mirage in Japan

With Joe making regular trips overseas, Wynn some-times had other errands for him to run.

One morning, Joe received another call to meet in Steve Wynn's office right away. Wynn asked Joe when he was going back to Japan on a collection trip. The answer: two weeks.

Apparently, a nightclub was using the Mirage logo. He wanted Joe to acquire anything the club had that depicted the logos and bring back the evidence, so he could have the lawyers take legal action.

"Where's this nightclub?" Joe asked.

"Japan."

"What city?"

"Japan."

Damn, Joe thought. All I have to do is locate one nightclub in a country with a population of 125 million. Hell, Tokyo alone has 25 million residents and probably 20 thousand unlicensed nightclubs.

Joe took off for Tokyo to try to make some collections and find the Mirage nightclub. On a whim, he contacted some police officials in Tokyo to see if they could help find the nightclub, but even as he was asking them, he knew they were thinking, this guy is nuts. He asked anyway; he wanted to go home someday. He also got in touch with gamblers he'd met who frequented Las Vegas and would recognize the Mirage logo when they saw it. Sure enough, it didn't take long for a customer to call him with the address of the club, telling him it was a private establishment with restricted access that opened at 10 p.m.

Joe took a cab to the club, arriving at nine o'clock. There it was, in an alley surrounded by about 30 other clubs, with the exact Mirage logo over the door. He snapped photos of the exterior signage, then walked up the exterior stairs and found the front door unlocked. He knew he didn't have much time to gather any other objects containing the logo before the club opened. When he entered, he saw the hostess station with logo matchbooks and cocktail napkins, which he just managed to slip into a pocket before a male employee in a suit came from a back room and started talking to him in Japanese.

"*No comprendo, no comprendo,*" Joe found himself saying, then caught himself speaking Spanish in Japan and said, "No speak Japanese." He went into his dumb lost tourist act, taking a cigarette from his pocket and motioning for a light.

The employee went behind the hostess stand looking for a matchbook, but Joe had taken them all. Behind the glass of the station were lighters bearing the Mirage logo, which Joe pointed to. The employee took one out and handed it to Joe, while Joe continued with his patter in pidgin English. The guy was so confused that Joe put the lighter in his pocket, said "*Domo arigato,*" and left.

Now, he thought, I can get on with collecting gambling debts.

Two weeks later, on his first day back in Las Vegas, Wynn called and asked about the nightclub. Joe told him he'd found it and gathered the logo items.

"Take them to the lawyers immediately."

"I already did."

Joe was waiting for Wynn to ask about the collections, thinking he could blow his own horn about collecting

$310,000 in unpaid markers. But Wynn was much more interested in pursuing the nightclub than the paltry three hundred grand. After all, he'd paid $700,000 to the Mirage Motel in Las Vegas for the rights to the name and logo — he wanted to protect his investment.

A few days after his return, Joe received a phone call from the Tokyo police. They'd finally located the Mirage nightclub — nearly three weeks after Joe did. He learned a good lesson from the experience: If you want to find someone or something really fast in Japan, ask a gambler.

A Quick Trip to Singapore

Joe received a call at the Golden Nugget — Steve Wynn again, asking him to come to his office at the Mirage ASAP. When he got there, Wynn handed Joe a customer's personal check for $650,000 that was written to cover a gambling debt, then asked him to travel to Singapore to cash the check and wire the funds back.

Joe left for Singapore that afternoon. He called one of his friends there, a retired government official, and informed him he was on the way, then asked if they could have lunch or dinner after he presented the check at the bank and wired the funds. His friend asked about the location of the bank, then Joe told him he'd call him in the morning.

The trip took 24 hours from his house to the hotel. Joe arrived in Singapore at 1 a.m. local time and went directly to bed, knowing he had to be up in six hours. He proceeded to the bank at 9 a.m. and presented the customer's check to the bank manager, who returned to her office. Just then, Joe's friend showed up at the bank and before Joe could ask what he was doing there, the bank manager returned and informed them that the account the check was drawn on had insufficient funds for the amount written.

Joe's friend asked the manager if he could speak with her in her office. Joe remained outside and watched through the window until his friend returned; he didn't say a word. Joe saw the manager hang up her phone. She returned to Joe and his friend and informed them that a courier was en route with a new check drawn on a different account with sufficient funds.

The new check arrived as promised and the manager hovered around them while they made the wire transfer to the Mirage. In fact, Joe was informed by the Mirage CFO that the transfer was received in record time.

Joe spent the day with his friend visiting historic sites and sharing lunch and dinner. He never asked for, and his friend never offered, any information about his interaction with the bank manager. But Joe was elated that he didn't have to call Steve Wynn to tell him the check bounced; he knew he'd want him to stay there and continue to attempt to collect the debt.

One good thing about Singapore was that you could file civil litigation to collect debts. The case would be adjudicated in three weeks and the court would order immediate payment. But this collection case was even better. Joe returned to his hotel, packed his bag, and caught a flight back to Las Vegas, having spent only 23 hours in Singapore.

Not even enough time to experience jet lag.

Meanwhile, Back in Vegas

$200,000 Chip-Exchange Theft

Joe's phone rang, waking him up. A call at a late hour

was never good news. Security Director Rick Santoro told him that the graveyard-shift security supervisor was missing during an exchange of foreign chips — chips from other Las Vegas casinos that wound up in the Golden Nugget's cage.

A foreign-chip run was initiated when the cage notified security that chip exchanges needed to be made at various casinos. An officer took the chips in the security vehicle to the various casinos, where he exchanged them and brought the cash back to the cashier.

"The supervisor was with one of our security officers at the Hilton," Santoro explained. "It was their last stop. The officer entered the casino and made the exchange, but when he returned, the van and the supervisor were nowhere to be found."

"Jeez. He was probably robbed," Joe said.

"That's what I'm thinking too."

"Have you notified Metro?"

"That was my first call. This is my second."

Initially, Joe was concerned that the supervisor had been murdered and the van dumped somewhere. But as more information was collected, it started to look like an inside job.

The supervisor had been contacted several times recently about foreign-chip exchanges, but had declined to make the run, claiming he was short of staff. By the time he agreed to make that night's exchange, the van contained around $200,000. Also, the supervisor going along on the exchange was anything but routine, even for that amount of money. Later in the day, the van was found empty.

Joe also learned that the supervisor had a gambling addiction and believed he had terminal lung cancer. Joe and Santoro quickly changed course: Now, the supervisor was no longer a victim, but a suspect.

Joe dreaded breaking the news to Steve Wynn; when you steal a man's money, it tends to piss him off. Joe got lucky this time: He notified Dennis Gomes, while Rick Santoro met with Wynn.

"Rick, I don't care how much we have to spend," Wynn told him. "I want you guys to get the son of a bitch. Go anywhere you need to. Just get him back here for prosecution."

Wynn authorized $20,000 for expenses and posted a $20,000 cash reward.

Joe concluded that the key to getting this guy was through his wife. He immediately set up round-the-clock surveillance of the suspect's home, which Santoro supervised. Rick was not only young, intelligent, committed, and wanted to learn all he could about everything, but he was like a junkyard dog; you didn't want him chasing you. He wouldn't rest until the supervisor was in custody. Also, like Joe, he felt betrayed; they'd placed a lot of faith in the night supervisor to run the property when most managers were sleeping.

The surveillance team had been keeping track of the wife's activities, but on the Sunday after the theft, Joe and Jim Mydlach took over their duties to give them a break. Surveillance can be extremely boring duty.

Mydlach and Joe set up in their personal cars at 6:30 a.m. A couple hours later, the wife and kids left and drove through Boulder City, across Hoover Dam, and south on US 93 toward Kingman, Arizona. Giving her the benefit of the doubt, Joe wasn't ready to declare her on the lam until she got onto Interstate 40. He knew that the security supervisor was from Arkansas and believed he'd been in law enforcement there. By the time she started heading east on I-40, Joe and Jim were well out of radio range with Las Vegas and couldn't notify the other surveillance teams of their location. Joe had Mydlach pass her, then use a telephone to notify the others to head their way. They could communicate via radio because they were close to each other. But the radio batteries wouldn't last long; the chargers were in the other vehicles.

Later, Joe learned that the previous Friday, the wife had purchased a new set of tires. Had he known that beforehand, he wouldn't have filled in for the surveillance teams. He'd have considered her a flight risk.

After about 10 hours and with dead radios, Joe and Jim followed the wife into a motel in Albuquerque. In the office, Mydlach learned she was staying only one night. They watched her unload the kids and kept an eye on her and the vehicle from a room they rented there.

By now, the surveillance team from Las Vegas was only a couple of hours behind them, calling into the motel room from pay phones. Joe was relieved to see them when they arrived to take over the surveillance. He and Mydlach were completely unprepared for long-distance traveling; they didn't even have toothbrushes. And Joe was still recuperating from double-bypass heart surgery two months earlier.

In the morning, he and Jim headed back to Las Vegas. Partway there, Joe started to experience chest pain as he breathed, which kept getting worse. He told Mydlach to take him to Desert Springs Hospital where they found that his heart sac had filled up with fluid and as his lungs expanded while breathing, they pushed against the healing heart muscle.

Joe spent the next seven days in the hospital recovering.

In the meantime, Santoro's surveillance teams ended up outside a house in a very small town in Arkansas. After a rebuff from the local sheriff, he printed up and distributed wanted flyers with the security supervisor's photo and description, plus the reward amount. With all the attention focused on him, the security supervisor surrendered to the sheriff and was brought back to Las Vegas to stand trial. He was sentenced to 12 years in prison. The money was never found.

Kashiwagi Part Two

While walking through the Golden Nugget lobby one day, Joe saw Akio Kashiwagi and his bodyguard at the VIP check-in desk. It was strange that the whale hadn't been whisked to his suite or a private table by a senior host. So Joe approached and asked him, "Was anyone from the casino aware that you were coming to play?"

"No. This is what you call in English a spur-of-the-moment visit to Las Vegas."

"I'm sure your host will be humbled when he learns that you're here and he didn't know about it. Let me try to contact him."

When Joe couldn't locate him, he called Dennis and told him Kashiwagi was on site and his host was unreachable.

Dennis knew that Joe had a good rapport with Kashiwagi and asked him to handle getting the high roller situated. Joe secured a suite and arranged for him to be escorted to the cashier's cage, where he wanted to put $2 million on deposit.

Joe asked the bellman to take Kashiwagi's bags to the suite, but Kashiwagi held back a large steamer trunk. As they approached the cage, Joe asked him for the cashier's checks he normally put on deposit, but the gambler pointed to the trunk. Joe asked him the amount of cash in the trunk and he responded, "All two million."

The cage manager, Patty Franks, led them to a room

in the back and took possession of the cash. She informed Kashiwagi that it was going to take a bit of time to count all the money. He agreed, so Joe accompanied him back to his suite to rest from his long flight from Japan.

Kashiwagi was aware that Joe was doing international collections and told him to contact him next time he was in Japan, so he could show him his Samurai-sword collection. Joe recalls that Kashiwagi left breaking even on that gambling trip.

A couple of million here, a couple of million there ... All in a day's work for a gambler and a hospitable casino staff.

Moving on Again

Dennis Gomes left the Golden Nugget in 1991 after receiving an offer to run the Taj Mahal in Atlantic City for Donald Trump. Gomes still had a year to go on his contract and Wynn sued both Gomes and Trump — Gomes for breach of contract and Trump for stealing Gomes away. Even so, Gomes asked the executives who had followed him to the Golden Nugget, some of them from the Hilton by way of the Aladdin and Dunes, to go the Taj. That included Joe.

Joe was conflicted about going to New Jersey. Though he would have liked to continue working for Dennis, Atlantic City was depressing and reminded him of the projects he grew up in. He spoke many times to Dennis about relocating and even received a generous contract, but he held out until a week before he had to activate or turn down the contract. That was when his phone rang. It was Steve Wynn.

"My office. Ten o'clock tomorrow morning. Sharp."

When Joe sat down in the hot seat, Wynn asked him point blank, "Are you abandoning me, the Nugget, and Las Vegas to go the Taj?"

"Gomes has made me a generous offer, but honestly, I'd rather stay in Las Vegas working for you."

"What are you being offered?"

When Joe cited the figure, Wynn said, "I'll match that," then stuck out his hand to shake on the deal. "Now that you're staying, I want you to look out for the new Golden Nugget president, Barry Shier."

Joe called Gomes and told him that he was staying put. He didn't leave Dennis high and dry, however, recommending Rick Santoro, who was now back in Atlantic City helping to care for his elderly parents.

Four years later, Dennis Gomes was back in Las Vegas again, managing both the Tropicana on the Strip and in Atlantic City.

Joe rejoined him at the Trop in September 1995 — and began his most exciting and demanding adventure to date.

11

The Tropicana

Dennis Gomes worked for Trump at the Taj Mahal for four years before moving on to become the head of the Tropicana properties in both Las Vegas and Atlantic City. It was a good deal for Gomes; he liked the New York/New Jersey area, his kids could stay in school there, and he initially spent six months in Atlantic City and six months in Las Vegas, where he had houses. Gomes was always capable of getting generous contracts for his services, which were in major demand.

Joe had left the Golden Nugget after three years to become a consultant for International Game Technology, the world's largest gaming-device manufacturer, holding 169 gaming licenses worldwide.

Dennis had been back in Las Vegas at the Tropicana for around a month when he began calling Joe. They spoke several times and Dennis finally prevailed on him to compile a list of employment terms that, if they were met, would persuade Joe to move to the Tropicana. They finally got together in person at the Trop in December 1995 — right in the middle of the National Finals Rodeo, when Las Vegas was teeming with cowboys and rodeo-fan spectators.

"Okay, what's on your list?" Gomes got right to it after they sat down.

"The usual," Joe began. "Compensation, life insurance, car allowance, bonuses."

Gomes motioned for him to keep going, knowing that the more important items were lower on the list.

"Chain of command—I answer only to you and the chairman of the board of Aztar. I also want the same health-care package that you and the board members get, along with four-weeks' vacation."

Again, Dennis nodded and waited.

"I know for a fact you're going to send me out into the world to do collections, so I want first-class airfare and I keep the accumulated points I earn, plus first-class hotel accommodations and I keep those points too. Also, I alone decide which collections I'll make."

Finally, Gomes spoke up. "Is that all?"

That was when Joe remembered that Karen had inserted an item onto the list. "One last thing. Two NFR tickets for this weekend."

"You're serious? This is the final weekend. Those tickets are like gold."

Joe knew that the casinos purchase blocks of rodeo tickets years in advance for their best customers and that they often have a few left over. "Yes." He smiled. "Deal breaker."

"Deal breaker?" Gomes exclaimed. "More like ball breaker!" But he called Bill Cleek, the Trop's vice president of marketing, whom Joe knew well from all the previous casinos they'd both worked at with Dennis. When Cleek came on the phone, Joe yelled, "Cleeker, I don't want the cheap seats!"

Cleek responded, "Yeah, I've got two tickets in great

seats for both nights. I'll deliver them personally to your office, Dennis." Then he asked, "Is Joe coming back to work with us?"

"He is now!" Dennis told him.

"When?"

"Monday."

Joe reminded Gomes and Cleek that he had to resign from IGT, then find a replacement, which would take longer than just the weekend.

"The sooner the better," Cleek said. "We've got a lot of crooks in this joint."

That was Joe's first indication that he had his work cut out for him when he returned to Gomes' employ. He didn't, however, have any idea how bad it was at the Tropicana and what he'd be confronted with immediately after he arrived a couple weeks later.

Tropicana Day One

"The Tropicana had had its problems over the decades and had changed hands many times. The previous management was weak to begin with," Joe recalls, "and they'd lost control of the casino. Essentially, the inmates were running the asylum. Put another way, a 'we're-family' attitude had been taken to extremes. Even as late as the nineties, the Mob had gone home — or to prison, or the cemetery — but the employees hadn't gotten the memo."

There was no leadership, no management oversight, and no discipline had anyone been caught, which no one was. The surveillance system was the weakest Joe had ever seen; a number of table games had no camera coverage whatsoever. He discovered these things on his first day on the job, even before he met with the directors of the security and surveillance departments. He also learned that rumors of mass firings were swirling around the property.

Joe met with his department heads and told them what he expected of them and their respective departments. He asked about their staffing levels and if they were short of manpower, then scheduled further meetings to discuss other issues. Finally, he informed them of his role as international marker collector and told them that he needed to count on them while he was off traveling.

He then proceeded to the marketing office, where Bill Cleek started right in on improprieties in the pit. He brought up the play from the past weekend on his computer and showed Joe a crap player's average bet of $250 over 18 hours of play at a table.

"This player better be in a wheelchair," Joe commented, not knowing anyone who could stand and play at the same crap table for 18 hours — who wasn't a camel.

He went directly to the surveillance room and watched the video of the crap game over that 18-hour period. Sure enough, not only was the reported $250 per hand false, but the game had been closed for many of the hours that the player's bets had been logged for his comp rating.

Joe also noticed that the players were being subjected to a hard hustle by the crap crew, coercing them into making side bets for them. Further, the dealers were placing those bets on hard-way numbers, but didn't take them down when the number rolled the easy way and hard-way bets lost. Instead, they left them in play until the numbers hit the hard way, then dropped their "winnings" into the table toke box.

Joe suspected that the Trop's pit and shift bosses were in on the tokes. He quickly had them open up a crap game to accommodate an undercover player that Joe sent in with

$1,000, instructing him to do everything the dealers and bosses asked in terms of putting up bets for them. In one hour, he shut the game down and examined the contents of the drop and tip boxes. The drop box contained $48. The tip drop held $462.

It's true that dealers work for low base pay, often minimum wage. Yet dealing in a casino has always been a coveted job. Dealers also receive tips, or "tokes" as they're called in casino speak. The tokes from a good casino job in the '90s could easily produce a six-figure annual income, most in cash. Promoting tipping, naturally, is in the best interests of the dealers. It's called "toke hustling."

The hustling is mostly what's termed "soft." For example, after a couple of player wins at a blackjack table, a dealer might comment about a "run of good luck," implying that he or she is partially responsible for the outcome and should be rewarded. No one worries much when the hustling is soft, but it becomes a concern when the efforts escalate to "hard."

The toke-hustler's paradise is the dice table, where a hard hustler blatantly asks for "a bet for the boys," possibly on every come-out roll. Many players don't want to look cheap, so they shrug and go along with it. This works especially well for a good-looking female dealer (who's also one of the "boys") when she plays up to a male customer. Some players don't understand all the payouts and lingo, so a dealer can take money directly out of the chips paid for a winning bet without the player knowing he's been shorted. Worse, on a dice table, the players' chips are on the rail and aggressive dealers can actually grab them and make bets for themselves. This is blatant "strong-arm hustling." It's not common, but it happens, and Joe saw it at the Trop's dice tables.

Tips are split among dealers in two ways: by envelope or table-for-table, also known as "going for your own." The envelope method is an even split among all the dealers at all table games on a shift. Everyone's tips are pooled, then divided evenly and disbursed in cash in envelopes. This method was implemented in part to inhibit hard hustling, since the fruits of a dealer's direct efforts must be split with everyone. Since the envelope is used almost exclusively today, hard hustling is much less of a problem than it used to be when table-for-table (dealers keep whatever they make at their own tables) was much more common. That creates a direct incentive to hustle, which is why table-for-table jobs have all but disappeared over the years.

The strong-arm hustling Joe observed as soon as he showed up for work at the Tropicana sent him to meet with Gomes. "How's it going so far, Joe?"

Joe responded, "Pretty good. I've been here two hours and already uncovered a couple of scams in the pit."

Dennis just smiled and said, "That's why I wanted you back with me. What's your plan for stopping them?"

"Well, I need to buy some time, so while I'm getting to the bottom of everything that's going on here, I'm going to spread the word that the new security guy is investigating table games."

"That should slow it down a little, anyway," Gomes said. "By the way, I have auditors going through the bad-debt accounts that you'll be collecting and I want you there when I review them."

"Music to my ears," Joe responded. "I have a taste for some raw-chicken sashimi and fried whale blubber."

Gomes laughed, knowing full well of Joe's aversion to Asian food.

Joe proceeded to place several trustworthy people in

various positions on the table games. He quickly discovered that the floormen were opening player accounts in made-up names and swiping their phony players cards through the electronic tracking system on all the games. With non-existent controls, the pit bosses felt so immune that they even swiped cards on games that were closed. Then they sold the cards for several hundred dollars to guests who could stay on full room, food, and beverage comps for pennies on the dollar.

Joe then turned his attention to the problem at the crap tables. He learned that dice dealers at the aging Tropicana were earning more than those at Caesars and the Mirage.

The first to go was the surveillance director. With these two scams going on right under his nose, he was either implicated or incompetent, maybe both; Joe could only imagine what else was happening on his watch. He hired a new surveillance boss he knew and trusted and they came up with a plan to put undercover players on the crap games at various times of the day and night. Their play would be monitored live by surveillance and recorded for later review.

The tapes clearly showed the dealers intimidating the players to place bets for them, as well as not collecting those bets on losing rolls. Joe could see that the Tropicana wasn't only losing revenue through phony comps and out-and-out theft, but also from players being driven away by heavy-handed dealers and pit personnel.

Joe presented the surveillance tapes and undercover-player reports to Human Resources and was taken aback when the HR director objected, claiming that with no audio, they didn't know what the dealers were saying.

"What?" Joe demanded. "Why do you have to know what they're saying? You can see right there: The dealers' bets aren't taken down after they lose."

"Look," she said, "you just got here. It's like you married into the family and now you want to show all your new in-laws the errors of their ways. You might want to rethink that."

"Fair enough. But I'll tell you this. You might want to rethink standing up for thieves—if you don't want to be implicated as an accessory to their crimes."

On his next visit to HR, Joe brought the audiotape of the intimidation recorded by an undercover player. Confronted by irrefutable proof, the director had no choice but to fire the first group of dealers. Joe knew that this would slow down the problem, but only for a while; the crap-pit personnel who shared in the tips would have to start up again, because they were accustomed to living on six figures a year and they'd be coming up short very soon.

He told the HR director, "I'm just getting started here. There will be plenty more terminations and if you balk again, I'll start having your employees arrested, rather than just sending them down the road. What might that do to your reputation in this town?"

Immediately on the heels of the mass firing, Joe called a meeting of all the crap dealers, floormen, and pit bosses; the surveillance and HR directors attended.

"You people have had a nice long run, but that's history," he told them. "The false-rating scam is over. So is the hard hustling at the tables. Both are violations of Nevada criminal law and if they don't stop here and now, and I mean immediately, I'll not only turn you over to my friends at Metro for theft, but I'll also notify Gaming Control, where I used to work, and your employment in casinos anywhere in the world will be over. That's the bad news. The good news is that when you stop driving players away and start providing good customer service like you're supposed to, it'll increase play and your legitimate tip earnings."

While this was simmering down, Joe was contacted about a slot customer who apparently lost $40,000 over a weekend playing a dollar machine. He went to marketing and obtained the information on the player; coincidentally, she was from San Diego. Looking at her home address, Joe knew that it wasn't an area from which a player could drop 40 Gs in one weekend. He further learned that she was an unmarried schoolteacher who didn't earn $40,000 in an entire year.

A deeper dive revealed that not only was there no rating of the player in the slot system, but the machine on which she supposedly lost in the mid-five figures had a problem and didn't register any wins or losses through the tracking system. The loss was recorded manually by the slot host who brought in the customer and received a commission on his player's losses.

Next stop, surveillance. The tape showed the player inserting dollars into the machine at a rate that would take her three months to lose $40,000.

Finally, Joe talked to the slot host. "Why would a big slot player stay at a machine that wasn't tracking the play for casino comps?"

The host responded as if talking to a two-year old. "Why does any player stay at any machine? It's her favorite!"

"Really?" Joe played along. "So this machine doesn't track play for comps and kicks the player's ass to the tune of a year's salary and she still plays it till she leaves. Am I understanding that correctly?"

"Duh."

"Well, if that's true, your player should be named Dumbshit of the Year. But," he stuck his finger in the host's face, "she'll have to share it with the moron in charge who thinks it's a good idea to allow a host who gets a commission on losses to report how much his players lose." Joe stood up, went to the door of his office, and opened it. "Let's go."

"What? Where are we going?" the host asked, alarmed.

"To HR. Where else?"

"What for?"

"To get your walking papers."

Next stop, VIP services, where Joe read the host supervisor the riot act. He was only one of the department heads Joe confronted with the employee gravy train that defined the culture at the Tropicana.

When they challenged him, all he had to say was, "Take it to Gomes." He was well aware that was the last thing they wanted to do. Some of this stuff was so blatant, it couldn't be defended or even explained. They knew Dennis had come from Gaming Control and that his first reaction would be, "You're the boss. If you didn't know this type of activity was happening, you're incompetent. If you did, you're complicit."

Joe was too busy to actually launch an investigation, but by firing a host, putting the supervisor on notice, and starting a rumor that he was auditing all the manual ratings in the slot department, from that time until he left, not a single questionable player rating was submitted.

Joe and Dennis cleaned house at the Tropicana. All this took place in the first two months Joe was there. And he wasn't done. But in the meantime, he happily went off on his first collection trip for the Trop, getting away from the non-stop casino problems. "Oh, the serenity!" Joe laughs about it today.

A Little Bit Every Day

Even after all the initial dust had settled, problems with the staff stealing continued to surface. On one occasion, the surveillance director called and requested a meeting. It turned out that he had highly reliable information about an employee removing silver dollars from sealed 500-coin canvas bags stored in the main casino change booth. The bags were used to fill dollar slot machines when they ran out or were running low on coin for payouts.

"A slot floorman requested a bag of coins from the change booth to make a slot fill. He presented all the necessary paperwork to track the coins leaving the booth. But as he grabbed the bag and began to walk away, he realized it was light; he didn't feel the weight of a full bag of five hundred silver dollars," the surveillance director explained.

"The bag had the metal seal on the neck from the hard-count room?" Joe asked.

"Sure. It would've been extremely suspicious if it didn't."

"So he returned the bag to the change booth?"

"Yes. He told me that the booth attendant seemed nervous, but she quickly gave the floorman another sealed bag."

Joe found out that the coin-booth cashier was on vacation and would return in four days. He met again with the surveillance director and together they came up with a plan to watch the employee when she returned. They trained nearby cameras on the booth to give it extra coverage. They were ready when the cashier came back to work, since Joe suspected that she would make a move immediately, needing the money after her time off.

Four hours into the shift, surveillance observed suspicious activity with the coin bags and security removed the cashier from the booth. Joe was notified and he viewed the surveillance video showing the cashier moving coin bags around for no apparent reason and exchanging coin for paper money with no customers at the booth. He then proceeded to the interview room, where the surveillance director and cage supervisors were already waiting and the elderly cashier was cooling her heels, all but ready to confess.

"How much did you take today?" Joe came right out and asked.

"Around two hundred and twenty dollars."

"And how much do you take on average per shift?"

"Four hundred and fifty dollars."

Joe knew he had to find out how she removed and replaced the metal seals after pilfering the bags, if someone in the coin count room affixed the seals on the bags to facilitate the thefts, and if other change-booth attendants were in on the scam. But having his hands full with all the other investigations, he didn't have the time that this one would require if the cashier didn't cooperate fully. So when she clammed up, refusing to implicate anyone else, he made a decision. "If you come clean and answer all my questions, the casino will not prosecute you."

The cashier took Joe at his word and explained all aspects of the coin theft to his satisfaction. It turned out that she'd devised a method of spiraling the neck of the older and less stiff canvas bags, making them small enough to twist off the metal tie; she reversed the process and replaced it in the same way. Every day the booth normally had 30 to 50 bags containing 500 coins, so several of them at least were vulnerable to the method.

He told her that she would be terminated immediately, but no legal steps would be taken against her. Then he asked, "How long have you been doing this?"

"Eleven years."

Holy fuck! Joe tried to hide his surprise. "Who else is involved in these thefts?"

"No one," the cashier responded quickly.

The cashier was removed from the interview room and Joe said, "Someone get me a calculator!" Stealing between $400 and $500 per shift for 11 years—he couldn't begin to do the math, but it had to be more than a million dollars, tax free. Then he said, "Screw it. I don't even want to know."

With the surveillance director looking at him, Joe said, "Almost all of the losses were sustained long before anyone in this room was here and under different management. Even though numerous audits were conducted by the company and regulators in the past eleven years, no investigations were conducted that I'm aware of. So I say let's let sleeping dogs lie." He paused, then added, "But how about if we post signs in all the employee break rooms that say, 'Really, the mob has left the building, so please stop stealing!'"

And the Scams Kept Coming

Early one morning, the surveillance director contacted Joe after his agents had observed some suspicious play by three Asians, two men and a woman. The trio was winning thousands of dollars at blackjack and surveillance operators believed they were counting cards.

Joe began his investigation by looking into the players' backgrounds and their activities since they'd arrived at the Tropicana. He learned that, prior to their arrival, one of them had put $50,000 in cash on deposit using a Hong Kong passport for identification. Joe inquired at other casinos about the three gamblers, but could find no information.

Early that evening, the three returned to the high-limit

blackjack tables and began to play. Joe observed them from the surveillance room. He had a manager print the passport photo and quickly realized that the person who presented the passport at the cage wasn't the player drawing funds from the deposited cash. Joe instructed security officers to remove the players from the game and bring them to the interview room.

Joe was correct; neither of the male players was pictured on the passport. It was a close match with one of them, but not close enough. The player could spout off all the passport information from memory, but it wasn't him.

Joe interviewed all three players, who tried to convince him that the actual person to whom the passport belonged had come in and placed the money on deposit for them to play with. The trio continued their story, claiming that the passport holder routinely traveled to New York City on business, allowing them to play on his deposits. But by then, Joe had figured out the scam. So when one of the players suggested that they take their $7,000 winnings and the $50,000 on deposit and leave, Joe said fine to their $7K winnings, but only the guy whose photo was on the passport and who'd put the money on deposit could collect the $50K — and it had to be in person.

When Joe insisted that the three players show their identification, they all handed over New York state IDs. When he'd asked them previously, they stated they were from Hong Kong. Joe copied their driver licenses, gave them his business card, and told them to ask the guy owning the passport to contact him at the casino.

Joe was confident he had figured out what the four of them were doing. One of the team put the money on deposit, then the others drew markers on that money. If they won, great. But if they lost, the guy with the passport came in, played for low stakes for a short time, then requested his $50,000 deposit back. When he heard that those funds had been drawn down at the tables, he claimed he didn't know the players and hadn't authorized anyone to make the withdrawals. In other words, the casino gave the money to the wrong people. Technically, he would have been right. They might have pulled it off at other casinos. But it didn't happen at the Tropicana.

Two days later, Joe received a call from the passport holder, who wanted his money back. Joe told the caller to bring his New York identification.

"But I'm a citizen of Hong Kong."

"Look, I've been to Hong Kong. I know that a lot of Hong Kong Chinese hold dual citizenships. I highly recommend you bring your New York identification. Otherwise, you'll have to litigate the release of the money, which will certainly cost more than fifty-thousand."

Under Nevada law, the $50,000 that was placed on deposit had to be given back to the depositor in the exact bills sitting in the cage; this was mandated to prevent money laundering. Dennis Gomes concluded that they had no alternative but to give the money back exactly as it was received.

"Not so fast, Dennis. I have another idea."

"I'm listening."

"We might have to give him back his front money, but I'm going to negotiate the seven thousand in winnings."

When the passport holder from Hong Kong showed up looking for his deposit, Joe addressed the situation with him. "Here's how it looks to me. You and your cohorts have come up with a pretty good scam."

The man responded emphatically that there was no intention to take money from the casino. Once again, he claimed that the players had no authorization to use his deposit.

"Oh yeah?" Joe asked, not bothering to hide his skepticism. "Who gave them access to your deposit if it wasn't you?" Joe went on to explain that the casinos were heavily regulated, not only by the state of Nevada, but also by the IRS and other federal entities. He said that he was aware of four people with Hong Kong passports and $50,000 in U.S. cash and he was concerned about immigration issues, to say nothing of Customs, if the money came into the U.S. without being reported.

"Now, I can call these agencies for assistance, but it will take a long time to release the funds and the whole situation could get sticky. But I do have an alternative plan, if you're interested."

The man nodded, all ears.

"You can repay the seven thousand your friends won. If you agree, we'll give you back forty-three thousand and call it even."

The man went for the deal, an agreement was drawn up and signed, and he left the casino with $43,000.

Joe didn't make the card-counting policies. He simply enforced the rules put into place by the casino managers. He ensured that, in the casinos in which he was in charge of security and surveillance, the surveillance departments were staffed with employees who were proficient in following the count at blackjack games. Joe was notified when a counter was removed from the property and tried to review the surveillance tapes of the incident. He wanted to make sure he didn't have an overzealous surveillance employee who misidentified an unskilled blackjack player who happened to be winning as a dangerous card counter, especially since in those days, suspected card counters were "interviewed" in back rooms before being 86'd, often against their will.

A misconception in gambling that endures from Joe's time is that card counting is illegal. It's not. Even many in the gambling industry who know it's not illegal still consider it cheating. It's not that either.

Card counting is a strategy that requires nothing outside of knowledge and skill—no marking of cards, use of devices, or assistance from the dealer (called "playing with the help").

All that said, information on card counters, cheaters, and other casino undesirables was shared via fax through a system organized and operated by the Metropolitan Police Department; Metro relayed any pertinent details to participating casinos. And Joe's casinos always subscribed to the Griffin Book, published by private investigator Robert Griffin, which contained mug shots and IDs of counters who'd been barred from a Las Vegas casino. By the 1980s, nearly every major casino in Las Vegas and Atlantic City (plus, it was rumored, illegal ones around the country) subscribed to the book, so they could give card counters the bum's rush when they were identified and caught.

Casino Debt Collections

At the Tropicana, based on his experiences abroad at the Golden Nugget, Joe's responsibilities expanded to include international casino debt collections. Most of his assignments were at the behest of Dennis Gomes.

In the days when Joe was collecting, it was difficult to recoup money owed to casinos from international gamblers. The number of reasons an international casino customer didn't or wouldn't pay were numerous. For example, the gambler might dispute the amount owed. Or he'd hold out in order to negotiate a discount if he didn't already have one or a better rate if he did. Or he wanted a face-to-face meeting with a high-level casino representative as a sign of respect; he was ready to pay, either in full or on the installment plan, but wanted to do so in person. Or he simply didn't have the money to pay. At the time, Japan especially, but also Asia in general, had experienced a sustained financial crash that wiped out a number of gamblers with outstanding markers in Las Vegas.

International marker collection for the Tropicana had an added dimension: The debts Joe took on were so old that they'd long ago been written off as losses by the company. As far as Dennis Gomes and the Trop owners were concerned, this was found money that, when it was brought back, went directly to the bottom line. But for Joe, the age of the markers made them that much more difficult to collect from gamblers who believed they'd gotten away with stiffing the casino.

Right after the Tropicana auditors completed their bad-debt analysis and aging report, Joe met with Dennis about dozens of uncollected markers totaling $13 million, 90% of which were more than two years old. Joe knew he needed, thus insisted on, full control over the collection process to increase his chances of success. Fortunately, Dennis gave him that latitude, allowing him to conduct negotiations, grant discounts, and spend travel and incidental funds without prior approval.

Creative Marker Collection

Joe's first overseas trip for the Tropicana was to Japan to collect a million-dollar debt that was more than five years old. He researched the debtor and discovered the man was having cash-flow problems after a dicey golf-course investment. But Joe also uncovered a $5 million asset the man held in Georgia: a one-of-a-kind 99-foot racing yacht. The expensive craft had been constructed in Maine, titled in the Cayman Islands, and was now moored in Savannah.

Joe traveled to Tokyo to meet this customer and found him to be honest and friendly. He explained to Joe that the golf-course project had failed to yield the expected profit that he planned to use to pay back the Tropicana.

Joe mentioned the yacht and reminded the man that it was not only sitting in the water not being kept up, but was uninsured. He recommended the customer sign the title over to the Tropicana. The casino would then sign an agreement that it would foreclose on the yacht and Joe would get it ready for resale. The debtor agreed to this plan.

The agreement stipulated that any amount over $1 million from the sale would be given back to the customer. Joe made it clear, however, that this agreement came with no guarantees, because his main objective was to satisfy the casino debt.

This was a complicated foreclosure transaction involving the U.S. federal courts and the government of the Cayman Islands. It took six months, but Joe finally foreclosed in federal court in Savannah and gained the title of the yacht, which was transferred into the Tropicana's name.

Joe hired a broker in Savannah who was to ready to offer the yacht for sale. The "Ferrari of sailing crafts," it was constructed out of carbon fiber that required a federal inspection of the hull as it was being built. It was custom-designed and included a sauna, lounge, state rooms, salons, and crew quarters.

The broker warned Joe that the yacht might be difficult to sell, due to its highly customized features. They planned to display it at the Fort Lauderdale Yacht Show and Joe looked forward to sailing the craft from Savannah to Fort Lauderdale for the show. However, the broker received a million-dollar offer just before the show opened.

The broker was ready to complete the sale in one day, but Joe explained that he represented a licensed gaming company and had to investigate the intended purchaser, who was from the Caribbean. With his narcotics experience, Joe knew that all types of vessels are used to smuggle narcotics from Colombia and other countries into the region. He imagined the headlines: "Former Tropicana Yacht Seized with Tons of Dope Onboard," or even worse, "Former Narc Sells Tropicana Yacht to Drug Smugglers."

Joe's investigation involved contact with the DEA, U.S. Customs, and other agencies. After he was satisfied with the results of his inquiries, the yacht was sold for $1 million. Prior to completing the sale, Joe flew to Tokyo to discuss the offer with the customer. The man was glad that his casino debt was finally settled.

A Down-and-Out Millionaire Can Rise Again

Joe's trips abroad had a subtext underlying the collection of bad debt. Especially with gamblers who paid up in full, the Tropicana coveted their return business — perhaps even issuing them credit after a period of cash-on-deposit action, known in the business as "pay and play."

Mr. S owed the Tropicana $1 million. He was a long-time

good-pay customer who'd been devastated in the Asian contagion, wiping him out completely. Joe was fully aware of his financial position before and after the crash; he also knew that ex-millionaires can become current millionaires if given enough time.

"I understand and sympathize with your predicament," Joe told Mr. S. "So even after traveling a long distance and departing empty-handed, I'll leave you with this. Please feel free to call me anytime in the future if you can make even a partial payment."

Mr. S agreed and the two shook hands.

Five years later, Joe had forgotten about the visit. He wasn't even working at the Tropicana any longer. But he wasn't surprised when Mr. S called to thank him for his patience and tell him that he could now repay the million dollars in full.

Joe arranged for the payment to go to the Tropicana from Mr. S, who became a valued customer once again.

Cleaning up More Credit Messes

Next up was a customer from Taiwan, Mr. W, who refused to pay a $300,000 debt. The gambler claimed a casino executive had berated him when he lost. Dennis asked Joe to investigate the details and do what needed to be done to collect.

Joe reviewed Mr. W's history. He was a major player at other resorts and always honored his credit play, often in the millions. Joe found it strange that the Trop was having trouble getting payment from this customer, as it wasn't his usual pattern.

His casino host shared with Joe that the customer, during his first trip to the Trop, had lost $300,000 in cash and $300,000 in credit. After he lost, he wanted his credit limit raised. The host called the president to request another $300,000. Problem was, the host made the mistake of calling the executive while standing next to Mr. W. The president, not knowing the gambler could hear him, actually did verbally berate him to the host. When Mr. W overheard the insults, he left the hotel and flew back to Taiwan. When his debt came due, he insisted that because he'd been humiliated by the president, he wasn't going to pay.

Joe called Mr. W, arranged a meeting in Taipei, and immediately flew to Taiwan. Mr. W invited him to dinner, which Joe knew wasn't the best idea. He was a fan of neither Asian food nor dinner meetings, which often lasted for hours before the customer admitted that he couldn't pay the debt at the time. And he always left hungry. But he knew that this was a delicate situation, so he agreed.

The dinner conversation revealed that Mr. W was a multi-millionaire who owned factories all over Taiwan. He'd felt disrespected in front of the host; the president's remarks included critical comments about the way he dressed. Indeed, when Joe met him for dinner, he was wearing working-man's khakis and a polo shirt.

Sure, the man didn't appear as coiffed as other millionaires he'd seen, but so what? If he had the means to spend $1 million in a casino, he should be able to wear whatever he wanted.

After listening intently to his complaint, Joe asked him for a bottom line. What could he and the casino do to make amends? Joe expected him to ask for a discount on the debt. Instead, he requested a written apology from the president.

Knowing that respect, called "face," was of the utmost importance in Asia, Joe suggested a written apology from the board chairman of the parent corporation as well. With that, Joe and Mr. W formed an unlikely friendship and he told Joe that if he ever left his position at the Tropicana to let him know; he would bring all of his business to whatever casino Joe was employed by.

Mr. W had plans to visit Las Vegas 30 days from their meeting and said he would be staying at Bally's. Joe told him he'd contact him when he obtained the written apologies and they could arrange payment of the $300,000. Joe then flew back home and met with Dennis Gomes to report what the customer had requested in order to satisfy his debt.

Dennis was surprised and asked Joe, "That's it? No discount?"

Joe said, "No discount. Just the apologies."

He then reminded Gomes of a collection trip he'd taken for the Golden Nugget when he needed Dennis' approval to grant discounts. Joe had called Gomes from Asia, explaining that a customer with a three-year-old debt of $200,000 requested a 50% discount. Dennis granted the discount, because the debt was so old. When Joe returned from that trip, he and Gomes went over the collections he'd made. When they reviewed the case of the customer given the 50% discount, Joe reported a figure of $180,000. Dennis was surprised; after all, he expected a payment of only $100,000, since he'd approved a discount of 50%. Joe said, "Yes, but I gave him only ten percent." From then on, it was mutually agreed that Joe would decide the discounts when traveling.

When Mr. W returned to Vegas, Joe showed up at his Bally's suite with the apology letters in his possession. One of Joe's security supervisors brought with them a bill-counting machine to verify the amount of the cash. Mr. W placed the bills on the dining-room table and Joe asked the security supervisor to begin counting. He told Mr. W it would be more efficient to use the machine.

The customer insisted on a manual count of the money, which took about two hours. When the counting was completed, the supervisor placed the cash in a briefcase and returned Mr. W's markers. Joe and the supervisor headed back to the Tropicana with the cash. On the way back, he asked Joe, "Is this what you do overseas?"

Joe replied, "Yes."

And his only response was, "*Jesus!*"

Will That Be Cash, Cash, or Cash?

Most of Joe's successful collection efforts resulted in a briefcase full of cash, U.S. dollars on the barrelhead, carried back to Las Vegas. In the early days, he didn't accept personal checks. The markers on which he was attempting to collect were the same as checks, which had either already bounced or never been put through the debtors' bank accounts. Or the gambler had written a personal check to cover his losses before leaving the U.S. that turned out to be from a closed account or one that had insufficient funds. He was holding more than enough markers and checks and didn't want any more.

In addition, the gamblers themselves didn't want to pay with checks. Doing so left a distinct paper trail to be followed by tax authorities and other investigators. Especially in Japan, gamblers were often charged by the government, not only for undeclared gambling winnings, but also losses, as they investigated where the money lost to the Las Vegas casinos came from — often sources that weren't legitimate. So the gambler had a hard time explaining major losses on reported income.

Also, in the early days of Joe's international collection efforts, wire-transferring foreign currencies wasn't permitted by most countries and where Joe was traveling, U.S. dollars were foreign. Later on, when it became legal to wire foreign currency, Joe began to accept checks, but he immediately took them to the issuing bank to verify the funds, which he wired back to Las Vegas before he left the country. Prior to that, however, customers preferred to pay in dollars, even though they had to go through the trouble of converting the local currency, and leave the movement of all that cash to Joe and the casino.

More Messes in Thailand

Realizing he needed assistance to clean up Tropicana collections in Thailand, Joe contacted Phil Needham, a DEA agent stationed in Bangkok he'd worked with in San Diego. Joe trusted Phil and knew he'd do anything possible to assist him.

On his next trip to Bangkok, Phil introduced Joe to a three-star general in the Thai National Police Department. Phil had nothing but good things to say about the general, so Joe felt good about how things were unfolding.

The general greeted Joe. "Phil tells me you need some help."

While the three sat together and Joe explained his efforts to collect on casino debts, he had a strange feeling that he'd met the general previously, perhaps a long time ago. Brushing aside the déjà vu, Joe gave the credit applications from the gamblers with overdue debts to the general, who handed them to his aide. "Call these people and set up meetings for tomorrow in my office at the police headquarters."

The aide soon returned. "Sir, some of these people say

they've already paid their junket representatives and have receipts to prove it. I told them to bring the receipts to the meeting."

At the meeting the next morning, the casino customers showed Joe receipts for various payments to a particular international junket rep, the same amounts that Joe's paperwork indicated were never received by the casino. He easily saw the pattern, so he planned to cut his trip short in order to return to Las Vegas and meet with casino executives on how they wished to proceed, including any criminal charges against the junket rep.

The next time Joe returned to Bangkok, Phil Needham contacted him and said that the general wanted to take them to dinner and "eat a lot of bread." Joe knew this was slang for "drink a lot of alcohol." The general took them to a Chinese restaurant, along with five of his bodyguards. In order not to have to eat the food and not insult his host at the same time, Joe drank and frequently stepped outside to smoke. Each time he left, the general sent a young bodyguard with him.

After one such trip, Joe told the general, "Your captain doesn't need to accompany me every time I go outside. I can protect myself."

The general laughed and said, "The captain isn't there to protect you from our people, but to protect our people from you!"

They all shared a laugh and continued drinking at the restaurant and a number of bars owned by the general till the wee hours. Sometime that night, Joe learned why he'd recognized the general: Joe had worked a narcotics case with a young Thai lieutenant in his NTF days, in which a former law-enforcement officer had been arrested in

Bangkok with two kilos of China-white heroin. The young lieutenant who had assisted in the heroin case in Bangkok many years before was, in fact, the general.

Joe finally got back to his hotel room at three in the morning, feeling no pain. The general was only five-foot-five, but he drank Joe, Phil, and all his young bodyguards right under the table. Joe returned to Bangkok on occasion and made it a point to get together with the general — but only for lunch!

Traveling Abroad

For international flights and hotel reservations, Joe used his travel agent from the Gaming Control Board, Jackie Vohs. Jackie was a first-class travel expert; she roamed the world extensively herself, in order to understand the problems that could and would come up during trips abroad.

At the Tropicana, Joe was traveling so often that Customs and Immigration officials began complaining that his four-year passports were all filled up with stamps and visas after two years; they ordered him to have pages added.

The collections themselves could go on for an unanticipated amount of time, so Joe had a challenge in estimating the time necessary to meet with customers. He also had to factor in their ability to pay while he was in their countries. On many of his international trips, he combined collections from gamblers in various countries. A delay in one collection meant a possible delay in all the following legs. Flights, hotel reservations, and appointment days and times with other customers all had to be adjusted.

There were, of course, good trips and bad. Most were routine, though one was the worst trip of them all.

He was asked to take a Tropicana casino-credit executive on a collection trip to numerous countries to train him. This was a stupid decision made by an executive who had literally no concept of how Joe went about collecting on markers. But he couldn't say no.

First, this guy had no law-enforcement contacts in the United States, let alone offshore, and he had absolutely no idea what awaited him on this lengthy trip—from Las Vegas to San Francisco, then on to Taiwan, Jakarta, Singapore, Thailand, Osaka, Frankfurt, and Paris over an entire month. Second, the trip was planned by the executive's assistants, not Joe. Jackie had to clean up the nightmare.

And third, he was one of those people who had never been in a foreign country, but knew everything. He had an overbearing personality and in every country, he became angry with people, mostly hotel employees, but also Customs and Immigration officials, because they didn't speak English and couldn't understand him. Joe tried to explain that you have to speak slowly and softly in an unpatronizing manner. But he was really hoping the guy would piss off an immigration official in a country they were trying to enter, so his entry would be denied and Joe could send him home where he belonged.

Joe didn't allow him to speak to the customers at all. He never introduced him to any of his law-enforcement contacts, for fear he'd insult them while they were out having cocktails and he'd get his ass kicked.

Toward the end of the trip, at the airport in Osaka, Japan, where they were boarding a flight to Frankfort, Germany, they had to change planes, after leaving earlier than expected. The ticket agent was trying to explain in extremely fractured English that they needed to buy new tickets. Joe had airline tickets totaling $25,000 and could have flown twice around the world without buying new ones. His traveling companion started butting in and screwing up the discussion.

Joe walked away, called Jackie in Las Vegas, and explained the situation. She told him to hang tight and she'd call back. He sat in a chair near the phone and observed his traveling companion attempting to sort out the problem, with no idea of what would get them onto the Lufthansa flight. He kept gesturing for Joe to assist at the counter, but he ignored the signals, while laughing under his breath.

Jackie called back and said that two tickets were waiting at the first-class check-in counter. Joe grabbed Dumbass (DA) and they boarded the flight to Frankfort. They were the only two passengers in first class and Joe had him sit on the other side of the aisle, so he wouldn't kill him.

After making contact with the gambler in Frankfort, they went on to Paris. Arriving a day early, Joe called Jackie again for hotel accommodations. Jackie called back before they left Germany and said there were no rooms in Paris, not one, due to an International Air Show taking place there at the time. Joe asked if she could change his flight from Paris to San Francisco, then on to Las Vegas. He then asked Dumbass if he also wanted his flight changed, since he was flying to a different destination in the States. When he said he could handle it, Joe muttered, "Good luck with that" and let it go.

They arrived in Paris, where the airport was a madhouse, with the Air Show going on all around them. In the cab lane, DA said he'd grab the cab. Joe said, "Be sure you find a driver who speaks English."

When Joe got into the cab, the driver didn't speak a word of English. Meanwhile, DA was trying to communicate with the driver and screwing things up further.

Then he showed the driver a personnel check from one the customers, pointed to his address, and said *"Içi"* ("here").

By then it was 7 p.m. on a Friday night during the height of rush hour with the biggest convention in history overwhelming Paris. Joe knew exactly what was going to happen, but he just sat there for the two-hour ride. The driver pulled up in front of a closed bank and announced they were *"Içi,"* and pointed to the closed bank. DA was attempting to tell the driver in no uncertain terms that he went to the wrong location when Joe shouted what he'd wanted to say for four weeks, "Would you shut the fuck up for once!" Then he explained, "When you showed the driver the check, your fingers were covering up the customer's address, so he took us to the bank's address instead. I want you to stop blaming other people for your own stupidity."

Joe knew they couldn't get a room anywhere, so he had the cab driver take them back to DeGaulle Airport. The total cab fare was $250. When DA insisted that Joe stiff the driver, Joe said, "You made so many mistakes in this fiasco, I should make you swim back to the States." He kicked DA to the curb, tipped the driver nicely, shook his hand, and pointed to his partner and said, "American asshole." The driver smiled and nodded; those were two words of English he clearly understood.

They entered the airport and Joe explained they'd have to spend the night in the first-class lounge. When DA started to follow him, Joe happily reminded him that he was booked on a different airline that was located in a different terminal and, since he'd refused to accept Jackie's offer to change his flight, he had to make his own arrangements. "Go to that terminal and find the first-class lounge for your airline. Good luck." Finally rid of his month-long ball and chain, Joe was laying odds that he'd get his arrogant ass thrown out of DeGaulle for being a poster boy of the Ugly American. This guy had pissed off half the world.

Joe got onto the plane and flew back to Vegas, finally rid of his clueless traveling companion. With a briefcase full of cash, he spent much of the flight preparing his currency declaration for U.S. Customs on all the collections he'd made.

A Normal Trip

For most trips to Asia, Joe left Las Vegas and arrived at his destination exactly 24 hours later. After checking into a hotel, sleeping, and freshening up, he started making contact with customers. These, of course, were delinquent debtors, who owed six and seven figures, sometimes for years, and weren't exactly anxious to hear from the casino's representative who had suddenly appeared in their city. He often enlisted the help of interpreters to surprise the customers and get them to set up meetings in an attempt to negotiate the debt. The typical response was, "I'll call you back." The interpreter was instructed to tell them, "You better, because if you don't, Joe will seek other avenues to collect, which you'll like even less."

From that point on, Joe was stuck in a hotel room, waiting for the call-backs. He knew from experience that if a customer called and Joe didn't answer, the customer would never call again during that trip.

The televisions broadcast shows only in the country's language. If he was lucky, he could get CNN. But after watching headline news for hours, he could have filled in for the anchors, reporting the news completely from memory.

Joe typically holed up for five days waiting. During that time, he met with customers in the hotel coffee shop or tea room. He was very careful in keeping the hotel operator apprised of his whereabouts on the property; going to eat or meet with a customer was the only time he strayed from the room phone.

Some meetings were successful in the first go-round; at others, Joe and the customer agreed to negotiate. For the customers who were adamant about not paying, Joe used other methods to get them to at least meet and discuss the outstanding debt on his next visit, usually the following month.

If it hadn't been for the Hard Rock Cafés all over Asia, Joe would have starved to death. But he does have the biggest collection of Hard Rock polo shirts in the West.

Target: Americans

While making frequent trips in the mid- to late 1990s, Joe flew in and out of Hong Kong when the airport was still located in Kowloon. On one trip, the Royal Hong Kong Police were patrolling the airport with submachine guns and their fingers on the triggers. He noticed these things automatically. He thought maybe some foreign head of state or Communist party leader was arriving.

He flew from Hong Kong to Narita Airport in Japan, located 45 miles outside Tokyo, where he saw full-on security manning checkpoints about a mile from the airport. He had to show his passport and airline ticket, then remove all his luggage from the cab, which was searched. While that was happening, buses arriving at the checkpoint were stopped, all the passengers had to offload, and all luggage was removed and searched.

When he got back to Las Vegas, he contacted some friends and learned that security was heightened all over

Asia, due to some intelligence information authorities in the various countries had received threatening U.S.-based airlines flying from Asia to the United States. Joe was happy to be home.

A few days later, Dennis Gomes called. "The board of directors has ordered me to Indonesia to settle Ms. Y's outstanding two-million-dollar debt."

"I know it well. The three-year-old markers, right?"

"Right. And since you've been dealing with her and have your contacts in Jakarta, you'll be going with me."

"Damn, Dennis, I just got back from Asia. Besides, it's not safe to travel there at the moment."

"Why not?"

"Red-level threats against American carriers flying from Asia to the States."

"Fine. I'm not going either."

Joe laughed. "Tell you what. Since the threat is against U.S. airlines, why don't we just fly on foreign carriers? I'm not worried; the security I saw in Asia is as tight as a frog's ass. Plus, I'll be in contact with the feds here and in Asia before we leave and again before we come home."

Flying on foreign airlines opened Joe's eyes to airport conditions, especially in Tokyo. When they arrived, they parked at a terminal he'd never been to in all his trips to Japan. The arrival area was spacious and beautiful with many amenities and services. He thought they finally built a new terminal, but it was simply the one for non-American arrivals and departures.

Joe and Dennis changed planes and continued on to Jakarta. As they were taxiing out, Joe saw that the American carriers were parked at the crappy terminal he'd always had to use—with the leaky roof, panels falling from the ceiling, only one restroom, and people sitting on the floor due to the lack of seats. It reminded him of an abandoned building filled with homeless squatters.

The terminal Joe and Dennis pulled into, on the other hand, reminded him of the Honolulu airport, with mixed inside and outside spaces and all the modern conveniences. Again, various military personnel were crawling all over the airport.

After all that traveling, Joe set up a meeting with Gomes and Ms. Y. They were extremely solicitous of her, but she jerked them around for a couple of days and they left without any money.

Gomes gave Joe the green light. "Joe, next time you're here, do your thing." He was ready for Joe to play hardball with Ms. Y.

Joe kept flying foreign carriers for a while, until he got the all-clear from his contacts. It wasn't until many years later that the American public was told of the threats.

Giving Advice Can Turn You into a Suspect

While at the Tropicana, Joe met John Chiero, the president of marketing, for the first time. Gomes had replaced Chiero as the president of all Tropicana operations in Las Vegas and New Jersey, but due to his multi-year contract, Chiero made a lateral move over to marketing. While he was president of the Trop, John brokered the deal to sell its country club and golf course to Kirk Kerkorian for the new MGM Grand.

He also had the most knowledge of the history of the Tropicana and Las Vegas than anyone Joe had ever met. And the collections Joe was making overseas were from credit given to gamblers when Chiero was actively running the Tropicana. Chiero had an excellent memory when it came to delinquent players and any collection efforts made in the past.

When they first met, Joe let him know that he didn't blame him for the bad debts. He knew that any casino operator is at the mercy of the hosts and junket representatives who recommended players coming from all over the world. At first, Joe detected a little doubt from Chiero about his ability to collect on the long-outstanding markers. But as Joe retired more and more old debts, Chiero began to believe in his abilities to negotiate and bring home the cash — and the two became good friends.

At one point, debt collections in Korea became a problem. Joe was well aware that it was against the law to collect gambling debts there. The Korean government actually arrested a casino host from Las Vegas for collecting on a marker, hoping to make an example of her.

Chiero came to Joe and said, "I'm going to Korea with one of the Korean hosts to visit existing customers and bring in new ones."

"Okay, John, but don't try to collect while you're there. And definitely don't allow the Korean host to collect. He'll get in a lot of trouble if he's caught."

"Understood. But what about the protocols of visiting existing customers and meeting with prospectives?"

"That's okay," Joe assured him. "It's normal for casinos to send marketing representatives to drum up new business."

A little later, Joe happened to run into the host accompanying Chiero to Korea and reminded him that he could wind up in jail if he attempted to collect on outstanding markers. Most hosts of Joe's acquaintance were highly ethical, though after meeting any number of junket reps, he always checked for his watch and wallet when leaving their presence.

Sure enough, Joe received a call in the middle of the night from Chiero, who was still in Seoul. "The Korean host showed up a little earlier in my hotel room with a briefcase full of Korean *wan*."

"What color were the *wan*?"

After Chiero described the bills, Joe said, "Korea has two types of currency, one for use in Korea, the other that can be used only outside the country. The stupid host has the in-country currency in his possession. It can't be taken out of Korea, even if the host wants to, because it's worthless beyond the national boundaries."

"Yikes. What should I do?"

"You tell that host to put the *wan* in a hotel safe-deposit box until the Trop's lawyers contact a Korean lawyer who can instruct us on how to proceed. Also, I think you should leave Korea, but have the host stay for his events with the customers."

Joe then left the matter up to the lawyers in both countries.

A short time later, the Korean host was arrested in Seoul and sentenced to a couple of months in jail.

Chiero came to Joe after the host was arrested, telling him that Gaming Control agents wanted to interview him about his trip to Korea with the now-jailed host. Joe told Chiero to just tell them what happened on his trip and not leave anything out. After Chiero was interviewed, the GCB agents called Joe for an interview, which left him puzzled.

Joe didn't know the two GCB agents, a male and female, who showed up for the interview. The agents asked Joe why the head of Tropicana marketing would call Joe to seek information on what to do while in the currency situation in Korea.

Joe explained what had transpired.

"Why didn't he contact one of the Tropicana's lawyers?"

"Because it was the middle of the night and the lawyers don't have my experience in traveling around the world collecting casino debt. I'm sure," he added, "Chiero wasn't too keen on violating Korean law and spending time in their jail eating fish heads and rice."

"What are you," the woman agent asked, "some hidden big shot who pulls the strings here at the Tropicana?"

Joe laughed. "Me? No, ma'am. I'm just a San Diego PD ex-cop and former Gaming Control background investigator doing my job as an international debt collector."

"You better be telling us the truth," the male investigator said. "We'll be looking into you and if we find anything amiss in your story, you'll be in some very hot water."

Joe called a friend at the GCB and learned that the two agents were married — *to each other*. He couldn't believe his ears. In all his years as a detective and GCB investigator, he'd never seen a married couple conduct an investigation that could possibly result in criminal charges. Talk about a conflict of interest! He could just about guarantee that both would hear the same "confession," even if one of them wasn't even in the room.

At the next meeting, Joe got impatient with their antics. When the male agent told him, "I'm tired of chasing you around the table," Joe responded, "Hey, I'm sitting here nice and easy in a chair. You're the one running around the table chasing ghosts." Essentially, he was challenging them to make their move or stop wasting his time.

The Mrs. agent left first, leaving Joe in the room with the Mr. He tried to give Joe some last grief, but Joe wasn't having it. "Did your wife give you that tie? It had to be a gift from her. It's the ugliest tie I've ever seen."

That was the last time Joe heard from them.

Detailed Assistance Guidelines

Joe had been back from Asia for a nice long respite of three weeks when he received a phone call from the Thailand national police. The caller was a major whom Joe had visited on his trip the previous month. While in Bangkok, Joe was having trouble making contact with a customer, Mr. P, who owed $250,000. The police major had taken Joe to the customer's house a few times, but it appeared he wasn't home. Joe suspected the customer was away on business, as he traveled often, but there was no record that he left Thailand, so it was likely he was traveling domestically. As Joe was leaving, he asked the major if he could have his men check the house every now and then to see if Mr. P had come home. Joe gave the major his business cards and asked him to have Mr. P call him in Las Vegas. Joe assumed the call from the major was to inform him that they had made contact.

The major said that his men had been surveilling the residence for three weeks and finally saw the lights on and movement inside. So they kicked in the front door. When they questioned the resident, he was calm and understanding. He claimed he'd paid the junket representative the outstanding debt three months earlier and could get proof from the bank.

Joe said he'd be in Bangkok in four days and asked the major to pass along a message. "Please tell him to get his door fixed or replaced and when he shows me proof of payment, I'll reimburse the repair or replacement costs."

Joe thanked the major and hung up, baffled as to why the cops knocked down the door when they could have knocked and been allowed entry in a civilized way. He also didn't understand how a homeowner could remain "calm and understanding" after his front door came crashing in on him. The only thing he could come up with was Mr. P was relieved that first, it wasn't a home invasion and second, he wasn't going to jail.

Joe left two days later for Bangkok with a newly activated collection in Pattaya Beach, 65 miles south of Bangkok. He was concerned about this collection, because the player was brought in by the same junket representative the player in Bangkok claimed he'd paid.

Arriving in Bangkok, Joe and the major met with Mr. P. He handed Joe a canceled check made out to the junket representative for 7.5 million *baht* ($250,000). He explained that the junket rep told him the debt payment had to go to him. Joe made a copy of the check and apologized profusely for the door, but Mr. P said reimbursement wouldn't be necessary; he felt the damage was minimal.

Joe began to understand that while having your door kicked in by law enforcement in the U.S is a big deal, it's not that uncommon in Asia.

Joe returned to his hotel where he contacted a DEA agent at the U.S. embassy and asked if he knew any foreign service nationals (FSN) who could translate and drive Joe down to Pattaya Beach to do an interview and collection. Since Thailand has the second-most traffic deaths of any country in the world (Libya is first) due to bad drivers, Joe asked for a driver who'd never operated a cab.

An FSN named Samchai contacted Joe and arranged to pick him up. On the trip to Pattaya, Joe and Samchai discussed payment; the FSN didn't want money other than gas, but he requested that on the way back, they stop at a Thai military base. Joe agreed, but insisted on paying him for his translation services with the customer.

During the trip, it was easy to see why Thailand was notorious for traffic fatalities: Samchai was doing an exceptional job of keeping other drivers from killing them. Cars were going twice the speed limit and passing on the right shoulder of the two-lane road. Tractor-trailers carrying petroleum were also using the shoulder as an active traffic lane.

Joe mentioned the name of the customer. The FSN replied that the customer was well-known in Thailand for owning the Royal Jomtien Resort, a multi-story hotel on the beach where they were meeting him.

When they arrived, the customer was very cooperative in furnishing information about the junket rep. He showed Joe a copy of the check for six million baht ($200,000) with which he'd paid the rep. Joe now knew beyond a shadow of a doubt that he had a bigger collection problem than he'd originally anticipated — further confirming his rock-bottom opinion of junket reps.

Joe and Samchai headed back to Bangkok and stopped at the Thai military base to visit a Samchai relative who'd recently returned from a deployment with the Queens Guard on Thailand's border with Burma. The unit had been involved in numerous armed clashes with drug traffickers.

Joe found the base to be similar to any in the U.S., except that the barracks, including the family housing, were minimal at best. A group of cinderblock buildings consisted of very small kitchens and living rooms; the dining areas were outside and each unit had a concrete table for eating. The bathroom consisted of a toilet, shower, and a large concrete basin filled with water; residents used a bucket to pour water into the toilet, flushing it manually.

Joe sat outside and Samchai introduced him to his cousin, who in turn introduced him to everyone. They drank some Thai beer and the wives brought out food. Of course, Joe didn't want to eat the food, but seeing how welcoming and poor the Thai soldiers and their families were, he wasn't about to insult them by refusing.

The longer they were there, the bigger the crowd grew to meet the American from Las Vegas. None of the military could speak great English and Joe didn't speak any Thai, but they half-understood one another. They were aware that Joe also served in the military, which seemed to make them want to close ranks. And like most military, these guys were putting away some serious beer.

When it was getting to be time to leave, Joe asked Samchai if there was a PX on base where he could replenish the beer supply. He led Joe to a building the size of a small garage selling soft drinks, beer, and "Mekong whiskey." Merely an annex to a larger PX on the base, it contained about four cases of soda, seven cases of beer, and four bottles of whiskey. Joe had Samchai inquire about the prices, then asked him to go get some guys to help carry some things.

When the FSN returned, he asked, "What needs carrying?"

Joe said, "All of it. Everything in this room is going to the soldiers and their families."

The total cost was US$50. Joe knew he'd gotten off easy — until the soldiers insisted he take the first shot of whiskey. Having paid $5 a bottle, he knew it was going to be rough. It was.

Just before leaving, the soldiers asked what Joe was doing in Thailand. Samchai informed them he was there to collect some gambling debts for a Las Vegas casino.

That launched a flurry of sudden discussion and activity.

Joe watched as the FSN gestured in a way that stopped the soldiers. After a couple of minutes, everything calmed down and the FSN explained what had just happened. "They wanted to repay you for the drinks by getting their weapons and a two-and-a-half-ton troop transport to go with you and collect the money."

"Tell the guys that I really appreciate the offer, but the gambler already paid."

It took 30 minutes to shake all the hands and hug the wives and kids.

Driving back to Bangkok, Samchai said, "You know they would have gone with you to collect the money."

Joe laughed. "Well, I don't think that's a collection method that's approved by the gambling authorities in Nevada."

"I guess not. But I'm sorry that the visit was supposed to be only thirty minutes and it lasted three hours."

"Listen, don't apologize. I loved every minute of it."

But Joe was reminded of a valuable lesson by the FSN episode and the Bangkok cops kicking in the customer's door. When you ask for assistance from law enforcement in other countries, you have to give Extremely Detailed and Specific Guidelines when they offer help.

On the drive back to Bangkok, he asked Samchai to stop at the first place they came to that sold Rolaids or some type of antacid to kill the fire in his belly. Once again, he remembered the reason that he abstained from extremely spicy Asian food. Back at his hotel in Bangkok, he got ready for his 6 a.m. flight to Hong Kong and San Francisco, totaling 18 hours of flying time.

When Joe returned to Las Vegas, he handed off the copies of the checks paid to the junket rep, the corroborating documents, and the information he'd uncovered about the rep to the casino lawyers for their follow-up.

A few weeks later, Joe received a fax from Bangkok. It was horrific news. The Royal Jomtien Resort in Pattaya Beach had experienced a devastating fire on July 11, 1997.

The fire was still under investigation, but the reports were that a large number of injuries and loss of life were expected. Weeks later, Joe learned that the owner of the hotel, the customer he'd met with in June, and the managing director were being charged with negligence and illegal modification of the building.

The investigation revealed that the practice of locking the emergency-exits doors to prevent people from leaving without paying had kept many of the victims from escaping the fire. Up to 90 people had perished. Numerous other violations were discovered and emergency response had totally collapsed.

Macau Raccoons

Gomes and Joe were sent to collect a $4 million debt from a Hong Kong customer and a half-million-dollar debt from one in Macau.

When they arrived in Hong Kong, they were told that the customer had an emergency and had to leave. Not believing it, Joe called a source at the Royal Hong Kong Police, who found no immigration records indicating the customer had left. Gomes and others finally contacted the customer and eventually reached a compromise concerning the debt via lawyers.

They proceeded to Macau and met with David, who owed the $500,000. David worked at the Lisboa Casino, where he leased a baccarat table. This was Joe's first trip to Macau and he found it to be reminiscent of a 1930s' Charlie Chan movie. Walking into the casino, he first noticed the players standing in line waiting to play baccarat. The cigarette smoke created a heavy cloud from ceiling to floor and burned Joe's eyes, even being a smoker at the time.

Everyone in the joint had a lit cigarette, all of which had three inches of ash waiting to fall. At numerous table games in each area, a representative of Macau's organized-crime Triads was extending credit to the customers. Joe said to Dennis, "I bet the Triads don't have any problem collecting their casino debts."

David also owned a restaurant and the three went there for dinner. Yet again, Joe had to make up an excuse for not eating, though Gomes ventured out and at least tasted all the served food. Joe could tell that David didn't have the funds available to service his debt, so he didn't want to eat anyway; he was ready to leave immediately. Still, Gomes kept eating while he got David to commit to making the payment and asked when Joe could come back to collect. Christmas was only a few days away and neither of them was anxious to stay in Macau over the holidays.

While Dennis and David were negotiating, Joe was drinking Crown Royal. After he'd had a few, he headed to the restroom. On his way, he noticed a cage in front of the hostess station containing two live racoons hugging each other. Or was it the Crown Royal?

Back at the table, he asked David, "What are the racoons for?"

He smiled and said, "They'll be served as meals."

Joe went back to the hostess stand and there they were, still hugging each other and shivering.

"How much does a raccoon dinner cost?" he asked David when he returned.

"A hundred dollars each."

Joe pulled out $200 and told David he wanted both raccoons.

"Really? How would you like them prepared?"

"I'm going to keep them in the cage—and will you have

your driver bring the Rolls Royce around to drive me into the foothills where I can release them?"

"Are you serious?"

"Yes, and will you please tell your driver that if I hear he went back to get them where I drop them off, I'll shoot him in the ass when I come back to collect your debt?"

They all had a good laugh and Joe was still laughing as he rode around the foothills of Macau in a Rolls Royce with two rescued raccoons. When he released them, they scurried off into the brush — without so much as a thank you.

Joe and Dennis returned to Hong Kong via hydrofoil and made it back to Las Vegas in time to celebrate the holidays with their families.

Years later, Joe heard from David, who called from Hong Kong asking him to assist with a licensing matter. The Dunes was coming up for auction and his friend Stanley Ho was considering bidding on it. David asked if Joe could help Ho get licensed in Nevada.

Joe knew that Stanley Ho owned all eight Macau casinos and controlled all aspects of them, including the credit at his tables issued by the Triads.

He also remembered a Royal Hong Kong Police official relating a story about a Triad accountant who was caught misappropriating some of their funds. The accountant was found in Kowloon Harbor missing his arms and legs. His extremities had been cut off with a blow torch, which cauterized the wounds; he was alive when he was thrown into the Kowloon Harbor.

Their termination process was a little too strict for Joe and he informed David that he had a better chance of becoming the pope than Stanley Ho did of obtaining a gaming license in Nevada.

Larry Hahn

Joe met DEA attaché Larry Hahn through some agents he knew. Larry became a close trusted friend as Joe went about the business of collecting casino debts internationally. As an embassy attaché, Larry covered Singapore and Indonesia for the DEA. He connected Joe with local officials who always had his back when he worked in their respective countries. Without Larry's support and contacts, Joe would never have attempted to collect casino debts in either jurisdiction. Indeed, without Larry Hahn, on at least one occasion, his collection effort could have been a fatal mistake.

Joe traveled to countries where police officers made the equivalent of $200 a month, while he was there to collect anywhere from hundreds of thousands to millions of dollars. Some of these countries were plagued by police corruption. But every local law-enforcement official that Larry introduced to Joe was beholden to Larry and the DEA for assistance in their countries. They were so grateful, they couldn't do enough to assist Joe.

One example of that was when a local contact called Joe in his Jakarta hotel room one afternoon to warn him of an insurrection in progress. He urged Joe to pack up and head to the airport, because Indonesians were staging violent protests at the U.S. Embassy and killing people of Chinese descent. The contact wasn't sure it was going to stop there.

Joe packed his bags and a hotel car drove him straight to the airport, going through roadblocks and armed checkpoints along the way. As people fled the country, flights were full, but he found a seat on a plane headed to Manila. Mel Gibson fans most likely remember his character's departure from Indonesia in the film *The Year of Living Dangerously*. Joe's experience mirrored this dramatic escape during yet another murderous time in Indonesia.

Safely in Manila the next day, Joe learned that the Indonesian government closed the airport shortly after his flight departed. If not for Larry Hahn and his local connections, Joe isn't sure what he would have done or what might have happened to him during that trip.

A Customer's Dispute

During another collection trip, a casino host traveled with Joe to Kuala Lumpur, the capital of Malaysia, to meet a customer who was disputing his casino-debt balance. Gomes requested the trip, knowing the customer wouldn't be satisfied unless someone from the corporate level came to listen to his perspective on the debt agreement.

The customer was a Tan Sri, an honorific signifying a highly regarded citizen in Malay society, comparable to a knight in England and highly influential in the Malaysian culture. According to the Tropicana, he owed $280,000. The dispute was over the discount on his loss; the player claimed it was 20%, while the host insisted it was only 10%.

Joe and the host arrived at the customer's office building, where they were kept waiting for two hours in a reception area one floor below the Tan Sri's office. At the end of the second hour, Joe tried to joke with the host. "Jeez, you must have really pissed this guy off." But the host had a hard time finding any humor in the situation. He knew the player's powerful standing in Malaysia.

Soon after, a large man approached them and asked that they follow him to an elevator. The host asked Joe, "Where is he taking us?"

Joe could see him start to sweat. "I don't know. He didn't say he was taking us to your player, that's for sure."

As the three of them got into an elevator, Joe caught a

glimpse of a stainless- steel .357-magnum revolver tucked inside the large man's waistband under his coat. He silently alerted the host to the presence of the gun; the host started to breathe heavily, in addition to staining his shirt with perspiration. This all caused Joe to laugh to himself. The poor guy was clearly out of his element.

As the elevator door opened, they saw numerous staff members going about their business. Joe said, "Well, it looks like business as usual. So we probably won't be killed ... yet."

After waiting another 20 minutes, Joe couldn't help himself. "You know, we're probably waiting for his staff to clean up the blood and gore from the last guy who challenged him."

When they were finally called into the Tan Sri's inner sanctum, Joe introduced himself, saying he'd been sent by the president of the Tropicana casino and that he and the host had traveled halfway around the world to meet with him personally to resolve the dispute fairly.

After some back and forth, Joe showed the Tan Sri the agreement he'd signed, which clearly specified a 10% discount. "However, the Tropicana and your host here value you highly as a customer. We don't often receive players of your prominence. Thus, I'm authorized to extend the twenty-percent discount you thought you were receiving — under one condition."

"And what is this condition?"

Joe knew that the host desperately wanted to keep the player as his customer, as he was single-handedly responsible for the lion's share of the host's commissions. Still, fun-loving guy that he was, Joe had to bite his tongue to stop himself from saying, "The condition is that you don't have him executed." Instead, he said, "Your host has to agree to the discount. He's the one who signed the agreement with you for the ten percent. This impacts not only his status in the casino, but also his salary."

Both Joe and the player turned to the host. Joe figured that the host was so relieved he'd come away from the meeting with his life, he'd have agreed to a 100% discount.

All parties were satisfied and they visited for another twenty minutes with the customer. He told them that his daughter was a student at the University of Southern California and he liked to golf at the La Costa country club outside San Diego.

After leaving, the host, whom Joe respected, admitted that Joe had made him even more nervous than he already was.

Joe grinned. "Really? Even with your advanced belts in karate and kung fu? I figured you could easily disarm that giant bodyguard. So I wasn't concerned." But then he added, "Just in case, on my flight here from Bangkok, I learned how to say, 'Call 911!' in Malay."

Singapore Connection

One of Dennis Gomes' collections was a three-year-old case. The customer, a well-known gambler, Ms. Y, had an outstanding debt of $2 million. One of her three sons, who had accompanied her on the casino trip, owed an additional $165,000. That son lived in Singapore, while her other two sons lived in Jakarta; all three were graduates of the University of Southern California. Ms. Y herself lived in Jakarta, where she had an extensive real estate portfolio, including a restaurant and disco. She also owned property in Hong Kong, as Joe learned during his pre-collection investigation. In addition, her reputation preceded her: She had a long history of being a big gambler, but prior to this collection, had always paid off her markers.

Her visit to the Tropicana concerned Joe, because she hadn't played there before. It was a common practice for high-profile customers to abruptly switch from a regularly frequented casino to one down the Strip when the other casino determined she was tapped out and didn't want to extend her additional credit to gamble.

He contacted DEA attaché Larry Hahn in Singapore and arranged to meet him there. Larry introduced him to a high-ranking Indonesian law-enforcement official who agreed to assist him in Jakarta with his collection efforts.

Upon Joe's arrival in Jakarta, he was driven from the airport to the Grand Hyatt Hotel, where he met again with the official. After an initial briefing and review of the casino-credit documents, the local guy informed Joe that a lot of the information was incorrect. The woman no longer owned the restaurant and disco and her home address had changed. In fact, he said, no current address was available for her in Jakarta. But to assist Joe, he would send a captain and major to pick him up in the morning to help locate the woman.

The captain and major arrived on time the next morning and politely introduced themselves. Joe briefed them, providing what information he had. Both men spoke English and one of them read English sufficiently to look over Joe's documents.

They drove to the woman's restaurant and disco properties, but found both businesses closed.

As they were leaving, the major noticed someone inside the restaurant sweeping the floor. Since Joe didn't speak Bahasa, Indonesia's national language, the major went in alone; when he returned, he had the woman's address. Sure enough, she no longer owned the restaurant and disco. Joe knew this wasn't good news. Ms. Y was in financial trouble.

As they drove away, Joe asked the major, "Are we going to Ms. Y's residence or to a tailor shop first?"

The major responded, "Why a tailor shop?"

Joe said, "Well, while the captain and I were watching your conversation in the restaurant though the picture window, we saw you put both hands on the janitor's shoulders at the bottom of his throat. I just assumed you were taking his neck size for some new shirts."

They drove to Ms. Y's home, located in an affluent gated community in Jakarta. At the front door, Joe said, "Please, major, no tailor shops."

The major smiled back at him just before the door was answered by one of the sons who invited them inside to meet with Ms. Y.

Everyone began conversing in Indonesian, so Joe requested the son interpret for him. The son was surprised that Joe knew he spoke English, but Joe pointed out that USC courses were taught in English. The son was further taken aback that Joe knew he had attended USC, but he agreed to interpret the conversation, even though Joe knew what Ms. Y was saying before he heard the English; he'd been on the receiving end of the same excuses Ms. Y was coming up with from big gamblers the world over. She claimed that her assets in Hong Kong had been sold, but couldn't provide proof.

Joe returned to Singapore to locate the son who owed the $165,000. When he reached him by phone, he heard, in perfect English, "Fuck you! I'm not paying you and my mother isn't either!"

Joe figured this son's degree from USC wasn't in public relations.

He returned to Las Vegas, devised a plan, and briefed

Dennis. He requested an arrest warrant for non-sufficient funds for the son, knowing that the warrant was good only in the U.S., but since the son went to USC, he would surely return to the States at some point to see friends. Joe obtained the warrant, returned to Jakarta, met with Ms. Y., and as a courtesy showed her the arrest warrant for her son. Joe tried to warn her about the consequences of the warrant, but she was unfazed by both the warrant and him.

During Joe's first trip for this collection, he'd noticed a vacant billboard just outside the gated community where the woman lived. With the major's assistance, Joe arranged to rent the billboard for 30 days, posting a big banner on the board that read: "Ms. Y Doesn't Pay Her Debts!" Joe had used this tactic in Japan, where face is critical, with great success.

Joe then visited an attorney to determine if a civil-litigation case could be filed for debt collection.

The attorney explained how things worked in Indonesia. "A favorable filing is possible, but you have to pay the judge fifty thousand U.S. dollars, all in cash."

"I work for a reputable licensed gaming company, so I simply can't make that kind of payment."

On his way out of the building, Joe deposited the attorney's business card where it belonged — in the trash can.

Next stop, Singapore. There, he was contacted by a Tropicana lawyer who was adamant about filing a civil suit against the son. Joe flatly refused. He wasn't worried. He simply called Dennis Gomes and reminded him of their contract, which gave Joe *full* control over assigned collections and that included not having to listen to interference from aggressive lawyers sitting in their comfortable offices in Las Vegas.

"Well," Dennis asked, "you got an alternative?"

"I happen to know that this son in Singapore has a trip scheduled to the U.S. and will have to clear Immigration. The arrest warrant is now outstanding and all we have to do is wait."

A month later in Las Vegas, Joe informed Dennis that they'd see activity on this collection the next day.

"How do you know? Have you heard from Ms. Y?"

Joe replied, "No."

"So what's going to happen?"

"The Singapore son will be arrested tonight in Los Angeles when he tries to enter the country off a Singapore Airlines flight."

"How do you know that?"

"Do you want the flight number? Just trust me."

"Maybe we should get a second warrant for the mother."

"Waste of time," Joe said. "She'll never come back to the U.S. She comes here only when she wants to gamble and no one will extend her credit while she still owes. Besides, we want her free and able to send us money." He knew a mother with spoiled sons wasn't going to sit around and let one of them rot in a county jail.

As expected, Joe received a phone call from the son in Jakarta in the middle of the night, complaining that his brother had been arrested in Los Angeles.

Joe said, "I tried to warn you and your mother about this happening, but you blew me off."

"Well, can you get him out of jail?"

Joe said, "Why would I do that? I'm the guy who put him there."

Joe offered a detailed description of the L.A. County Jail and how things worked. "If your mother pays off her markers, I can see what the casino might want to do next."

"We told you, my mother isn't paying you."

"Fine, but the jail doesn't have a section for rich Indonesians with college degrees, so your brother needs to be prepared to do some hard time. I can't help you," he said and hung up.

A couple of days later, the son called again to tell Joe that they were getting the bail lowered.

Joe called a prosecutor in L.A. with whom he'd worked on an undercover drug case. Joe explained the case in detail and the prosecutor said he would take care of it.

The next night, Joe received another call from the brother in Jakarta.

"How'd the bail hearing go?" Joe asked him.

The question was met with silence.

"Look, I'll tell you what. If your mother settles her debt for two million, we'll forgive your brother's debt and have him released."

The next day, the son called and asked Joe to return to Jakarta, so his mother could pay up.

Joe gave instructions that the mother bring the funds, drawn from a Hong Kong bank, and meet him in Hong Kong instead. Given the level of government corruption in Jakarta, Joe had no intention of transferring a large amount of money there. Also, Joe was friends with the chief superintendent of the Royal Hong Kong Police.

The debt was settled in Hong Kong. Joe returned home and the son was subsequently released from jail. No one ever mentioned the billboard.

Mr. O

Some of the international customers became Joe's friends over the years. One customer, Mr. O, came to the casino from Japan with $700,000 in cash to put on deposit.

Mr. O told Joe he had one stipulation: *no credit*. He didn't want to be offered any markers should he lose his deposit and he wanted his request shared with the casino managers and credit executives. He said, "Even if I beg and plead, I do *not* want to be given credit."

Joe honored the request and informed the casino vice president. Mr. O stayed for 10 days, then returned to Japan.

Later, Joe was talking to the CEO when the marketing VP approached and overheard them discussing Joe's upcoming collection trip to Japan. The VP asked Joe to collect a debt from Mr. O.

"What debt? He brought cash and insisted that he never be given credit."

The VP said, "Well, he asked, so I gave him a credit line of three hundred thousand."

Joe was understandably angry and told the VP, "*You* gave him the credit, *you* collect it!"

That practice was known as "burying the customer": granting credit that the casino knew the customer would have difficulty paying back.

Joe met with Mr. O. He too was angry that he'd been granted credit after specifically requesting that the casino not do so. He further explained that he hadn't initially been drinking, but as he began to lose, he drank more, then requested the line. He said it would be a couple of months before he was in a position to pay off the $300K.

Joe told him he understood and that he could take all the time he needed.

About three months later, Joe was collecting a million dollars in Hong Kong when he received a message that Mr. O was now able to pay, so Joe arranged to meet with him in Tokyo.

A company lawyer in Hong Kong with Joe accompanied him to meet Mr. O at one of his clubs in the Ginza entertainment district of Tokyo. Mr. O walked up to the table carrying a brown shopping bag filled with $300,000 in cash. He set the bag on the table, removed the cash, and placed it on the table to be counted. Joe immediately stopped him and placed the money back into the bag. The lawyer looked astonished.

Joe assured Mr. O that he trusted him, as they'd been dealing with each other for years and it wasn't necessary to count the money. He also told him that he would send the markers via Federal Express back to Mr. O as soon as he returned home. In most collections, only after the markers were returned did the gambler turn over the money. But Mr. O trusted Joe as much as Joe trusted him and he completed payment without the markers.

The corner of the club where they met Mr. O was relatively secluded, but Joe noticed a Japanese man in a suit walk in and sit down nearby in another dark corner. Mr. O immediately excused himself, then sat with the suit. Because of Mr. O's quick response to the man's entry, Joe knew he was to be respected and he looked at him closely.

After finishing their drinks, Joe was ready to leave. The lawyer started to walk over to say goodbye to Mr. O. But before he got far, six other guys in suits walked in and joined Mr. O and the other man; Joe knew that these were the man's bodyguards. Joe grabbed the lawyer's arm and hustled him out of the club. While they walked down a narrow Tokyo street looking for a cab, Joe carried the $300,000 in the brown shopping bag. The lawyer's head turned one way and the other, nervously looking for whoever was going to kill them and take the cash.

When they were safely in a cab headed back to the hotel, Joe explained to the lawyer why they didn't want to disturb

Mr. O before leaving. "The man in the suit looked similar to the head of the Tokyo Yakuza, the organized-crime syndicate. If someone happened to snap a photo of Mr. O and you shaking hands with the Yakuza in the background, it would raise eyebrows all over Gaming Control."

"Who would take a photo?"

"Local law enforcement could be watching. You never know."

The lawyer excitedly fired questions at Joe. "You do this stuff all the time? You think the guy was being followed by the cops? How could you be so nonchalant walking out of the club with all that cash?"

"As the man met with Mr. O and the bodyguards walked in, I saw all seven of them glance back at us two Americans. It looked to me like Mr. O was explaining who we were and what we were doing there. If those guys had anything to do with the Yakuza, anyone within a five-mile radius knew the boss was in the area. No one would dare commit a crime against a 'friend' of Mr. O's."

"You saw all that?"

"I also saw the man nod to one of his bodyguards, who followed us out to the cab. With him watching, I wasn't worried. Just before we got into the taxi, I nodded at the bodyguard, to express our thanks, and he walked back to the club."

Joe's investigative training and undercover experiences will always be a part of him. He's never lost the undercover sense of constant awareness of his surroundings. He also knew that answers to the lawyer's questions would lead to more nervous inquiries, so he thought it best not to elaborate further.

The debt money was wire-transferred the next morning and the two headed to the airport to return home. Joe noticed the lawyer appeared weary and asked if he'd gotten any sleep. The lawyer replied, "How do you do this stuff all the time?"

Joe responded, "Very *very* carefully."

Joe waited for the lawyer to ask the most important question, "How did you know the guy looked like the head of the Yakuza?" But it never came.

Joe's answer would've been, "By doing my homework."

Joe hated homework in school, but as an adult in his line of work, homework had kept him alive more times than he could count.

Kashiwagi Part Three

In fall 1991, Joe received a call from the president of the Trump Plaza in Atlantic City, who explained that Akio Kashiwagi had been playing there, but left abruptly, owing nearly $4 million.

He asked if Joe was still in contact with the whale.

Joe said, "Actually, yes. I had contact with him recently."

"What about?"

"Well, I was trying to collect three hundred thousand from a player in Japan, but he told me he couldn't pay, because he owed Kashiwagi four hundred thousand. He told me that Kashiwagi took back a signed deed to the house of his parents as collateral."

"Jeez," the president said. "Those are some harsh terms."

"Yeah, but I can tell you that this customer is the worst degenerate gambler I've ever seen and God knows I've seen a few. He didn't even tell his parents he hocked their house. And he had to pay back the four hundred G's in ninety days."

"So you got in touch with Kashiwagi to confirm all this?"

"I did. I was told that he had already begun proceedings to have the degenerate's parents removed from their home."

"So let me guess. You gave up on trying to collect the three hundred large."

Joe laughed without humor. "Hell yeah. Why bother? This guy was in big trouble with everyone. I was the least of his worries."

"What about a lawsuit?"

"Nope. Lawsuits for gambling debts aren't allowed in Japan."

"Do you think you can contact Kashiwagi over the four million he owes us?"

"I can try. I was certainly successful getting in touch with him the last time."

"Okay," the president said. "I'll get back to you if I can get the terms approved by Trump."

It was now January 1992 and while awaiting an answer, Joe was contacted by a law-enforcement associate in Japan. Kashiwagi had been murdered.

He was at home alone one day while his bodyguard was driving Mrs. Kashiwagi on an errand. The police were investigating the following scenario. A friend of Kashiwagi's son, who owed him money, visited him in an attempt to get a better payment agreement. But Kashiwagi refused. The son's friend became enraged, removed from the wall one of Kashiwagi's prized Samurai swords, and used it to stab him 150 times, then hack up his body.

Joe relayed the news to the casino president at Trump Plaza, who responded that he thought they could go after Kashiwagi's estate. Joe reminded him again that gambling debts were not enforceable in Japan and wished him luck with further collection efforts.

Later, while in Japan, Joe was shown a photo of the

murder scene and he remembers thinking that the number of wounds suffered by Kashiwagi clearly demonstrated the out-of-control rage of the perpetrator.

Mock Retirement

In 2002, a new president was hired at the Tropicana to oversee the Las Vegas operations. He was well-known and highly regarded in the casino industry, having built a great reputation as a fair and well-qualified executive with the knowledge and skills necessary to manage a successful operation. After a couple of months at his new position, the president called Joe into his office and told him that due to budgeting issues, he had to let the director of security go. Both the directors of security and surveillance still reported to Joe, who reported directly to the president. The president could see the expression on Joe's face and asked him, "What's the matter?"

Joe responded, "He's been a loyal employee here for sixteen years and managed the security department in an exemplary manner. I know him to be a good, honest, hard-working man who doesn't deserve to be laid off like that."

"Be that as it may — "

Joe broke in, "Just hear me out. Before you began working here, the previous president tried to renege on some collection commissions we agreed on and I have the signed agreement."

The president was shocked and asked, "How did he do that?"

"He promised me a twenty percent commission on an

old marker I collected on one trip, but he never paid me."

"Frankly, Joe, that surprises me."

"It surprised me too. But if you speak to the CFO, she was part of the deal and signed off on the twenty percent I never received."

With that, he had the president's attention. "So here's what I'd like to do. As I said, my man has been a loyal employee to this company and its various management regimes for nearly two decades. It's going to be tough for him to find a new position with another casino at his age. He also has some children in college, or they soon will be."

"Well, what do you suggest?"

"Here's what I suggest. Put out information that *I'm* retiring. That will solve the budget issue, he keeps his job, and I go away." Joe knew the president would agree, as Joe's salary and benefits were a much bigger expense to the company. He also knew that the rest of the long-term outstanding markers were uncollectable and he'd no longer be traveling. He felt good that he'd brought in millions that had been viewed as uncollectable.

The president responded, "Well, okay ... if that's really what you want to do."

"You know, myself, I've never had a problem getting jobs."

As part of the deal, the president was to tell no one the truth, so it would never get back to the security director that he'd been given this gift. (The president would later share with Joe that he thought that was the finest thing he'd ever witnessed any executive do for one of his subordinates. Especially since Joe had only been there for seven years.) The president also agreed to pay Joe the thousands owed to him per the collection agreement and to make it all look good, he'd throw him a retirement party.

Joe contacted Dennis Gomes at the Atlantic City Tropicana and explained the deal.

"It's unbelievable the way you care for your staff."

Joe responded, "I learned it from you, Dennis."

After leaving the Tropicana, Joe ran into his old friend
and colleague from the Hilton, Dave Austin, who was
now the vice president of security for the MGM and a very
good friend of the security director at the Tropicana, whom
Austin had worked with at the Las Vegas Hilton. Austin
asked Joe why he left the Tropicana and Joe stuck with the
retirement story, though he felt pretty guilty about lying.

A few years later, Joe got a call telling him that the Trop's
security director had a pacemaker implanted a couple of
years earlier due to a heart condition, but he'd passed away
on vacation playing golf. Joe was now doubly happy about
his decision to leave, because the health insurance from the
Tropicana had been available to the security director for
all his medical needs.

Later, when Joe was discussing the news with Austin,
he told him the truth about his "retirement" years earlier.

Austin said, "He never told me that."

Joe answered, "He didn't know. I didn't want him to
know. I didn't want him to learn that after sixteen years of
busting his ass, they would just let him go."

Joe felt comfort in letting Austin know, as he too unex-
pectedly passed away sometime later, knowing the truth.

The Tropicana was the last gaming property at which
Joe ever worked.

Between 1992 and 2012, Joe was a consultant for the
governments of Greece, Panama, Mpumalanga (a province
in South Africa), the island of Tinian, the Ontario Gaming
Commission, Wynn Las Vegas, Pechanga Tribal Council,
IGT, Konami Gaming, and numerous gaming attorneys. He

also did a stint as an instructor at the Gaming Institute at the University of Nevada teaching courses to hundreds of gaming agents from all over the world on how to conduct international investigations.

Life After the Casinos

Joe retired for good in 2012 at age 71, but health issues started to dog him. After surviving a heart condition and surgery, he had a bout of prostate cancer, then abdominal surgery that went badly wrong. He developed an incisional hernia, caused by an incompletely healed surgical wound. That led to another surgery. Then, an infection from that operation led to a third, which kept him in the hospital for more than six months; he was there for so long that the hospital's CEO came down and introduced himself. He had a total of five abdominal surgeries and was placed on life support three different times.

Father Doug

One morning, Joe woke up and found Father Doug Koesel, his priest friend from Cleveland, sitting in the hospital room. Joe suspected that his condition had to be pretty serious for the priest to be at his side, ready to administer last rites.

That wasn't the case. Father Doug loved Las Vegas and traveled there every chance he could, visiting Joe and

Karen each time. During one of his annual trips, the priest told Joe that he sometimes organized casino nights at his parish and he considered himself knowledgeable about casino games. Later, Father Doug called Karen and asked if she could help a friend land a blackjack dealer position at Ellis Island.

"Well," Karen tried to let him down gently, "our usual practice is not to hire break-in [new] dealers, but as a favor to you, Father, I'll ask the shift boss to evaluate your friend."

When Father Doug showed up the next day, Karen looked around for the potential new dealer, but seeing the priest dressed in standard dealers' attire of a white shirt and black pants, she was blindsided upon realizing that Father Doug himself was the new dealer requesting the interview. She actually wondered if she was on "Candid Camera," then tried to figure out how to say no to a man of God!

Father Doug smiled and said, "After twenty-seven years in the priesthood, I'm taking a year's sabbatical and I've always wanted to try dealing cards."

All Karen could think about was the strong language often used by losing players. But stranger things than a priest dealing blackjack happened every day in Las Vegas.

When the shift boss auditioned Father Doug, just to see if they could help him secure a position at another casino that hired break-in dealers, he hired him on the spot—he was that good.

So Father Doug became a blackjack dealer at Ellis Island for his year's sabbatical. He was very skilled at his job and well-liked by everyone. The only people who knew he was a priest were Karen, the shift boss, Gary Ellis, and Joe.

In fact, he was also good for the casino, as he tended to beat the players a little more often than the other dealers. One time Gary inquired how Doug was doing and Karen told him that he was winning more than losing.

Gary responded, "That's because he's got God backing his play. Come to think of it," he added, "do you know any more priests who want to be dealers?"

When his sabbatical ended, Father Doug returned to Ohio, but still visited Vegas as often as he could and sat with Joe in his hospital room and at home as he healed.

The Long and Winding Road

The doctors were unable to close Joe's wound. He went home with an open abdomen and endured wound care every day for more than a year until it healed — after another two surgeries.

One of Joe's saving graces was Gordon Dickie. Gordon retired from the San Diego Police Department and they worked together at the Gaming Control Board. He never missed a day in the hospital and was by Joe and Karen's side during the darkest hours. He also kept the police community and friends informed on Joe's medical updates via a blog and made himself available for them any time of the day or night.

They were also fortunate that Karen has a boss who was very concerned about Joe's survival and care. From the very first day Joe became ill, Gary Ellis, owner of Ellis Island, told her, "You take care of Joe and we'll take care of the business."

Throughout his ordeal, Joe always took interest in the nurses, nursing assistants, and other staff. He learned about their families and how many children they had. He appreciated the long hours they worked to care for so many. He was grateful to be alive.

Each day as Karen arrived at the hospital, she never knew

what to expect, unsure of which "Joe" from his past would be greeting her — and the medical staff — that day. All the medication he was on wreaked havoc on his mind. Karen had always admired the way he could recall the details of most events in his and their lives, including names, dates, and places. But now she was witnessing what a mind is truly capable of and it was both fascinating and terrifying. It was as if each Joe from past decades emerged at random, beyond any conscious control.

Most intriguing was the disbelief expressed by the nurses as they listened to what Joe was recalling involuntarily from his past. All the events, people, and places from his life were factual, yet many were so incredible and implausible that the medical staff doubted their validity.

Karen began bringing in photos and documents to show them that this was not a drug-addled patient spewing fiction. This was a man who had experienced events few could fathom, performed actions that could very well have impacted their own lives or those they loved, and witnessed things they'd probably only seen on TV, in movies, or in their worst nightmares.

And so the idea of this book was born.

Finally, in 2017, Joe was in good enough shape to start physical therapy, which he still undergoes three times a week. At age 77, Joe says he feels better today than he did in his forties.

Karen is still working at Ellis Island and they take RV trips around the country during her time off. Joe plans the trips, works on the RV, and does things around the house.

From time to time, he consults on security issues for casinos. He was recently approached and asked if he might be interested in consulting for the Japanese on their three new "integrated resorts," large-scale entertainment complexes with casinos, hotels, restaurants, conference centers, retail spaces, theaters and showrooms, and theme and amusement parks, which are expected to cost up to $15 billion and to open by 2025. For Joe, it would've been a multi-year project in Japan — way too much work and too far from home. So he respectfully declined. Besides, he still doesn't care for Asian food.

Ellis Island

In 1990, after the Aladdin and Dunes fiascos, Karen Dorsey went to work for Gary Ellis, the owner of Ellis Island Casino (and now Brewery), as his assistant. Ellis Island is a popular locals casino on Koval Lane just south of Flamingo Road, right behind Bally's. Karen quickly became a part of the Ellis family and was invited to all the family events, such as Christmas Eve and Easter Sunday dinners. Joe, of course, accompanied his wife to all of the events and eventually, they met the whole extended family.

Frank Ellis, Gary's father, came to Las Vegas with his parents in the early 1950s. His father purchased a small motel in downtown Las Vegas and announced his intention to move his family there. He believed the town would grow, so Frank and his mother sold their businesses in West Virginia and returned to Las Vegas. Mary Jo, the love of Frank's life, soon joined him in southern Nevada, where they were married.

Over the years, the motel struggled, so Frank took a job dealing cards at the Golden Nugget. Frank could see that dealing was a dead-end job for him, so Mary Jo attended real-estate classes. At home, she taught him what she'd learned each day and eventually, Frank took and passed the real-estate test and received his license. Frank was extremely successful in his new career and invested in various properties that increased his family's prosperity. Frank and Mary Jo raised two boys, Frank and Gary, and two girls, Michele and Tina.

At the family events that Joe attended, Frank held court and Joe listened intently to his stories about the real history of Las Vegas and how things happened in the years when the mob ran the town. Subsequently, Joe often found Frank in an oversized recliner in the living room of the home he (literally) built with Mary Jo. Frank had an incredible memory for names, dates, and events and Joe always picked his brain when doing consulting jobs if names of old-timers came up.

The story that stands out most in Joe's mind concerned an attempted bombing of a restaurant that Frank had opened in 1976, the Village Pub. At the time, a major labor strike was taking place on the Strip and it didn't seem that it would end anytime soon. Frank opened the Village Pub as a non-union establishment and began to receive threats to his safety.

On the night of January 24, 1977, a security guard at the Village Pub noticed a vehicle parked in front of the restaurant that was emitting a strong odor of gasoline. The fire department was called for a routine gas washdown and it was discovered that the vehicle had been booby-trapped with an explosive device. A big 55-gallon drum full of gasoline was set to detonate inside the vehicle when the door was opened. Luckily, it failed to explode.

While the booby-trapped vehicle was being dealt with at the Village Pub, a second call came into the fire department concerning a similar vehicle at another non-union restaurant, the Starboard Tack. The fire marshal attempted to disarm the device and was burned on his face and hands when the device went off. Fortunately, again, the drum full of gasoline didn't detonate.

The union leader, Al Bramlett, was suspected of having some involvement in the attempted bombings. In the same year, 1977, he was reported missing. Three years after the report, he was found under a rock pile in a rural area. Later, it came out that he'd hired Tom and Gramby Hanley, considered the two deadliest hit men in Las Vegas at the time, to place the car bombs at both locations. The information concerning their involvement came from Tom Hanley's wife. The Hanleys were later prosecuted for the murder of Al Bramlett after the union leader reneged on the fee for the bombings they'd agreed upon.

Gary Ellis later bought the Village Pub from his father and renamed it Ellis Island. In honor of his father, however, Gary went on to open 12 more Village Pubs.

As Joe sat with Frank at family celebrations, he realized that he was seeing something quite remarkable. By then, the Ellis Family had expanded to grandchildren and great-grandchildren and they all enjoyed one another to the point that Joe never heard any arguments or fighting among them. It was as if the family had a rule that the older children took care of the younger children and it seemed to Joe to transfer from generation to generation. Joe could plainly see a genuine love of family among the Ellises and he credited it to the love Frank and Mary Jo had for each other and always showed their children.

In 2015, Frank's health was waning. Late that year, Frank went to the hospital, where Joe visited him. On one such occasion around Thanksgiving, he could tell Frank was struggling. Frank motioned Joe to come close and said, "I have to make it past Christmas, because I don't want my passing to be a sad memory for every holiday to come."

Joe had zero doubts that Frank would make it through the holidays, because he always put family first, even through the end of his life. He passed away on January 25, 2016.

Joe and Karen

As can be expected about a man whose career included the Navy, Coast Guard, law enforcement, and casino collections, Joe isn't exactly an emotionally expressive kind of guy. He learned early that the jobs he'd been hired to perform didn't have room for emotions. He had to become an expert at compartmentalizing. When he went to work, he left his emotions at home. That's not to say he didn't feel and care — in fact, it was quite the opposite. Though he tried to wear an impenetrable shield to protect his interior life and family from the cold cruel parts of the world he was subjected to, it didn't work. Unless he'd been made of steel, Joe couldn't have experienced all the things he did and not have them penetrate and permeate his heart and soul.

Through it all, by his side, has been his wife, Karen. When Joe tries to remember his life before she entered it, he asks himself, Why? His life took on new meaning when she came into it and a heart that was used to denying emotion began to experience feelings it couldn't ignore.

Joe's life changed forever when he met Karen Rose in October 1975. People believe in different things; they attribute good fortune to faith, fate, karma, or just luck. Joe experienced all of the above when Karen walked into his life. To this day, he's grateful that he had the good sense to marry her on June 30, 1979, because he's been blessed every day since.

Karen had previously introduced me to Joe. We began

initial discussions about a possible book collaboration someday.

In October 2017, with Karen's hopeful and persistent persuasion, I spoke to Joe and offered to assist him in a biography project. Joe told her he'd think about it.

That night Karen asked Joe, "Are you going to do the book?"

Joe, knowing how large a task it would be, said, "I don't think so."

"Would you do it for me?" Karen asked sweetly.

Joe knew he couldn't refuse. He responded immediately, "Yes, Karen Rose, I will. This one's for you!"

About the Author

Linda Ellis started writing poems as a child, a talent inherited from her Irish grandmother. She grew up in Florida and then lived in New York for several years. However, her southern roots kept calling her home so she settled in Georgia where she now lives with her family and a menagerie of pets. She spent years working in the corporate world, but after her first poem was shared on a syndicated radio program in 1994, an alternative career began to emerge and she soon came to the realization that her true passion was in creative writing.

Keep up to Date on
All the Developments in Sports Betting

Go to GamblingWithAnEdge.com to access the blogs and podcasts of the world's top advantage players, including professional sports bettors who cover the subject from every conceivable angle. Shop lines on our live odds feed, get analyses of the latest online incentive offers, track the progress of newly legalized sports betting jurisdictions, and learn about new sports betting technologies, e.g., plans for the VBX betting exchange. Visit often for the latest information and opportunities in the explosion of sports betting nationwide.

Visit
LasVegasAdvisor.com
for all the latest on gambling and Las Vegas

Free features include:

- Articles and ongoing updates on gambling.

- Real-time odds for all major sporting events.

- Sign-up and free-play bonuses.

- Question of the Day offering in-depth answers to gambling and Las Vegas-related questions.

- Active message boards with discussions on blackjack, sports betting, poker, and more!

Become a Las Vegas Advisor Member and get our exclusive dining, show, and gambling coupons and members-only discounts.

Whale Hunt in the Desert
by Deke Castleman

This definitive exposé reveals the shrouded world of ultra-high rollers and the Faustian pacts they forge with their hosts, the casino representatives whose job it is to part them from their fortunes, using an arsenal of "weapons" including complimentary suites, private jets, diamond jewelry for their wives (and/or mistresses), front-row seats to sold-out events, and other shadier "tricks" up their sleeves.

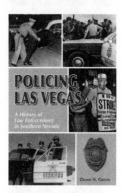

Policing Las Vegas
by Dennis N. Griffin

Policing Las Vegas chronicles the evolution of law enforcement in Las Vegas and Clark County from the days of night watchmen and cops who carted drunks to jail on horseback to today's acclaimed Metro Police. It's filled with stories about the colorful characters on both sides of the law, drawn from history, legend, and the personal accounts of many men and women who policed Las Vegas.

The First 100
edited by A.D. Hopkins and K.J. Evans

The First 100 brings to life the incredible men and women who ushered Las Vegas to the forefront of popular culture. From Mob boss Bugsy Siegel to Howard Hughes, Rat Pack crooner Frank Sinatra to showman Liberace, Bob Martin, considered the dean of all bookmakers, to Benny Binion who founded the World Series of Poker, and Bob Stupak, Kirk Kerkorian, and Steve Wynn.

Fly on the Wall
by Dick Odessky

A chronicle of Vegas during the glamorous '50s and '60s by a newspaper reporter and publicist who was in the thick of it—the proverbial fly on the wall. As a reporter for two of the city's most respected newspapers and a publicist for two of the city's most infamous casinos, Dick Odessky tells his recollections of Las Vegas' good old bad old days.

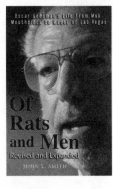

Of Rats and Men
by John L. Smith

Was Oscar Goodman only what he claims: an attorney who defended his clients based on the simple principle that they, too, have constitutional rights? If so, how did he manage to mingle with the mob for decades without becoming part of it? Pulling off an unlikely career change, from legal spokesman for the notorious crime figures of our era to being elected twice, and winning, mayor of Las Vegas.

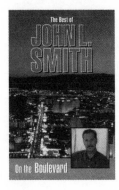

On the Boulevard
by John L. Smith

On the Boulevard is from the *Las Vegas Review-Journal's* most popular columnist, John L. Smith. Smith provides singular insights into the fast, fluid, and often funny town he's chronicled for nearly 20 years. Subjects include: former Las Vegas mayor and Mob mouthpiece Oscar Goodman, legendary slot cheat Bill Land, and seldom-chronicled gambling icons such as Mel Exber (Las Vegas Club), Si Redd (IGT), and Big Julie Weintraub ('60s junket operator).

About Huntington Press

Huntington Press is a specialty publisher of Las Vegas-
and gambling-related books and periodicals, including the
award-winning consumer newsletter, *Anthony Curtis' Las
Vegas Advisor.*

Huntington Press
3665 Procyon Street
Las Vegas, Nevada 89103
E-mail: books@huntingtonpress.com